PRIVATE EYE ANNUAL 2016

EDITED BY IAN HISLOP

*"His Lordship sends with compliments a photograph of his genitals
to The Lady Mary. Is there to be a reply?"*

Published in Great Britain by
Private Eye Productions Ltd
6 Carlisle Street, London W1D 3BN
www.private-eye.co.uk

© 2016 Pressdram Ltd
ISBN 978-1-901784-64-0
Designed by Bridget Tisdall
Printed and bound in Italy
by L.E.G.O. S.p.A

2 4 6 8 10 9 7 5 3 1

PRIVATE EYE ANNUAL 2016

EDITED BY IAN HISLOP

THAT ALL-PURPOSE RESIGNATION LETTER IN FULL

It is with a heavy heart that I have announced my decision to resign from whatever position I currently hold in the Government/the Labour front bench/UKIP/ the England World Cup squad/*Top Gear* *(delete as applicable)*.

Whatever I am resigning from, I am painfully aware that, despite my efforts, what remains is a shambolic mess, which, I would like to emphasise, has come about through no fault of my own.

I have done a lot of good in my time inside the organisation I am resigning from and can take full credit for whatever success has been achieved. I cannot, however, hand on heart enumerate all my achievements at this time.

But now I must make way for someone else who can be arsed to do this thankless job in impossible circumstances, while I either move on to a well-paid part-time job criticising that person in a national newspaper column, or instantly resume fighting to get my job back.

Thank you,

I.M. QUITTING

Today we begin the serialisation of the most sensational and explosive political biography ever written

Lord Cashcroft exclusively lays bare the astonishing secrets of prime minister David Cameron's shocking and scandalous life

LORD Cashforhonours reveals for the first time, in his devastating portrait of the man who must surely now be considering resignation in the light of this world-shattering book serialised exclusively in the Daily Mail, that:

■ Cameron went to Eton with a lot of very rich boys.

■ Cameron went to Oxford with a lot of very rich boys.

■ Cameron took drugs when he was a student with a lot of very rich boys.

■ Cameron always wanted to be prime minister to spite his old school friend Boris Johnson.

■ As prime minister, Cameron is always on holiday and never does any work.

■ Cameron watches lots of low-brow television, particularly box sets of popular series.

■ Cameron is utterly ruthless and believes in nothing except being prime minister.

■ Cameron is incredibly disloyal to his supporters, particularly those who have given him a great deal of money and might have expected, if he had an ounce of decency, to be

rewarded with at the very least a place in the Cabinet, possibly as Chancellor of the Exchequer, rather than being stabbed in the back on some paltry excuse that they are trying to avoid paying taxes by living in Belize and therefore have no alternative but to get their revenge by hiring some pliable journalist to put the boot into Cameron by finally exposing all the dirty secrets that the world needs to know, such as the fact that he wouldn't give a job to a distinguished entrepreneur who had generously donated vast sums of money without which the posh little bastard would never have become prime minister in the first place.

TOMORROW

Lord Cashpoint exclusively reveals that he was told by a very good source that someone who knew someone who had known Cameron at Oxford remembered some story that involved a pig's head.

We should warn readers that they may be deeply shocked to discover that we have no idea if this story is true or not, but we decided to publish it anyway because it is the only half-interesting bit of dirt we could come up with that hasn't already been published somewhere else.

Lord Cashpile's book "Call Me A Pathetic, Vengeful, Rich Bastard" is available from Lord Cashdowndrain's own publishing house Bitehand, in association with Dacretrash Productions.

Man Found Guilty of Revenge Pork

by Our Westminster Correspondent
Douglas Hogg

A 69-year-old man has this week been found guilty of committing the new offence of "Revenge Pork".

After their relationship went sour, Lord Ashcroft sent a mental image to everyone around the world of his former partner, "Dave", indulging in a lurid sex act with a dead pig.

Said one regular browser of Mail Online, who saw the image in his head, "I know it's probably not true, but it's disgusting, and now I've pictured the scene I'll never be able to forget it. Though I will be sure to pass it on to all my friends."

The victim, known only as David Cameron, Prime Minister and First Lord of the Treasury, said, "This is a shocking and hurtful breach of trust. I used to love Lord Ashcroft's money, and just because I couldn't satisfy his unorthodox desires, that is no justification for him getting his own back in this disgusting way. He should be locked up, and forced to take part in a prison initiation ceremony in the shower. How's that for a mental image, you bastard?!"

HOW RUTHLESS ORGANISATIONS EXACT REVENGE

The Mafia	The Conservatives

Horse's head in bed	Pig's head in book

"I sometimes wish he'd never gone to drama school"

Coe breaks new record

LORD COE, the athlete and politician, has made history by breaking the world record for the fastest sprint away from damaging allegations about doping athletics.

"It was incredible," said a bystander, "I've never seen anyone move like that. One minute he was standing right by his predecessor as head of the International Association of Athletics Federations, and the next he had put an enormous amount of distance between them."

Indeed, questions are being raised about exactly how Coe managed to sprint so extremely fast, after which he announced an immediate and thorough review into himself.

EU SUMMIT 'TO DECIDE ON AGREED COURSE OF INACTION'

by Our Man in Brussels **Phil Refugee-Camps**

BRUSSELS said an emergency EU summit this week would pave the way for an agreed course of inaction on the tens of thousands of Syrian refugees pouring into Europe, as one by one countries shut their borders.

"We want to ensure that the refugees are treated with respect and compassion as they are shunted from one country to the next," said an EU spokesman. "We hope that by combining the inaction of various countries into a unified course of inaction we can have these refugees wandering the train stations of Europe for many years to come."

The EU denied that it was callous and uncaring towards the refugees' increasingly desperate plight as winter approached.

"Far from it... who couldn't fail to be moved seeing just how much reaching Europe means to these bedraggled men, women and children crossing into Hungary with tears streaming down their faces, though that may have something to do with the tear gas the riot police were firing at them before the baton charges and the rubber bullets began."

"So what exactly are we – refugees or migrants?"

MIGRANT CRISIS

Where in the world do you propose to put these refugees?

How about Syria?

POLICE DEFEND OPERATION GUMTREE

by Our Paedophile Staff
Hugh Tree

INSPECTOR Knacker, the man leading the investigation into an alleged Westminster VIP paedophile ring today defended his decision to proceed on the basis of the evidence of the controversial source, codenamed 'Dud'.

Said Knacker, "Dud came into Neasden Police Station and told us an entirely convincing story about nefarious goings-on in Dolphin Square in the 1970s. Dud was a credible witness, who told us in great detail about how he'd been murdered by Edward Heath, whilst he was Prime Minister. The account was deemed by ourselves to merit a full investigation due to its coherence, and high level of plausibility."

The inspector continued, "When Dud told us that he'd also been murdered by Harvey Proctor, the case took an even more sinister turn. And we felt clearly it was time to arrest Paul Gambaccini before Dud was murdered for a third time. We would urge anyone else who has been killed by high-profile paedophiles not to suffer in silence, but to come forward."

There were doubts last night about the credibility of Inspector Knacker.

Jeremy Corbyn WRITES

A LOT of journalists from the Times, the Telegraph, the Mail and the Sun stop me and ask me: "Why do you consort with members of Hamas, Hezbollah, and the IRA?".

To which I say to them, "My philosophy is always to talk to everyone, even those peoples you profoundly disagree with, because it's only that way you can get your message across."

Or I would say that to the journalists of the Times, the Telegraph, the Mail and the Sun, if I were talking to them.

But I'm not, at the moment.

So if you do see any of them, pass on the message from me would you, thanks so much!

LIB DEM CONFERENCE LATEST

Delighted supporters leave packed venue after speech

POETRY CORNER

**In Memoriam
Denis Healey,
Last of the Great
Generation of
Politicians**

So. Farewell
Then Denis Healey,
One-time Labour
Chancellor of the
Exchequer and
Would-be Leader
Of your party.

For 40 years you
Fought to prevent
Labour from being
Taken over by the
Far Left.

When it finally
Happened, did you
Decide to die
In protest?

E.J. Thribb (97½)

**Also In Memoriam
Geoffrey Howe,
Also Last of the Great
Generation of
Politicians**

So. Farewell
Then Geoffrey Howe,
One-time Tory
Chancellor of the
Exchequer and
Nemesis of
Mrs Thatcher.

Denis Healey once
Compared you to
A dead sheep.

Now you are
Really dead.
As is he.
See above.

E.J. Thribb (17¾)

MUM'S THE WORD COUNT

The new feature that everyone's talking about

The brilliant new double column by Polly Filler and her mother, Polly Sell

Polly writes

Polly writes

There's always some point in the week when the working mum, desperately walking that old tightrope of career/life balance, has to make the call to granny.

This week I was in deadline meltdown as the editor rang me, saying, "Polly, there's a hole to fill in the back of the magazine. Can you do me 800 words taking a sideways look at modern motherhood? By lunchtime."

Of course I said "Yes", but with the new au pair Slava Laba already fired for putting the Useless Simon's underpants in the dishwasher (see previous column!), I had no childcare for toddler Charlie.

So it had to be my poor old mum, who always complains about having Charlie dumped on her, and my stepdad, Ron Seal... but I know they love it really, even though they once changed the locks and then moved to Inverness for a year without telling me.

Anyway, imagine my annoyance when Mum (formerly features editor of this paper!) said she couldn't take Charlie, as she was busy writing a column about looking after your grandchildren when your daughter is working!

It's the call every granny dreads! "Mum, Charlie is off school, sick..." (ie, the school is sick of him "expressing himself" by setting fire to the art room)... "Could you look after him while I finish my column about writing my column?"

Usually, my new husband, Ron Seal (formerly managing editor of this newspaper) and I come up with some excuse, like "Sorry, we're dead", but this time I wasn't quick enough and all I could think of was to say that I had to write a column about being a granny – which actually happened to be true.

The next thing I heard was the sound of crying and a 4x4 VW Tourette driving off, leaving me in charge of Charlie.

There was only one thing to do – call my mum, Polly Styrene (formerly women's editor of this paper), and ask if the nursing home minded me dropping off a hyper-active but gifted toddler for the day, provided I confiscate all his matches. And Bingo! (Tuesday afternoons in the TV room) – problem solved!

● *Polly and Polly's hilarious new book "We're in the Mummy" is published by Bryony Gordon & Gordon and the authors will be appearing together at the Wye-on-Wye Literary Festival (providing they can find some childcare).*

"She used to love sitting here, admiring the memorial benches"

Richard Howell

EXCLUSIVE TO ALL PAPERS

I Wept At Bake Off Final

by **Everyone**

I think of myself as pretty hard-bitten and cynical, but I confess that when my editor called me in and told me to write a thousand words by lunchtime about the Bake Off final, the tears rolled down my cheeks.

Cry oh cry

"Every other paper has a long piece about how Nadiya reduced the whole nation to tears," he said, "so bash one out now or you're fired."

Instantly, I found myself welling up and reaching for the tissues.

I suddenly found that I too was overcome with emotion at the thought of this 4'11" beacon of hope in a headscarf uniting the entire nation in a display of patriotic, multicultural tolerance and fair play, symbolising a new, optimistic, feelgood Britain and I too wanted to join in with all my colleagues in this mass outpouring of drivel. *(Surely "brilliant features"? Ed.)*

Yes, Britain will never be the same again. Nadiya has done more for race relations in Britain by baking one simple cake than anyone since Mo Farah, when I wrote exactly this same piece during the Olympics. *(You're fired. Ed.)*

QUEEN IN CORBYN SNUB

TV NEWS

NEW APPRENTICE LINE-UP REVEALED

HERE they are, the new contestants we will be following on the BBC for the next 94 weeks, as they vie with each other to become Lord Sugar's apprentice.

With their über confidence, their 150% commitment and their super salesmanship, which wannabe tycoon of tomorrow will be pushing the box and thinking outside the envelope to take the ultimate prize of helping Lord Sugar turn thousands of unsold Amstrad Dictafax ZL-197s into landfill before being fired?

"I walk the talk and talk the walk" *"I'm a salesman, not a failsman"* *"Wimps are for lunch"* *"Money is in my DVLA"* *"Failure is not in my Pictionary"* *"I'm a gun for fire"*

(That's enough arses. Ed.)

8

DANIEL CRAIG

Does James Bond have a favourite spoon?

Oh, for God's sake. Bond is so boring. Get over it.

But for your last appearance as Bond you were paid millions of pounds...

Big deal. I'd rather slit my wrists with a spoon than ever have to look at another Bond script.

Are there any spoons in the new Bond film?

No. I hate playing Bond. Bond is so misogynistic he wouldn't even know which drawer in the kitchen the spoons were kept. He's pathetic.

Does Bond prefer his martinis shaken or stirred with a spoon?

Look. Since I took the role of Bond I can't even go into a bar any more, because everyone stares at me. I hate it.

You said last month in Spoons and Spoonmen you would definitely go on playing Bond as long as you could.

Did I? *[checks]* Oh, I did. Well if you're going to compare every spoon-based interview I've done in the past with what I'm saying now, there's no hope for you.

Is it true the new film was going to be called Spoon rather than Spectre?

You're pathetic. You're worse than Bond.

Has anything amusing ever happened to you in connection with a spoon?

Next.

NEXT WEEK: Lord Sugar, "Me and My Sugar".

From The Message Boards

Members of the online community respond to the major issues of the day...

Britain's most 'boring' men named

Head's up re the funkiest book of the year! As youll know from the seriously serious media coverage, the iconic Dull Men's Club has published a book called 'Dull Men of Great Britain' and I am absolutely PASSIONATE about it! Why? Because speaking with my PR hat on it celebrates Brand Britain in it's world class eccentricity and passion in a way not seen since the Olympic's Opening Ceremony! Theres literally everything from collector's of toy soldier's, traffic cone's, vacuum cleaner's, lawn mower's, and beer can's to a man who photograph's bandstand's!! Special prop's to retired doctor Simon Barley, who collects handsaw's and did a cutting edge PHD and book on the subject! # GBPLC #TeamBoring – *Hattie*

i colect pound coin's i had 27 "BUT" I give my nan 2 pound's to get chip's so now i got 25 sumtime's i colect chip's "BUT" I always's end up eting them – *colin*

As a serious record collector, I collect mint vinyl (stored in optimal conditions which I have described before) and don't own any form of gramophone (records are not for "playing": styli damage grooves and turntable heat causes warping). The only non-mint discs I possess are valuable mis-pressings and mis-labelings: the Holy Grail of record collecting – nay, ALL collecting. Hence no such serious collectors appear in this rather silly book. – *PCS 3042*

If you don't play them, how do you know they are mis-pressed and mis-labelled? – *Jon*

i got some record's that are even more rarer i got a copy of the beatel's sargent pepper in the sleeve of dawns greatest hit's and a copy of disc one of elvis 40 greatist in the sleeve of cherish by david cassidy i got them at car boot's for 50p each but they must be worth a fortune – *Record Fan*

Those are neither rare, nor collectable or valuable. – *PCS 3042*

y not – *Record Fan*

Because they're not. – *PCS 3042*

your just jelous i bet you aint got them – *Record Fan*

I refuse to waste my time arguing with you. If you don't believe me, consult Record Collector or Goldmine. If you can't read, get a grown-up to read them to you. – *PCS 3042*

I have a phrase that I think sums it up nicely: there's nowt as queer as folk. – *Original Thinker*

give yer head a wobble mate i dont think these guys got a queer bone in there bodys 😊 gays dress to empress and these lot look like tramp's if u give them moisturizer they probly put it in a box and collect it lolz – *Hunny pot*

not bein funny but it wood be a dull old world if we was all difrent – *Hayley 321*

"I can't be bothered to microwave anything, shall we get a take-away?"

CAROL STOKES.

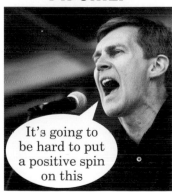
9

How to Win the Nobel Prize

Whether it's for peace, literature, science or medicine, winning the Nobel Prize is a great way to expand your contacts book and earn more money – as well as a valuable ticket to speaking at some of the most prestigious literary events.

Using his many years' experience in the communications industry, Steve Flopp will share advice on every aspect of winning the Nobel Prize, from researching the correct address for the Nobel Prize Committee, to composing your application, writing a cover letter to ensure your pitch gets read and insider tips on what to say in that all-important acceptance speech.

This course is for you if...

● You've almost finished work on your novel or chemistry experiment, and want to make sure it gets the recognition it truly deserves.

Saturday 14 November, 2pm-5pm,
Cost: £150 (incl. choice of still or sparkling water). Capacity: 200

How to Suck Eggs

Are you a mature woman with grandchildren? Is there a vital element missing from your life? This intensive 6-week course will teach you all the basic skills necessary to suck eggs.

During this highly informative masterclass with acclaimed international egg-sucking coach Jilly Smugg, you'll be guided through the key components of:
● picking your egg
● inserting it into your mouth
● sucking it, complete with insider tips on
● removing the sucked egg from your mouth
● replacing it in the egg tray
● clearing up the mess

This course is for you if...

● You have always wanted to be patronised by know-it-alls
● You're thinking of a career change, and hope to start an international egg-sucking clinic
● You have more money than sense

Saturday 21 November-January 4 2016, 4.30pm-7pm,
Cost: £720 (incl. six eggs)

Where to Place that Apostrophe

Whether you've come new to apostrophe's, or you've never felt quite sure where exactly to place them, theres' never been a better time to start learning.

Award-winning grammarian Mark Conman has over eight year's of experience working with apostrophes' and is keen to teach you to make it work for you in all situation's.

Monday 7 December, 6pm-8pm. Cost: £155 (incl. six apostrophe's)

How to Waste Precious Time

Wasting precious time is a fantastic way of responding to the increasingly complex and fast-moving digitalised world of the 21st century. If you're a tweeter or blogger, or if you just want to learn how to interact with an award-winning video game for hours on end, then this inspiring course, led by veteran time-waster Marcus Dullard, is tailor-made for you.

Using his vast reserves of sloth, Marcus might just get round to teaching you how to fail to act on your impulses, and how to counterbalance your early stirrings of creativity with apathy and indifference. Includes Q&A and group discussion.

In a further session for advanced timewasters, "How to Waste Other People's Precious Time", you will learn:
● The art and practise of tweeting
● Cold-calling for beginners
● Making your texts too long and dull to be worth reading

Tuesday 17 November, 10am-7pm, Cost £220

Coping with redundancy

It can be tough coming to terms with the news that the newspaper you work for is proposing drastic cutbacks to stem mounting losses currently running at £50m a year.

This masterclass, aimed specifically at journalists working for the *Guardian*, will take you through all aspects of life outside of Guardian Towers, including what it's like trying to eke out a single coffee all day as a freelancer in Starbucks (and how to nab the seat next to the plug for your MacBook!), plus how shopping at Lidl with the great unwashed isn't nearly as bad as you think – look on the bright side, there could even be a feature in it!

Conducted by famed redundancy expert Philippa Downsize, this is a "must attend" course for any journalists currently at their desks in the newsroom.

Saturday 13th February 10am-4.30pm
Room P45, Guardian Towers. Cost: £385

"God, I wish someone would shut that baby up"

"And, perhaps most poignantly, this post, from @minge634, 'Miss you bro, shag an angel for me'"

STANDING STONES

SITTING STONES

Brian Sewell reviews
The Pearly Gates

MUCH against my better judgement, I had the misfortune last night to find myself standing in front of one of the most tawdry, tatty and meretricious works of "art" I ever saw in my life.

We've all heard foolish and purblind panjandrums enthusing about the supposedly divine quality of the grandiose architectural folly colloquially known as the "Pearly Gates".

But nothing on earth could have prepared me for the unutterable vulgarity of this shoddy installation, with its absurd "pearl-themed" ornamentation, too fussily suburban even to merit the term rococo, masking what are only too obviously some dismally functional and perfectly ordinary gates.

And the real tragedy, as I pointed out to the bearded security man standing next to them – Peter someone, I didn't catch his second name – is that, behind those very gates are some of the greatest figures in the entire history of Western art, any of whom could have been relied upon to design something infinitely more elevated and aesthetically satisfying.

For heaven's sake, why the management couldn't have had the sense to commission that incomparable genius Michelangelo Buonarroti – with whom I'm hoping to sip a little vintage nectar at some point in the next million years *(continued for eternity)*

A Non-Doctor Writes

AS A non-doctor, I'm often asked, "Non-doctor, as you're here in Richmond Park, and I'm about to give birth beside this tree, could you lend a hand?" To which the simple answer is: "YES! I'M BRIAN BLESSED. I'M AN ACTOR. IF I CAN PLAY A POLICEMAN ON Z-CARS, I'M SURE I CAN PLAY A DOCTOR IN RICHMOND PARK!"

What I'm suffering from is *Luvvius delusionales grandiorum* – a common problem for thespians – where on the back of a few good reviews you believe you can do anything.

Symptoms include bellowing "PUSH! PUSH!! PUSH!!!", before biting through the umbilical cord, and licking the baby clean with your tongue.

If the baby's a boy, and called Gordon, the non-doctor may then shout: "GORDON'S ALIVE!", followed swiftly by inquiring of the patient: "HOW WAS I? NO, HONESTLY, WHAT DID YOU THINK?!"

In this situation, the patient may then say to the non-doctor, "I seem to have a very recently perforated eardrum." In which case, call an ambulance, like so: "AMBULANCE!!!" and hopefully they should hear you miles away in Casualty in Holby City, and give you a bit part. © *Anon Doctor*

The Alternative Rocky Horror Service Book

No.94 A Service to be held in Manchester Cathedral, to be led by the Very Reverend Leader of Her Majesty's Loyal Opposition, the Rt Hon Jeremy Corbyn, in support of the demands of the Communication Workers Union for action to protect the terms and conditions of employment of workers in the postal industry

(Mr Corbyn will be attended by other religious leaders, including Natalie Bennett, Chief Minister of the Green Party, and Ms Charlotte Church, leader of the Welsh Independent Campaign to Save Syria from the Effects of Climate Change [surely Regime Change? Ed.])

The President, Mr Corbyn (for it is he): Brother and sisters, we are gathered here today in this holy and ancient place to join together in solidarity against all the forces of wickedness currently holding their conference a few hundred yards over there...

(Here he may gesture towards the Sir Alex Ferguson Conference Centre)

Congregation: Tory scum!!

THE READING

(There shall then be a reading from the Letter of St John the McDonnell to the Morning Star)

"The rightful demands of our brothers and sisters in the CWU, which are being totally and sickeningly misreported by the right-wing captialist media, ie the Guardian and the New Statesman, are entirely consistent with the sacred texts of our Socialist faith in the inexorable unfolding of the Marxist dialectic which, er..."

(The reading may here continue for several hours)

HYMN

The President: We will now sing Hymn No. 94(a), "The Red Flag".

(The congregation will all sing all verses of this ancient hymn, out of respect for the overwhelming mandate secured by Brother Jeremy in the recent leadership election)

PRAYERS

(There will be no prayers out of respect for the deeply-held atheistic beliefs of most members of the congregation – apart from, of course, members of the Fraternal Delegations from Hamas, Hezbollah and the Former IRA)

THE PEACE

(The congregation shall then make the Sign of Peace, ie a raising of two fingers to a blown-up front page of the Daily Telegraph showing a picture of the late Baroness Thatcher)

All: Maggie, Maggie, Maggie, out, out, out.

(Or they may give some other time-honoured and sacred response, such as "No to the Poll Tax" or "Support Tony Benn for leader")

THE DISMISSAL

The President: You are free to go forth into the world from this place and to spit at any Tories you see in the streets.

(As the congregation leaves the cathedral, there shall be sounded "The Last Post" in tribute to the brave men and women of the Communication Workers Union who have given their lives to fighting the evils of privatisation)

© The Church of England 2015.

Exclusive!

CHINESE EXPEDITION DISCOVERS REMAINS OF ANCIENT CIVILISATION

by Our Imperial Expedition Leader **Admiral Zheng Hu-Hee**

I CAN report an astonishing discovery made by my intrepid band of Chinese explorers who lately returned from a small island off the coast of Europe.

We were amazed to find that this island had clearly once been at the centre of a great civilisation, remnants of which could still be seen wherever we went.

There were the ruins of huge palaces, factories and power stations dotting the countryside. We learned that the inhabitants of this island had even discovered how to make steel and nuclear energy long before the Chinese invented them!

The natives were clearly dazzled by the arrival of representatives of a civilisation so much superior to their own, and laid on a series of quaint tribal celebrations to show their immense respect for us.

We were treated by the ruler of this strange land, an elderly female styled as their "Empress", to a feast attended by all the tribal elders dressed in charmingly old-fashioned clothing.

The local food was almost inedible, and the banquet interminable, with the ruler of the country continually asking me whether I had come far... seemingly the only phrase she knew in our language.

Apart from this gathering, much of the rest of our time was taken up with attempts by the local headmen to ask us for money.

This became increasingly embarrassing, as their poverty and desperation drove them to bow lower and lower until they were lying prostrate at our feet, begging us to buy all that they owned.

Alas, we had to tell them that there was little in their decayed kingdom that was worth purchasing, but that out of charity, we would be prepared to give them an old-fashioned nuclear power station that might help them to keep their lights on.

We sailed away to the sound of them weeping and wailing in gratitude, as we headed off in relief to visit some rather more advanced nations, such as our successful colonies in Africa.

HEALTH BREAKTHROUGH LATEST

by Our Medical Correspondent
Phil Doorway

A MAJOR new World Health Organisation study has revealed that eliminating all red meat, bacon, sausages and alcohol from your diet can reduce the chances of there being any enjoyment in life to virtually nil.

Said an expert, "Simply by excluding all foodstuffs that taste delicious and all drinks that you might like, you can totally rule out the risk of experiencing any pleasure whatsoever at the dinner table."

He continued, "The great news is that eliminating all red meat and alcohol will add an extra five years to your life. The bad news is that it will seem much much longer than that."

"Can you see a bright light? If you can, go towards it"

That State Banquet Menu In Full

 BRITISH MENU

Large Steak (of UK)
Toady-in-a-Hole
Humble Pie
Appease Pudding
Chocolate Brown-nose
Coffee with sweetener (£2 billion)

To be eaten with the finest Sheffield stainless-steel cutlery made in China

❋

 CHINESE MENU

Spring Rollover
Crisp Oodles of cash
Bean shoots of recovery (not available)
Peking Duck tricky questions
Curried favour
Human Rice (off)

To be eaten with the finest Sheffield stainless-steel for-the-chop-sticks.

Entertainment will be provided by the Metropolitan Police Band with a selection of their recent 'hits' i.e. A Chinese Dissident and Two Tibetan Women Who Were Trying to Protest

---

BRITAIN WELCOMES CHINA

1　　　　**2**　　　　**3**

THOSE REASONS PARENTS CAN NOW SEIZE A TEENAGER'S PASSPORT TO STOP THEM FROM GOING ABROAD IN FULL

- They believe they are going to Syria to join IS.
- They believe they are going on a gap year around South East Asia and, if their two brothers are anything to go by, that means by month five they'll be constantly emailing home for more cash, having "mysteriously" spent every penny in Bali.
- Er...
- That's it.

DIARY

PETRONELLA WYATT: MY A-Z OF AMOUR

ATTLEE, Clement: Upon being introduced to the former Labour Prime Minister, I found myself taking agin' his unashamed moustaches, but the friendly way in which he rubbed them against my tender cheeks as his left hand tweaked my *derrière* convinced me that history would regard him as a leading world statesman, and so it has proved.

BUNTER, Billy: William Bunter was delineated of feature, slim and lithe. In the softly flickering light, he had the look of a young Valentino. I looked deep into his hamper. "Hands off my pork pie, you rotter!" he cried. Even at that tender age, I knew that men are inclined to say the opposite of what they mean. Something in his manner let me know how much he longed for me to handle his pork pie, to strip off its outer layer of pastry and to gorge myself on the meat below. "Yaroo!" he exclaimed as I did so, and at that moment I found myself drowning in his tears.

CIGAR: I thought he would never surrender. I was desperately young and, as the French would have it, *très gorgeuse,* and Sir Winston was well into his dotage, but that didn't stop him falling head-over-heels in love with me.

Perhaps It was that all-in-one boiler suit of his that, in the dreadful modern parlance, "did it for me". Over a late-night cigar, I graciously permitted him to place his hand on my lower knee as he told me things he had never told a living soul – his fervent patriotism, the little-known part he played in helping us win the war, and his strong dislike, amounting almost to animosity, towards the German Chancellor, Adolf Hitler.

DERRIERE: The French have a word for it. The neutrality of my derrière has oft been violated by a veritable plenitude of wandering hands, but none more welcome than those of William Ewart Gladstone, or "Ewie", as he begged me to call him. Considered somewhat severe by those who did not know him well, to me he was a little puppy-dog in a stiff white collar.

EDINBURGH, HRH Duke of: Philip always credited me with helping him overcome his struggle with self-doubt.

FEND OFF: *see Gordon Brown; President de Gaulle; Earl Mountbatten; Mr Pastry; Luciano Pavarotti; President and Mrs Ronald Reagan, Homer Simpson, Sir Cyril Smith; Sir Denis Thatcher; Gore Vidal et al.*

GANDHI, Mahatma: Those who did not know him well often considered this belligerent political firebrand a skinny figure. But for those of us privileged to see him without his trademark loin-cloth, he was in fact hugely well-covered, even veering towards the portly.

HEATH, Sir Edward: A big man in every way, with eyes of cobalt blue, Sir Edward oft begged me to marry him, but I was betrothed to another.

INCY WINCY SPIDER: He gained a reputation for repeatedly climbing up water-spouts, but the Wincy I knew was very different. "I truly detest water spouts, Petsy," he once confessed when we were sharing a bath, "and I would do anything to avoid them." But then the sun came out and when I turned my back he started climbing up that waterspout again. Like so many of us, Wincy was a mass of contradictions.

JOHNSON, Boris: He has gained a reputation as a ladies' man, and as someone who repeatedly cheated on his wife, but during our steamy four-year affair I learned a very different side to Boris Johnson.

KNIGHT, FRANK AND RUTLEY: All three of them know how to woo a lady, but it will always be Rutley who moves me.

LAMONT, Norman: Lord Lamont is not only recognised today as a distinguished and courageous Chancellor, but as a man without malice or side.

MAGOO, Mr: Mr Magoo is not only recognised today as a distinguished and courageous businessman, but also as a man of immense stature and clear vision.

NAVY BLUE: The colour of a moonlit night on a turbulent sea... the colour of *amour.* When I first set eyes on John Major, he was wearing HIS navy-blue blazer with bright gold buttons. I used to love the way he would do up his middle button, then undo it, then do it up again, and so on, with ever-increasing skill. When I got up close, I could clearly see my face reflected in that button. His fingers reminded me of well-drilled soldiers, but I would never, ever reveal the exact region of my *corpo* over which they completed their amorous march.

OSBORNE, George: His hair is nut-brown, his fringe seductively horizontal, his eyes the colour of Swiss chocolate, and, though his marriage to his gorgeously mousy little wife is famously secure, in his provocative red box he carries a photograph of... but my lips must remain sealed.

PHILOSOPHY: To fend off undesirables may not be a complete philosophy, but at the very least it's a start.

REFERENDUM: In, out, in, out. For me, it's always meant so much more than just that.

SOOTY: Though he makes much in public of his admiration for Sweep, Sooty was privately much aggrieved by Sweep's public following. Mefears these two glove puppets, each one so talented in his way, are oft at daggers drawn.

TELL, Kiss and: My deepest contempt has long been reserved for those who indulge in the despicable practice of "Kiss and Tell". For this reason, I have long eschewed the "Kiss and Tell" for the infinitely more dignified *"Baiser et Dire".*

U and NON-U: When dancing at a Winter Ball with a senior member of Cabinet, take care to ask them to remove their hand from your behind or *derrière,* but never your arse.

VLAD, Impaler, The: Not only recognised today as a distinguished and courageous ruler, but as a man without malice or side, and a lovely dancer.

WINTER BALL, Conservative: It was at this tumultuous event that I was first introduced to Jacob Rees-Mogg, I knew at once that he was mentally undressing me, and that he yearned to ravish me on my ancestral chaise-longue over a bubbling glass of Perrier-Jouet. "How do you DO?" he said, rolling his tongue around those words like a rope around the wrists of a willing young virgin.

XXX: I was most touched when the impossibly svelte Eric Pickles said he wanted to kiss me, but I was at the time kissing another, so was obliged to decline.

Yodel: It was when Harold Macmillan heard me yodel, over a dinner given by my then *beau,* Alec Douglas-Home, that he first fell in love with me.

Zzzzz: There was no time for sleep when John Selwyn Gummer was in the house, but that, as they say, is another story. *Mes lèvres son scellées,* as our French cousins might put it.

As told to
CRAIG BROWN

13

That Putin perfect 10-point plan in full

1. Bomb Syria
2. Create huge wave of refugees
3. Fill Europe up with migrants
4. Create huge demand for energy in Europe
5. Point out Middle East too unstable to provide energy, due to bombing by Putin
6. Suggest name of energy provider (Russia) who can help Europe with supplies
7. Make vast profit
8. Buy more bombs
9. Bomb Syria
10. You get the idea

Late News

YOUNG CONSERVATIVE IS REVEALED TO BE GHASTLY

On Other Pages
- Pope is a catholic **5**
- Bear "youngconservatives" in woods **6**

✗ EXCLUSIVE EYE POLL ✔

WHICH BULLIES DO YOU PREFER?

If there were an election tomorrow, would you prefer to be bullied by:

a) **Tatler Tories** threatening to blackmail you, film you having sex or to be really horrid to you in restaurants in the Kings Road?

b) **Corbynista trolls** threatening to shove pictures of dead babies through your letterbox or tweet that you are Blairite scum who deserves to die?

c) **Cybernats** threatening extreme physical violence and death to all "Judas traitor vermin" who voted the wrong way in the referendum?

d) **Lib Dems** who threaten to burst into tears because you didn't vote for them, although they realise that you are entitled to be disappointed with them after their mixed record during the coalition with the Conservatives?

Just tell us your bullying preference now – or we'll come round and kick your head in

---

Sarah Vain

It's all about me!

Poor old Helena Bonham Carter. Pictured by the cruel tabloids (see picture left), sporting hair that's not as fulsome as it used to be.

For Heaven's sake, let's not start laughing at people who, through no fault of their own, have to face up to the reality that they have "thinning" issues.

For many years, I myself have suffered the indignity of producing incredibly thin material and no matter how much I try to bulk it out, filling a page is always a struggle.

For some journalists, full, heavyweight articles come naturally, but for others like yours truly, every piece looks dull, grey and threadbare.

So, please, as you look again at the photo of Helena Bonham Carter *(see picture left again)*, do not mock the afflicted. That's my job and *(continued for most of rest of page...)*

Nursery Times

········· Friday, Once-upon-a-time ·········

WIZARD REVEALED AS 'PATHETIC FRAUD'

By Our Financial Staff **Nick Judy Garland**

THE most celebrated magician in Nurseryland, the Wizard of Ozbourne, was today exposed to be a complete charlatan.

Increasingly in recent years, the reputation of this almost legendary figure had been built up as an astonishingly clever and capable financial wizard, who had so brilliantly turned round the Oz economy that even the streets were paved with gold (or at least they looked gold, although they later turned out to be made only of yellow brick).

Wizard of Oborne

"George" Oz, as he was known, was admired and respected as one of the greatest masters of money ever known, who had solved the seemingly impossible riddle of how to balance the kingdom's books.

"I will make the debt disappear – just like that!" he said, waving his magic wand. "And within five years we will be in surplus."

Heidi-hi

But then, catastrophically, a small girl, only lately arrived in Oz, called Dorothy *(surely Heidi Allen MP? Ed)*, ventured into the Wizard's lair and pulled aside the curtain behind which the supposed financial mastermind was projecting an enormous larger-than-life image of himself.

What she revealed was a pathetic, frightened little figure who for years had been fooling the public with his talk of how he was going to make the Debt vanish.

But there behind him, visibly growing larger with every minute that passed, was the Debt, all £1.5 trillion of it.

Dorothy could scarcely believe what she was seeing.

Far from disappearing, the Debt was now twice as big as it had been when the Wizard took charge.

"Why, it's all smoke and mirrors," the little girl exclaimed.

"This so-called wizard is nothing more than a third-rate conjurer, who has been getting away with his cheap little tricks for years."

The Wizard of Ozbourne was unavailable for comment because he was dining with the Emperor of China whom he hoped would give him enough money to keep Oz going for a few more weeks.

On other pages

- Nurseryland Health Service (NHS) too bankrupt to give Tin Man a heart transplant **2**
- NHS says Scarecrow "doesn't qualify" for new brain **5**
- Cowardly Lion shot by Minnesota dentist – world outrage **10**
- Volume II of Charles Moore's highly-acclaimed biography of the Wicked Witch serialised **20-46**.

"Mavis, what's the password to turn on the toaster?"

HAWKEY.

BRITAIN DEVASTATED BY STORM ABI-NO-GALE

by Our Meteorological Staff **Clement Weather**

MILLIONS of Britons were left reeling yesterday by the failure of electricity to be cut off, trees to be felled in their thousands and roofs to be blown off their houses, as a result of "the worst storm in living memory".

For days, the Met Office had been warning the nation to stay indoors, preferably in their cellars, and to await the terrifying arrival of what they called Storm Abigail, under the new system of giving unusually violent weather events friendly-sounding names such as Tropical Storm Cheryl, Hurricane Michael Fish or Tornado Abi Titmuss. *(Is this right? Ed.)*

However, as the hours and days went by, the country remained unflattened, floodwaters failed to rise and traffic continued to flow normally without heavy goods vehicles being blown off the M25.

The Met Office remained unperturbed and downgraded Storm Abigail to Light Breeze Barbecue Summer.

But they then issued a fresh Disaster Alert as they forecast an even more powerful storm about to hit the Met Office, nicknamed Why Are We Paying You £220 Million A Year to Get Everything Wrong?

Dame Julia Slingo is 94.

I'm not wasting money on jigsaws. Here, put this potato back together

Moose

V&A Changes Mind Over Thatcher Collection

by Our Heritage Staff **Katie Priceless**

BRITAIN's leading storehouse of historical design and visual culture, the Queen Vic and Albert Square Museum in London, has dramatically reversed its earlier decision to reject the offer of personal memorabilia connected with the late Baroness Thatcher.

Having originally ruled that they wanted nothing to do with this "pile of tasteless, suburban tat, as worn by that ghastly right-wing harridan", they last night issued a new statement, declaring that "when it comes to the lady, the V&A is for turning".

Possibly as early as next year, the public can now look forward to an exhibition almost as exciting as the V&A's earlier sell-out blockbuster shows dedicated to the clothing and personal accessories of Mr David Bowie and Ms Kylie Minogue.

What you will see

- **one black handbag** slightly scuffed from hitting Geoffrey Howe over the head in 1983
- **another black handbag** historic provenance uncertain, but believed to have been carried by the late prime minister on the occasion of her famous "Rejoice, rejoice" speech after she had won a budget rebate from the EU
- **blue suit with matching blue scarf** worn by the future prime minister when addressing the East Finchley Conservative Association's annual bring-and-buy fundraising event in November 1961
- **three pairs of shiny shoes** (personally licked by Mr Parkinson)
- **one pearl-effect necklace** (gift of the Al-Yamamah Construction and Armaments Company)
- **one Betamax copy of Ronald Reagan's cinematic classic 'Bedtime for Bonzo'** in original cellophane.
- **one tin baked beans (unopened)** as used by Mrs Thatcher in TV election broadcast in 1977 to illustrate how Tories would bring down the cost of living
- **handwritten letter from Mr Charles Moore** asking if she would mind if he were to write her official three-volume biography, saying how marvellous she was.

All proceeds go to charity, namely the Charity for the Charmless Sons of Former Prime Ministers Called Mrs Thatcher.

Late News

Oxfam put in last-minute bid for Thatcher collection. Hundreds of pounds offered.

BILLION-POUND CHARITY 'SAVED HUNDREDS OF LIVES' BOTNEY TELLS MPS

by **Lentin Quetts**

"I AM proud of what we did," the £300,000-a-week arts chief of a multi-billion-pound charity Alan Botney told the Parliamentary Committee yesterday.

A startlingly uncharismatic figure with glasses and a stubbly beard, Botney was close to tears as he described the work of his fashionable charity, the BBC, supported by compulsory donations from members of the public.

"We were dealing with literally thousands of at-risk individuals," he told the MPs. "These people came to us looking for help and we were able to put them to work making cookery programmes and devising quiz shows."

MPs questioned why literally millions of pounds had been spent on providing taxis and expensive lunches for the "clients" – some were even sent abroad to film meerkats. "I am not ashamed of any of it," Botney told the committee. "If it had not been for the BBC, these people would have turned to crime and drug addiction."

Botney admitted that, inevitably, there were problems with some of the clients who "self-referred" to the charity. He instanced the case of a man codenamed "Big Mouth" who was provided with thousands of pounds and the use of fast cars, but who had assaulted his mentor when drunk. He was later dismissed.

"The media are to blame," Botney said. "We do not read about the hundreds of success stories."

DESPERATE SEARCH BEGINS AFTER PLANE CRASH

After the crash of a Russian Airliner over Sinai, all areas of Facebook are being scoured for any evidence of passengers' past lives.

"We must leave no stone unturned until we discover traces of the more attractive passengers smiling and posing with drinks," said a leading crash expert from ITV.

"Because if we don't do this, then people won't realise what a tragedy it is, and they might let it happen again."

"It's important to piece together the events leading up to the crash, particularly the events that involved women wearing bikinis on the beach at their resort hotel," said one crash expert from the Daily Telegraph.

"These discoveries are important, because it shows the passengers to be wealthy, happy and in no hurry to migrate to Europe. Therefore they did not deserve to die whilst transporting themselves to another country."

DEFINITIVE CRASH THEORY 'MAY TAKE SOME TIME'

Amateur crash investigators who logged on to Twitter in the weeks following the downing of the Russian passenger plane Flight KGL9268 say the confusion surrounding the crash means that, as yet, there's no definitive conspiracy theory for the disaster.

"Initial conspiracy theories saying Putin's security services planted the bomb to shore up support for stepping up Russia's military campaign in Syria have now been mostly discounted," said the well-respected conspiracy nutter @WinstonSmith6578.

"Besides, that was quickly shot down by an even more nutty theory that the plane was downed by the CIA to punish Putin for intervening in Syria," posted @911trutherr435.

"But in the end even this was considered not quite mad enough for the internet," said @mulderandscully4ever. "We're now thinking the plane never crashed. The footage you saw was faked on a sound stage in Vladivostok. Wake up sheeple, you're being played."

A theory proposed by the British government that the plane was brought down by ISIS terrorists who exploited shockingly lax security at Sharm El Sheikh Airport in order to plant a bomb in the luggage hold, was dismissed as far too sensible and completely plausible by the wider conspiracy community.

UNIVERSITY CHALLENGE

(Silly fiddly music plays)

Paxman: You all know the rules by now. Let's begin. What was the first civilisation to... Yes?

Student: You can't say 'civilisation'. That implies some people are less civilised than others, which is offensive towards people of different cultures.

Paxman: All right, fine. Which men were noted for their discovery, in 1926, of the structures underpinning...

Other student: I think you mean 'cis man'? Otherwise that's a microaggression...

Paxman: Alright, which 'cis men' were noted for their discovery of...

Third student: It's actually appropriating the discoveries of other groups to assume those two men were the only ones responsible. What about the women and other people of minority status who helped them?

Paxman: OK, let's try this. Which convicted murderer was also...

Students: Trigger warning!

Paxman: Right then. We'll go to a music round. Here's music by a classical composer. All I want to know is...

Yet another student: It's actually an act of class aggression to privilege classical music over other kinds.

Paxman: Right. I've had enough of this. You can all get out.

Students: Actually, this is our safe space, and we've decided to no-platform you.

(Students advance on Paxman. Silly fiddly music plays)

Downton Abbey Series 94

Next week's episode (ITV)

In the middle of dinner with Neville Chamberlain, Lady Cora and butler Carson are surprised when an alien bursts out of Lord Grantham's chest, showering the diners with blood and entrails.

"Oh really," says the Dowager Countess, "if I wanted something unpleasant to spoil my dinner, I would read Mr Ramsay Macdonald's Labour Party manifesto."

Lady Mary, however, is charmed by the newcomer at the table and remonstrates with her grandmother. "Times are changing, granny. Just because someone comes from a distant galaxy and looks a bit different, there's no need to be prejudiced against them. This is 1927, you know."

Kindly Lord Grantham then adopts the alien as his son and heir and appoints him as estate manager in charge of the pigs, hoping that one day he will marry magazine proprietor Lady Edith.

However, trouble starts when the alien goes on a killing spree, leaving a trail of half-eaten bodies below and above stairs.

When the police arrest Mr Bates for the murders it looks as if he will hang after all – instead of the real culprit, ie Julian Fellowes.

Eye rating: *At Downton no one can hear you ask the footman for more ice cream.*

"Very fetching"

"Even stronger than that, if possible..."

News in brief

Interest rates stay low

■ The Bank of England confirmed today that it would be keeping rates of interest in buying a house extremely low.

"Lots of young people are far too interested in buying a house," said a spokesman, "and we've got to make it clear that there's just no way it's going to happen for them. So these measures are purposely designed to keep prices nice and high, in the hope that young people will get the message and that any interest they might have had will fade away. Maybe they can develop an interest in something else, like getting that new phone they've always wanted or going travelling next summer?"

Pensions 'stark warning'

■ A new report has warned that people taking out large sums of money from their pension pot from age 55 could have to face up to ten years of really uncomfortable Sunday lunches with their children.

"Our figures suggest that the majority of selfish offspring will simply not understand what the hell Mum and Dad are doing behaving like overgrown children, taking holidays with money that could have been spent giving their grandchildren a decent education," said the report's author.

"Most of this will manifest itself in passive aggressive silence over the roast beef, but at any stage this could become a full-on fight as their daughter-in-law blurts out, 'So you're just going to spend all of John's inheritance are you, you selfish bastards?' and starts crying *(cont. p94)*

POETRY CORNER

Lines on the birthday of Twitter

So. Twitter,
You are ten
Years old.

I was going
To wish you
A very Happy
Birthday.

But then thought
I should say
Something more
In the spirit of
Twitter, instead.

So I hope you
Get cancer
And die.

> E.J. Troll (17½ characters)

In Memoriam Sir George Martin, record producer

So. Farewell
Then George Martin,
You were known as
"The Fifth Beatle".

Apparently, without
Your genius, we
Might never have
Heard of the
Fab Four.

Now you have gone
To join John and
The other George
(but not Paul or Ringo).

Will there be
Heavenly music?
Perhaps "Elysian
Fields Forever",
As arranged for
Three harps by
St George.

> E. Ray Connolly
> (17½ articles this week)

PS. In Memoriam Ray Tomlinson, internet pioneer

So. Farewell
Then Ray Tomlinson,
Yes, you invented
Email.

You gave new life
To the @ sign.
Now you are
@peace.

> E.J. Thribb
> (17½ spam emails per second)

THAT PARIS LEADER IN FULL

Allons, Enfants!

A defiant nation... we stand together... shoulder to shoulder... Strong links... Verdun... Mons... Entente... Nous sommes Paris... aux armes... Defiant... Eiffel Tower lit up... Powerful symbol... Lessons must be learned... French security blunders... Not so good... Hollande... empty gesture... France in crisis... National Front... open borders... panic on streets... history of defeats... Waterloo... Vichy... cheese-eating surrender monkeys... they had it coming to them... Altogether, God Save Our Gracious Queen.

"You hate music, football, eating out and drinking? Might as well kill yourself now"

LA MARSEILLAISE

A Handy Gnome Guide To Those Lyrics In Full

Da da da da de la patrie

Le da da da da est arrivé

Something something de la tyrannie

Da da da da da la di da

Mumble mumble mumble mumble mumble mumble

(This bit's a bit low, isn't it?)

AUX ARMES, OOH LA LA!!!

Formez vos blah blah blah blah

MARCHONS! MARCHONS!

La da da da

Dee dum dee dee dee da

(CHEERS AND APPLAUSE)

PARIS ONLINE UPDATE

Social media 'vital for spreading misinformation'

News organisations say the Paris terrorists attacks have revealed the important role that social media such as Facebook and Twitter now play in the rapid spread of misinformation as a disaster unfolds.

"Whereas old media sadly had to rely on facts checked and cross-checked by trained reporters, new media has no such constraints. Within minutes of the attack taking place, it is already awash with misinformation," agreed all media observers.

"From sharing fake photos to stoking up levels of panic, people are increasingly turning to Twitter and Facebook as the most trusted source for wild speculation and misinformation.

"In a rapidly changing media environment where facts are increasingly shunned, old media simply can no longer compete with the sheer speed of misinformation social media offers its millions of users."

Twitter fury

There was widespread fury on Twitter as to which was the most appropriate hashtag to use to show you cared the most about the Paris atrocity.

"Whilst some users opted for *#prayforparis*, others insisted they cared more about the dead by using *#jesuisparis*, others insisted it had to be *#standwithparis*, whilst others said the only way to show you cared more than everyone else was to use the hashtag *#icaremorethaneveryoneelse*.

Everyone on Twitter agreed it was vitally important they decided which Paris hashtag was the most appropriate one, as revealing their feelings in the wake of the tragedy was the most important thing.

God admits doubts about Archbishop Welby

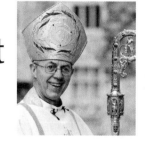

by Our Religious Correspondent
A. Men

A very senior figure in the Church of England, God, has shocked the faithful by confessing that "sometimes I don't believe in Welby".

The Almighty apparently made his comments following the Archbishop's revelation that he had suffered a crisis of faith after the events in Paris.

Said God, "What I find difficult to believe is that the Archbishop has only just noticed that terrible things happen in the world and that they have done throughout history. Having some sort of answer to this has traditionally been considered over the centuries as part of the Archbishop's job.

"I have to say, my faith in the whole Church of England has been seriously undermined."

Kay Burley's Animals of the Paris Bombing

Dog with sadness in his eyes

Defiant kitten refusing to be scared

Radicalised hamster

Silly bird

CAMERON DECLARES WAR ON ISIS

The plan is to degrade their military capability until it's impossible for them to fight

Like you did with us

Cameron announces thousands of new announcements

by Our Security Staff
Phil Frontpage

In the wake of the Paris massacres which have shocked the entire world, Prime Minister David Cameron last night hit back at the terrorist menace by announcing that he would be making thousands of new announcements every day until the ISIS threat was finally eliminated.

The first tranche of new announcements included:

● Recruiting 1900 cyber-spies to hack into Jihadi communications networks, to be operative by 2025 at the latest.

● Increasing the SAS budget by £10 billion to ensure that every street in Britain is patrolled by highly-trained Special Forces marksmen by 2035.

● Setting up a National Decoding Centre at GCHQ to train hundreds more computer experts in how to decipher Facebook messages and secret Jihadi emojis by 2045.

● Putting 10,000 troops on the streets of London by yesterday.

● Investing millions of pounds in two new Typhoon squadrons, 24 new F35 fighter planes, 20 new Protector drones, nine Boeing P8 maritime patrol aircraft and a partridge in a pear tree – all to come on stream by 2094.

Tomorrow, Mr Cameron is expected to come up with thousands more shock responses to whatever it is that has got into the news that morning, such as his plan to shown Britain's solidarity with Europe by holding a referendum on whether we should leave it.

Coalition of the Willy

OBAMA 'COALITION OF THE WILLING'

by Our Defence Staff **Jess Wee-Can**

SPEAKING at the G20 summit in Turkey, President Obama said he was close to achieving a coalition of the willing to let Putin do whatever he wants in Syria.

"Country after country is telling me now is the time for inaction and prevarication in the face of this terrible threat," President Obama told reporters.

"And as Putin is the only one willing to do anything, I say hell, yeah, you go for it, Vlad."

Obama also praised French airstrikes on ISIS in the wake of the attack.

"We all remember how effective in the wake of 9/11 just randomly bombing stuff for the sake of it is, and I have no doubt that France's bombing will be just as effective as ours was in bringing peace and stability to the region."

THE TIMES OF LONDON

November 27 1941

In common with other newspapers, we may have given the impression that the Soviet Union was in some way an evil, despotic tyranny dedicated to suppressing freedom around the world.

And that furthermore its leader, Vladimir Stalin, ruled with an iron fist and could not be trusted by the Western Allies under any circumstances.

We now realise, in the light of recent events, that nothing could be further from the truth and that Uncle Vlad, the leader of our oldest friend the Soviet Union, is an enlightened torch-bearer for freedom against an evil, despotic tyranny which wants to suppress freedom even more than he does, which he doesn't.

We apologise for any confusion our previous coverage of Joseph Putin may have caused and would like to reassure readers that he is a thoroughly good egg (at the time of writing).

Corbyn Unhappy About 'Shoot To Foot' Policy

by Our Political Staff
Michael White Flag

LABOUR leader Jeremy Corbyn yesterday buckled under a light grilling in the House of Commons, when he was asked whether he was in favour of a "Shoot To Foot" policy.

This would mean that at the first sign of trouble the Labour leader would have to shoot himself in the foot, without any hesitation.

Mr Corbyn was pressed on whether he would pull the trigger if necessary on his own foot, and immediately replied, "Yes, I mean no... Ouch! Call an ambulance!"

The "Shoot To Foot" policy dates back to the Seventies, when under the then leader Michael "Shoot To" Foot, Labour believed that leaders of the party should at all times respond to events by immediately saying something unpopular and inappropriate. They would thereby alienate even those voters who were trying to like them, and would make absolutely certain that there was no danger of the party ever getting elected for another couple of decades.

DEFINING MOMENT AS BRITAIN EXTENDS WAR A LITTLE BIT

by Our Diplomacy Staff Tommy Hawk

IN extraordinary scenes in parliament, British MPs last night took the most important decision since the country went to war with Hitler in 1939.

After impassioned speeches on both sides, the House decided to authorise the RAF to carry on doing what it had been doing anyway, except up the road a bit.

This momentous resolution takes Britain into uncharted waters, drawing a line in the sand just a couple of hundred yards further away and marks an unprecedented extension of the war.

Britain is now fully committed to continuing to bomb from the air a bit but not, of course, doing anything silly like putting troops on the ground where they might win or get killed.

The Prime Minister pointed out that historically the fight against fascism has always been won from the air and from as far away as possible, without taking any risks, so it was vitally important to commit a couple of extra planes to win the most important war, one that threatens our very civilisation.

LABOUR GOES TO WAR WITH ITSELF

We shall fight them on the benches

We shall never surrender

It's the beginning of the end!

HILARY BENN MP

IN

OUT

BERNIG

"These are all death threats from various pacifists"

LEN McCLUSKEY OPPOSES SYRIA BOMBING

Finally, some strikes that I don't support

'Syria – it couldn't be simpler' says Cameron

Exclusive to Private Eye – the Prime Minister explains where everyone stands in the current Middle East crisis

It's all perfectly straightforward.

Britain is against Daesh.

Daesh is against Assad.

Britain is also against Assad.

But Russia is for Assad.

And Iran is for Assad.

But Turkey is against Assad.

And Turkey is also against Daesh.

But now Russia is against Turkey.

And the Americans are for Turkey.

The Americans are also for the Kurds.

But Turkey is against the Kurds.

Iran is against the Kurds, also against Turkey and Daesh, and against the Saudis.

The Saudis are against Assad, but they and the Qataris are also thought to be behind al Qaeda in Syria, whom I have not mentioned yet, but they are against Daesh and the Kurds.

Britain is against al Qaeda, but for the Saudis and the Qataris, who are also against Assad.

So, as you can see, Britain has only one option to bring peace to Syria. And that is to send in some old RAF planes to fire British-made smart missiles at selected targets – ie not very smart British-made jihadis. (Will this do? D.C.)

This year's top ten names for missiles

Most popular	Least popular
1. Brimstone	**6.** Wendy
2. Buttkicker	**7.** Jeremy
3. Shitstorm	**8.** Gandhi
4. GutRipper	**9.** Adele
5. Arseblaster	**10.** Peregrine Worsthorne

STORM DESMOND SWEEPS BRITAIN

by Our Met Staff Del Huge

BRITAIN was swamped this week by a hurricane of filth pouring into the nation's high streets as so-called "Dirty" Desmond hit the country with a vengeance.

Millions of copies of the Daily Express, the Daily Star, and Asian Babes flooded newsagents and supermarkets, leaving members of the public "drowning in muck".

Said one resident, "We are up to our necks in Readers' Wives and MegaBoobs, thanks to Desmond."

There was no stopping the rising tide of sleaze, and the situation was made worse by the simultaneous deluge of smut from televisions in people's living rooms which rapidly filled up with overflowing torrents of Television X and Red Hot TV.

As the army was sent in to rescue members of the public, questions were being asked in parliament as to why there were no adequate defences against Desmond and why Desmond was allowed to burst through all the barriers and submerge the entire United Kingdom in rank streams of obnoxious *(We get the idea. Ed.)*

Nursery Times

Friday, Once-upon-a-time

ANOTHER TRIUMPH FOR THE WIZARD OF OZBORNE

by Con Trickster

ALL Oz was in awe last night at the latest brilliant feat of magic by the legendary Wizard of Ozborne.

For weeks, the Munchkins had been singing very rude songs about the Wizard, protesting that he was planning to take millions of pounds from the "poorest and littlest" people in the land.

Their chief spokesperson, Dorothy, had been leading mass protests against the Wizard's evil "tax credit" scheme – which was so fiendishly complex that no one understood it; not even the Wizard himself.

Hey Pesto!

But at the last minute, just when it looked as if the Wizard was about to be exposed as the most heartless villain in the history of Oz, he came up with an astonishing conjuring trick that had the whole country gasping in amazement.

In front of the entire nation, the Wizard smiled a crafty smile and produced out of his hat a huge pile of money, larger than anyone in Oz had ever seen.

"Look," cried the Wizard, "here is £27 billion, which I have managed to produce out of thin air."

As everyone reeled back in wonder, the Wizard went on, "And every penny of this I will then give to all those poor little people who would otherwise have starved to death."

The Tin Man wept openly at such a brilliant feat of prestidigitation. "I didn't think he had a heart," said the Tin Person.

The Scarecrow too joined in, "I didn't think he had a brain."

As for the Cowardly Lion, he said, "I didn't think he had the courage to scrap his ridiculous plan – but now he has done the bravest thing ever seen in Oz."

And the three of them joined hands with Dorothy to march off down the Yellow Brick Road, singing "Ding dong, the Wicked Tax Credit Scheme is dead".

Daily Mail

COMMENT

Hats on to Kate!

WHAT a great example the Duchess of Cambridge has set the nation.

While others moan about the tax credits they're losing, thrifty Kate cleverly recycled an old tiara, and wore it at a state banquet.

That's recycling the Royal way! Her make-do-and-mend attitude shames the so-called hard-working poor, hanging around on street corners, waiting for handouts so that they can buy new baseball caps!

Well done, Kate! Thank goodness someone in this country is taking austerity seriously!

There's a wise head on those young shoulders and it's got an old tiara on it.

Han-z-z-zard

HOUSE OF LORDS

Motion To Ask Her Majesty's Government To Delay In Order To Give Further Thought To The Issuance Of A Statutory Instrument Enacting Its Heartless Proposal To Cut The Tax Benefits Of Millions Of Hard-Working Families Just Before Christmas

Baroness Queen of Quango *(Very Cross Bencher)*: I wish to move a non-fatal motion against this totally outrageous example of the Tories' callous targeting of the poorest and most vulnerable in our society, including millions of toddlers who will have to spend this Christmas with no shoes and no food on the table except a bag of crisps, which will only increase the problem of childhood obesity, about which I have addressed this House on many occasions.

Lord Statelyhome *(Con)*: This is the gravest constitutional crisis faced by our country since the late Mr Lloyd George shamelessly abused his position as the elected chancellor of the day by forcing through a disgraceful budget which provided for giving huge quantities of public money to the lower classes, namely an old-age pension of 9d a week, which we hard-working landowners could ill afford. All I can say, 114 years later, after his notorious "People's Budget", is plus ça change, plus c'est la même chose – except that, of course, this time it's the other way round.

Lord Handintill *(Con)*: On behalf of many other noble Lords, I would like to point out that there are far more worthy recipients of public money than the so-called starving toddlers referred to by the noble Baroness – namely, all those of us in this Chamber, who need to be properly rewarded for the time and effort we put into coming to this place every day to claim our expenses and to offer our services to those lobbying companies who are rightly happy to remunerate us for advice on how to persuade ministers to see the wisdom of their case. Can I, at this point, just mention the very powerful arguments that can be put forward by my friends in the soft-drink industry that the small amounts of sugar contained in their products pose no threat whatsoever to children's health.

Baroness Buggins of Turn *(Lib Dem)*: As the former Deputy Leader of the Snoresbury and Dullsworth Borough, when that community still enjoyed the benefit of being served by Liberal councillors, I would like to express the anger and disgust of my 250 Lib Dem colleagues in this House that our views have been ignored and brushed aside in a way which makes a total mockery of democracy by outvoting our Fatal Motion which, if it had been passed, would have brought down this unelected Tory government and replaced it with one representing the true voice and interests of the British people, namely the Liberal Aristocratic Party which...

(At this point the Chamber emptied as Peers rushed off to give press or television interviews explaining what a superb example this debate had been of why we need an Upper Chamber that can correct the mistakes of idiots like George Osborne)

"They're William Morris dancers"

Mrs Angela Merkel An Apology

IN RECENT months I may have given the impression that, as German Chancellor, I was in some way only too happy to welcome a million immigrants from the Middle East to live and work in Germany.

I may have reinforced this impression by saying on a number of occasions that Germany wishes to lead the world in showing humanity and compassion for all these pitiful and tragic refugees, forced to flee from a dreadful crisis not in any way of their own making (not least because this would demonstrate that modern Germany is now a very different country from what it was during certain rather unfortunate periods in the past).

I now, however, realise that there was not a scintilla of truth or common sense in any of the above.

I further accept that the current levels of immigration into Germany are putting an intolerable strain not only on our resources but also on the patience and goodwill of the German people who, despite being in every way different from those responsible for certain regrettable historic events in the past, are nonetheless quite rightly getting seriously fed up with the sight of all these foreigners who think that they can just come into Germany and enjoy all the benefits of living in a well-ordered, well-run and prosperous economy.

It is time for Germany to close its borders, and anyone who says otherwise is simply giving way to thoughtless sentimentality which should never be allowed to cloud the judgement of a hard-headed pragmatic Chancellor who is hoping to get re-elected again in the near future.

I apologise to voters for any confusion that this misunderstanding may have caused and hope that when they enter the polling booth they will do the right thing.

And fröhliche Weihnachten to you all!

"...I'm afraid the price of oil is now almost as cheap as the price of human life, Your Majesty"

From The Message Boards

Members of the online community respond to the major issues of the day...

Sperm shortage

Please, please join my Facebook group SPLASH OUT FOR CHRISTMAS! The National Sperm Bank is desperately short of sperm, yet unofficial unregulated donors are producing dozens of children, risking disease and distress as well as the obvious consequences for local gene pools. One man has fathered more than 50 kids in the Middlesbrough area, as well as eight of his own! – **Supermum**

send him to norfolk he will broaden there jean pool ☺ #itfc – **tractor boy**

Love it, Supermum! My husband and I are in our sixties and have many hobbies, including real ale, non-league football, swinging and dogging. We had a fundraising event with the same slogan as yours, but it was a different sort of sperm donation! The local paper sent a photographer and he ended up joining in! We raised £3,000 for Help the Heroes and old people's charities. – **Gilfy Gracie**

Greetings and facilitations! I with respects of myself am a most honorable and wealthy gentle man from Nigeria and my most given name is Adebamgbe, meaning Royalty Dwells With Me. I am in position to offer most exellent and virile manly royal sperm's for English Lady's by postal return. I am also offer Personal Intimate Transaction service at my apartment in Royal Kennington during my regular Business Visit's to London Town. Furthurance of term's on application. – **The Honorable Adebamgbe Okonkwo**

iv nocked up 147 bird's this year in walsall. 15.283cm cock. no charge no string's. pm 4 detail's – **The Sperminator**

is it juss spurm they want or is it urin as wel? – **colin**

I'm sure there are thousands of women desperate to receive the "spurm" and "urin" of a socially inadequate chip-guzzling unemployed illiterate virgin who lives with his mother. Please send as much as you can, asap. Future generations will be in your eternal debt. – **Jon**

no worry's jon but i actially live with my nan not mum – **colin**

Killed herself when she saw you as a baby, did she? – **Jon**

no she dyed wen i was 10 she told me to be strong and look after nan – **colin**

That worked out well then. – **Jon**

thank's jon i do my best mery crismas to u and ur famly – **colin**

Yet another failing bank subsidised by the taxpayer. Apparently a third of its donors some from abroad. – **Brown out**

thats a long way to cum! lolz – **Hunny pot**

not bein funny but imagin gettin a muslim baby in a burker instead of a little princess romper? – **Hayley 321**

The EYE's New Year Charity Appeal

Poor Saudi Arabia is currently running a huge deficit due to a calamitous fall in oil prices which is not its fault and has left it desperately short of money.

Could you help in this tragic humanitarian crisis and give your money to Saudi Arabia in its hour of greed?

£5 Will buy a small stone to throw at adulterous women

£10 Will buy a lash to whip homosexuals

£100 Will buy a sword for beheading opponents of the ruling family

£1,000 Will help fund Islamic terrorism throughout the whole Middle East region

£5,000 million Will buy a diamond-encrusted solid gold private jet in which to fly to New York to ask for a loan

Controversy threatens Sparts Personality of the Year

by Our Media Staff **Clare Boring**

The prestigious Sparts Personality of the Year award, celebrating the greatest spartsman or spartswoman or spartstransgenderperson of 2015, was in chaos last night over objections to the comments of one of the leading contenders.

Dave Spart, who was the favourite to win in his role as Neasden convenor of the Stop the War Against the Stop the War Coalition Coalition, has angered members of the voting public after making a series of ill-advised comments about how he would like to "totally deselect all the sickening neo-Blairites with their proto-fascist agenda to make the Labour Party electable".

Mr Spart claims his remarks were taken out of context and were part of a 70,000-word essay he wrote for the New Spartsman, entitled *Is Corbyn Sufficiently Corbynite?*. Following his remarks, there were calls for him to be deselected from the shortlist. However, he was defended by Ken Leninspart, a previous winner of the award, who said, "Anyone who criticises Dave Spart is a lunatic, they must be mentally ill, no offence and no apology".

Dave Spart was also supported by the rest of the shortlist, including Corbynist Diane Abbspart, Stalinist Seumas Spart, Maoist John McSpart and Gallowayist George Gallowspart.

However, such has been the outcry over Dave Spart's supposedly offensive remarks that there are now worries that the award may be given to a compromise candidate, who is not really a true spartsman, but who ticks all the boxes of the politically correct competition and would be acceptable to the sparting community, ie Vladimir Putin.

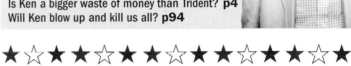

"So my New Year's resolution this year is to stop saying 'so' at the start of every sentence"

Tyson Fury
HIS CONTROVERSIAL STATEMENT

" I'd like to thank Barbara Slater, Head of BBC Sport, for including me on the shortlist for Sports Personality of The Year, as she's really fit and scrubs up well... unless she's a Lesbo, in which case she should burn in hell. No offence, darling, and if you get the hump then I'll be forced to give you a slap, you old minger. "

ISIS COMES OUT FOR TRUMP

by Our Election Staff **G. Hadd**

The front runner for the Republican Party presidential candidate received an unexpected boost yesterday from an unlikely quarter.

A spokesman for the caliphate issued a statement endorsing Mr Trump, saying that he had won an unofficial primary in the state of Syria and recorded an astonishing 99 percent of the vote.

The spokesman said, "Trump speaks to our people. He is a gun-crazed, reactionary, misogynistic, homophobic, hate-filled fanatic.

"He's our kind of guy. You gotta love him. Go Trump!" He continued, "We see eye to eye on many key issues, including bringing about the end of the world. It's what you guys call the last Trump!!"

THAT LABOUR DEFENCE POLICY IN FULL

1 If under attack, question enemy's mental health (particularly if he's had mental health problems).
2 When reminded they have mental health problems tell them to "get over it".
3 When told your remarks are indefensible, defend them.
4 When asked for an apology, refuse, unless the request comes from your own leader, who's sobbing and saying he's in enough trouble as it is.
5 Tweet an apology.
6 Go on television and attack your opponent again.
7 Repeat 6.
8 Say "If anyone was offended, then I apologise to those pathetic, depressed lunatics who can't take a joke".
9 Er...
10 That's it.

ON OTHER PAGES
Should Ken be decommissioned? **p2**
Is Ken too dangerous for a civilised society? **p3**
Is Ken a bigger waste of money than Trident? **p4**
Will Ken blow up and kill us all? **p94**

★☆★☆★☆★☆★☆★☆★

ALL-PURPOSE, READY-TO-GO 'AMERICAN SHOOTING' ARTICLE

America was reeling today from the latest shooting outrage in the sleepy town of *(insert name here)* in the state of *(insert name here)* when a gunman/gunmen went on the rampage, killing *(insert number here)* innocent victims at the school/hospital/church. Americans reacted in horror at the worst shooting since *(insert last shooting venue here)*, and an ashen-faced President Obama announced "something must be done about gun control/there must be a change in attitude to guns/this is a wake-up call for America/oh shit, I give up". The National Rifle Association insisted this was yet another isolated incident and had the victims in the school/hospital/church been armed themselves, then there would have been fewer casualties. Neighbours said the gunman/gunmen was/were quiet/unassuming/polite and kept themselves to themselves/did post some rather unnerving things on Facebook. *Continued for ever...*

"Of course, if you're takin' down a school, you'll be needing this..."

'We have saved the planet' agree world leaders

by Our Climate Change Staff
Dee Carbonise

There were standing ovations all round in Paris last night, as 194 world leaders applauded themselves on having agreed on what they all agreed was the most historic agreement ever agreed in the entire history of the world.

The cheers which went up as the French chairman, Monsieur Tedius, read out the final text on which they had all agreed could be heard all the way to the Eiffel Tower.

The final text of the agreement came after 94 days and nights of tense negotiation between 94,000 delegates working around the clock to secure what was being described last night as "the end of the fossil era and day one of the brave new world of tomorrow".

That historic text in full

1. We are all agreed that this is an absolutely historic agreement.

2. We are all agreed that it is vital for the survival of the planet that we should limit rise in world temperatures to 2 degrees or possibly 1.5 degrees or preferably to several degrees below freezing point.

3. We are all agreed that, in order to do this, all the fossil fuels which currently provide 94 percent of the world's energy should be discontinued immediately, or as soon as possible.

4. We are all agreed that every country should produce its own plan for how this is to be achieved, which will be reviewed by themselves every five years from now until the year 2100, to ensure that everyone is doing their best to meet the targets that they themselves have set.

5. We are all agreed that it is very important that all countries should make the greatest possible effort to achieve whatever it is that they have said they hope to do, whether they are a rich country like the USA, or even richer countries like China or India, unless there are special circumstances which justify them doing nothing at all, as in the case of, for example, the USA, China and India.

6. We are all agreed that this agreement is not legally binding, but that we will tell everybody that it is.

7. Er...

8. We are all agreed that that is it.

"So you see, it's vital that we go back to pub lunches and stop dropping acid"

The Daily Terrorgraph

How do we stop this sick propaganda?

by The Terrograph's Terror Staff **G. Hardy Junior**

ARE you scared? You should be!

Somehow Isis are spreading their message far and wide into all corners of the British media, with editors seemingly powerless to stop them using newspapers as a publicity tool to whip up fear and panic in the population.

© All British newspapers.

Is there any way that we can react to a video coolly and calmly, without doing exactly what they want us to do, which is to put an enormous terrifying still from it on the front page?

No.

ISLAMIC STATE EXECUTIONS – CAMERON SENDS IN THE BOMBERS

by Our Middle East Staff **Ed Less**

IN a dramatic response to news of a series of grotesque executions, the British Prime Minister has ordered a swift and ruthless reaction.

"They are going to pay for this," promised Mr Cameron, as he finalised yet another multi-billion-pound deal to provide military aircraft to the Islamic state of Saudi Arabia.

"We can't let them get away with this atrocity without selling them some more arms. After all, they're going to need them now that they've provoked the Third World War with Iran."

The Prime Minister continued, "Our message is clear. The Saudis have executed a lot of people, but then our friends the Iranians have executed even more than them. So perhaps we could sell arms to Iran as well. After all, they're going to need them now that they're fighting the Third World War with Saudi Arabia. One thing's for sure, British firms are going to make a killing."

SHOCKING NEW VIDEO RELEASED

by **Phil Boots**

THERE was widespread outrage after a new 30-second video surfaced, featuring a man identified only as "Jihardup John".

In the video broadcast straight after Coronation Street, "Jihardup John" is shown engaging in a brutal, violent act of beating a car – a senseless act that every civilised nation decided in 1982 wasn't funny any more.

Relatives later identified the man in the video as "John", a member of the extremist Monty Python Group, known to have been active in the 1960s.

In a bizarre rant released on his YouTube channel, "John" defended the video which has so sickened so many comedy lovers, insisting he found the script really "tickled his money bone", and adding "Praise be to Specsavers, who have written me an enormous cheque".

Friends of "John" say since fleeing Britain for the desert climate of California, he had become divorced from both reality and half a dozen blondes with extremely good lawyers.

Who's Who in 'Pwhoar and Sleaze'?

IT'S THE latest sexed-up epic drama that's got the nation gripped. Over a thousand pages long if you read all the newspapers, this sprawling masterpiece of love and loss (of trousers and dignity) has become an instant classic. Here's a guide to the characters, for those who haven't managed to keep up with this complex saga of family intrigue...

The Honourable Simon Danczuk – he's the scheming lothario, drunk, drug-user and moderate Labour MP, famous for his campaigning stand against paedophiles and Jeremy Corbyn.

Mrs Sonia Danczukova the First – 10 years his junior, she's the vengeful first ex-wife, who accuses him of harming their children through bad publicity, then sells her graphic story the next day to the Mail on Sunday.

Mrs Karenina Danczukova the Second – 17 years his junior, she's the slightly less vengeful second ex-wife, who in between tweeting pictures of her breasts, vengefully points out how vengeful Danczuk's other

exes are. She accuses the first Mrs Danczukova of being a lady of ill-repute and then tweets her breasts again for luck.

Councillor Clara Legova – 17 years his junior, she's the Labour politician who stands by her man in photographs, until another even younger woman comes along and she dumps him by tweet, interrupting Danczuk's flow of sexts to... (see below)

Sophena Dominyatriks – she's the 17-year-old ingénue who runs an online spanking agency and who lures the naïve, unsuspecting 48-year-old into sending inappropriate messages which she can then sell to the press, who are quite happy to print anything as ammunition in the great Circulation War, irrespective of casualties.

**DON'T MISS!
NEW EPISODES EVERY DAY!**
Eye rating. no one comes out of this very well.

THIS WEEK

TUPPENCE MIDDLETON

You do a lot of spooning in the BBC's "Phwoar and Peace", don't you?

I think what Andrew Davies has done is bring out the spooning that is implied in the text.

So you don't mind getting your spoons out?

If the part demands it, and the spooning is not gratuitous, then I think it is artistically valid, yes.

What about the infamous dining table spoon scene?

There is *more* to my career than just spooning. For instance, in "Dickensian", where I play Miss Haversham, she doesn't really get to do any spooning at all.

(silence)

Going back to "Phwoar and Peace", will there be more spooning with your brother? Now that he's had his leg blown off, he'll have a problem getting it over...

(silence)

Aren't you going to ask me if anything amusing has ever happened to me in relation to a spoon?

No. Now about "Phwoar and Peace"... *(continues)*

NEXT WEEK: *Tuppence Middleton, "Me And My Tuppence".*

How the TV version isn't nearly as good as the book I've never read

by All Hacks

LET me confess – I've never actually managed to get through the 7,832 pages of Leonardo da Tolstoy's epic saga *War and Peace*.

But I read enough to know that this TV adaptation which everyone's talking about can never capture the scale, the grandeur, the complexity and the insights into the human condition of the immortal masterpiece that was too boring to finish.

© *All newspapers*

OSCARS RACE ROW

The Academy has hit fresh controversy with its list of all-time best films, as chosen by its members. The list described by critics as "unrepresentative" of the total canon of filmography is given in full below:

SNOW WHITE

WHITE CHRISTMAS

MAN IN A WHITE SUIT

MR WHITE GOES TO WASHINGTON

THE WHITE STUFF

PALE RIDER

HEAVEN CAN WHITE

MEN NOT IN BLACK

(We get the idea. Ed)

More discrimination at Oscars

by Our Hollywood Correspondent
Walter White

THERE was outrage in the film world that despite *The Revenant*'s twelve Oscar noms, including Best Picture and Best Actor, there was no nomination for the much-lauded performance of Leonardo DiCaprio's co-star, Mr G. Bear.

"As usual, this is Hollywood yet again totally overlooking performers of colour," said Mr Grizzly Bear, speaking from his Bel Air cave.

"You just know if I was a white bear, I would have been nominated for Best Supporting Actor, but as I am a 'bear of colour', I don't stand a chance.

"Bears of my colour have long been the subject of discrimination in this town. And it's statistically proven that brown bears in the US get shot just for minding their own business, far more than white bears.

"It's like the Academy members don't see me, which is probably because I'm CGI."

"...an extra five pence for the bag, I'm afraid"

25

PM — TOWER BLOCKS TO BLAME FOR POVERTY

APOLOGY
Bank robbers 'turn out not to be very nice men'

IT WAS revealed today after months of investigation that the men who broke into the Hatton Gardens Safe Deposit are not, in fact, lovable old codgers who couldn't help being lured back for one more job, but a load of thoroughly nasty criminals who have threatened people with guns, doused guards in petrol, plotted to torture and kill people and stolen vast quantities of money.

We realise now that we may have inadvertently aided the former impression with our headlines since the robbery, which included "Diamond-edged geezers whose brilliant raid left bozo coppers clueless", "Silver heroes tunnel their way into a nation's hearts" and "Shame on you, Ma'am, for not honouring these old-fashioned British entrepreneurs with knighthoods".

We now recognise that it was grossly irresponsible to lionise these men and, now the trial is over and the details of their other crimes can be made public, we have corrected this with our new coverage, notably with stories headlined "Lock up scumbag grandads and throw away the key" and "Why haven't they been done for treason yet, Ma'am?"

ON OTHER PAGES
• Why all Britain loves a good old-fashioned crime caper
• Profile: the wily cockneys who cocked a snook at the super-rich
• What would YOU do with all that lovely wonga?

"*Of course you can have some help from the Bank of Mum and Dad, just as soon as we've had a word with the Bank of Grandma and Grandad*"

What should Jeremy Corbyn's nameless cat be called?
YOU DECIDE

1 Chairman Miaow
2 Fidel Cattro
3 Kit-il-Jong
4 Marxmaduke
5 Tariq Ali Cat
6 Vladimir Pusstin
7 The Proletaricat
8 Paws Four
9 Communist Purrty (*This is terrible. Ed.*)
10 Moggy Thatcher (*You're fired. Ed.*)

Jeremy Corbyn WRITES

HELLO! It's me again. You know, there's been a lot of talk in the right-wing media about my policy on Trident. That in trying to please everyone, I've created a policy which is, quite frankly, bonkers.

Well, here's a surprise, right-wing British media, nothing could be further from the truth. In fact, it's the most sensible policy there is!

I've consulted widely amongst the nicer members of our party, and I've discovered that while everyone I know agrees the armed forces are a good thing to have, for saluting statues, playing the theme from the "Dam Busters", remembering how awful wars are, etc… by far the most controversial parts of the armed forces are the bits that kill people. It's true! If ever there's a negative story about the army, you can bet there's a bullet, or a bomb, or a tank at the bottom of it.

So with that in mind, I've considered those options that would make the army slightly more palatable to the Labour members I like. For example, here's a thought… should we lose the submarines and keep the warheads? Sensible, you might think. Well I've been told (informally) that submarines are essential to stop sailors from drowning when they go underwater. This is against my principles, as I'm a firm opponent of needless casualties. Tricky!

So, the only logical thing to do is keep the subs and lose the warheads. Not only does that make our submarines less aggressively militaristic (a very good thing), it also creates platforms for tired seagulls to rest on. Sorted!

Cheerio!

 Dave Snooty AND HIS NEEDY PALS

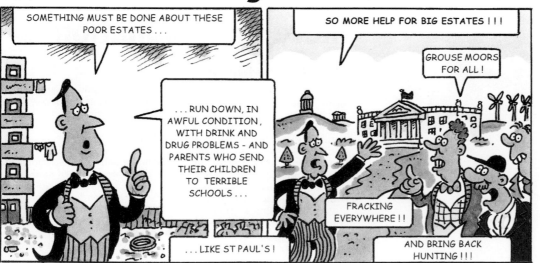

SOMETHING MUST BE DONE ABOUT THESE POOR ESTATES …

…RUN DOWN, IN AWFUL CONDITION, WITH DRINK AND DRUG PROBLEMS - AND PARENTS WHO SEND THEIR CHILDREN TO TERRIBLE SCHOOLS …

…LIKE ST PAUL'S !

SO MORE HELP FOR BIG ESTATES ! ! !

GROUSE MOORS FOR ALL !

FRACKING EVERYWHERE ! !

AND BRING BACK HUNTING ! ! !

LOST CITY OF KESWICK 'FOUND'

by Our North East Correspondent
Tori Rential

DIVERS say they believe they have located the fabled lost city of Keswick, thought to have once existed above ground in Cumbria.

"This involved extremely deep dives to hundreds of metres below sea level in the Lake District," the scientists leading the expedition told reporters. "We realised we'd stumbled across something extraordinary when we found the remains of this ancient building which we believe perhaps once housed the local M&S."

Amongst the items found during the historic dive were submerged roads, homes and the

Prime Minister still insisting that everything possible was being done to ensure that local residents were back in their homes in the New Year.

Floods ruin holidays

by Our Meteorological Staff
Sandy Bagg

ENVIRONMENT Agency boss Sir Philip Dilley has broken down as he described how a flood of emails and texts totally ruined his Christmas in Barbados.

"I was just enjoying my second Piña Colada on the beach when the flood of messages overwhelmed my smart phone's defences," the clearly shaken Environment Agency boss told reporters as he landed at Heathrow.

"I tried to move to higher ground where I thought there'd be no signal, but the deluge of angry messages demanding I return to Britain kept flooding in.

"You can understand my anguish, I had to cancel my scuba-diving day to return to Britain to coordinate desperate efforts to keep my job."

Meanwhile, the Environment Agency has reminded people in flood-ravaged regions of the UK that there are no warnings in place for rain anywhere in Barbados over the Christmas period.

"In future, we'd suggest that people leave the flood plain and board the same jet plane as Sir Philip Silley to fly to a sumptuous Barbados villa," said an Agency spokesperson.

"Once there, they will be able to enjoy sunshine and long lazy days on the beach, safe in the knowledge that their wellies are packed away for another year."

That flood coverage in full

Anchor: We go now to our local correspondent on the ground, Mike Bore. Mike, how is it over there?

(Shot of Bore standing waist-deep in some water)

Bore: Well, Sally, I'm here in the little village of Up-To-Its-Knees-In-It. As you can see, I'm standing in an enormous amount of water at the moment – to give you an idea of how much it is, I'm almost six feet tall, and yet only about three feet of me is visible above the water here. So that's almost three feet of water.

Anchor: That's extraordinary, Mike.

Bore: I know, Sally. The problem here is that the water has been rising far above its normal level – in fact, so much so that it's flowed out from the river, which is where it's meant to be, and is now flowing all through streets and houses, where it's not meant to be. I've been meeting local residents who've been affected by the floods.

(Shot of four firemen pulling old lady in an inflatable boat. Cut to interview outside house submerged in more water)

Bore: How do you feel about the floods?

Local: Well, obviously, it feels absolutely terrible, we've been...

Bore: Is it hard to believe that your home is ruined?

Local: Well, we've been through this before, but never quite...

Bore: What do you think the government's response should be?

Local: Well, it's quite complicated, I think...

Bore: So there you have it, Sally. These floods are worse than they ever have been before. It's impossible to believe that it's happening all over again, and people are absolutely furious with the government.

(Shot of water flowing over the top of an abandoned 4x4)

Bore: The waters are receding now, but when the army leaves...

(Shot of a soldier standing around looking worried)

Bore: ...it'll be up to the locals to help each other. Back to you, Sally.

(Shot of people passing sandbags in a chain)

CAMERON SHARES NORTH'S PAIN

These are my ee-bah-gum boots

NEW STORM OVER RHODES STATUE

by Our Colonial Staff **Jim Babwe**

Hundreds of angry demonstrators last night besieged Oriel College, Oxford, protesting at the campaign to remove the statue of Cecil Rhodes, the famous 19th-century British imperialist.

The protestors explained that Rhodes had been one of the most celebrated gay men in the British Imperial record and any attempt to airbrush such an iconic figure out of the history books could only be regarded as a "grotesque act of homophobic discrimination and cultural censorship".

Rhodes, who died in 1902 in the arms of his long time male lover, has long been viewed by sections of the post-colonial gay community as one of the most important early pioneers of an openly homosexual lifestyle; and his supporters are now threatening to mount a 24-hour guard round the controversial statue to halt any attempt *(cont. 1894)*

Why is UK broadband so slow?

by Our Online Staff
Phil Cyber-Space

IT'S the question everyone wants answered. With internet speeds failing to meet European standards across the country, what technical reasons are there for service providers to be falling so abysmally short? Determined to find out, and leaving no stone unturned, I've checked online, and can exclusively reveal that... That... Oh hang on. Give it a second. Or a minute. Shouldn't be long now. Just "buffering". Whatever that means... Is something happening or not?! Come on! Come on! I haven't got all day!... Darling, are you getting any signal in the kitchen?! Can I borrow your iPhone?... Oh, bollocks. I'll just make it up like usual. Thank God I've already downloaded all my porn. Whoops! *(Cont. 9.4 Megabits per second)*

AFTER THE LAST FLOOD I GOT OUT OF SHEEP AND CATTLE

CLIFF

'BOWIE MADE IT POSSIBLE FOR US ALL TO BE COMPLETELY DIFFERENT'

says Everyone

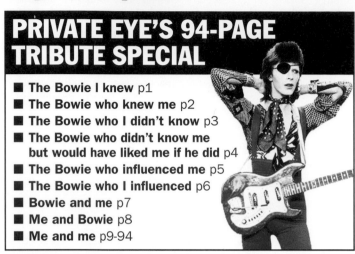

DAVID BOWTIE – NO TRIBUTES POUR IN

by Our Political Staff **Phil Space-Oddity**

THE word "genius" is often overused. But when it comes to David Bowtie, the former leader of the Conservative Party, one thing is absolutely certain. He was not in any way a genius.

As tributes to him yesterday did not pour in, and Twitter failed to go into meltdown, critics were queueing up to offer their interpretation of the extraordinary engima that was David Bowtie (as he became known after he changed his name from Dave Cameron).

All were agreed that Bowtie's greatest gift was his ability to "reinvent" himself every few years throughout his long career.

Originally, he was "Posh David", appearing in his trademark costume of white tie and tails. Then there was his "Tory Boy" persona, when he flirted with right-wing poses and borrowed ideas from Mrs Thatcher.

But then came the moment when his act went through its most dramatic transformation, when he suddenly appeared as "Green Dave", making an historic video of himself driving a team of huskies across the fast-melting ice.

Yet, only a few years later, he shocked many of his former fans by dismissing this pose as no more than "green crap".

Ch-ch-ch-changes

He adopted yet another new image, based on some avant-garde ideas he'd picked up from a fringe group called Ukip, claiming that he was now a fierce euro-sceptic.

He told the new fans that, as far as Europe was concerned, he was "out of it".

But within months there was yet another David Bowtie on show, when he came up with the haunting refrain "Look up here, I'm in Europe" and promised his followers that this was where he planned to remain for ever.

Now that Bowtie has passed into history, millions of people in Britain have not been plunged into mourning.

No one yesterday was saying "he defined a generation" or "he was an original, a one-off" or "there will never be anyone like him".

Thousands failed to gather at makeshift shrines (*We get the idea. Ed.*)

Why I wept at the death of Bowie *by all editors*

I WILL never forget where I was when I heard the news that David Bowie had passed or, as we say in Britain, died.

I was staring at my front page, which was full of pictures of Islamist terrorists blowing up the world, when suddenly someone said, "There's a starman waiting in the sky".

And I admit freely the tears welled up in my eyes and I wept uncontrollably – with relief.

"Scrap all the depressing jihadi stuff and let's go with glam-rock glitter and gush," I shouted.

And I was not alone. The entire newsroom was full of normally cynical grown men and women sobbing with relief, as they threw away their articles about the EU debate and NHS reform and started writing lists of their top 20 favourite Bowie songs, films, videos, hairdos, jumpsuits, shoes and, of course, spoons.

Music Legend Dies

■ STUNNED by his sudden death, Britain was in mourning yesterday for the musical icon who defined a generation from the 1970s onwards.

The country's leaders were queueing up to pay tribute, with Prime Minister David Cameron saluting a man who, he said, "provided the soundtrack to my life". The Archbishop of Canterbury echoed these sentiments, saying, "I grew up listening to him on the radio, I can't believe he's gone." Jeremy Corbyn added his thoughts: "He was a cultural phenomenon, we'll never see his like again."

As grief-stricken fans tried to come to terms with the death of Ed "Stewpot" Stewart, crowds began to form outside the former Crackerjack studio (now Yentob Towers, a luxury flat development) and there are plans for a minute's silence later in the week. When asked for a precise time, a spokesman said, "It's Friday, it's five to five!".

On other pages in our Stewpot memorial supplement:

● Who can forget his memorable Top of the Pops appearance, when he appeared wearing a tank-top and flares?

● How did Ed Stewart invent the incredible persona of "Stewpot"?

● And what is the correct way to pronounce Ed's unusual name? Is it Stew-pot, as in "hot", or Stew-pot, as in "pot-pourri"?

JUMP HORROR – CELEBRITY UNHURT

by Our Reality TV Staff **Phil Hospital**

THE Twittersphere went into meltdown yesterday at the incredible news that one of the celebrities taking part in Channel 4's "The Jump" had emerged unscathed from a day's filming.

The "ski-tainment" programme had previously delighted viewers by managing to injure a number of D-list celebrities in the opening weeks, including That-man-off-the-telly and That-woman-from-Holby.

But controversially, as the competition entered its third week, it was revealed that no celebrities had been hurt at all.

Furious viewers are now demanding that the show be axed on the grounds of excessive health and safety.

As one angry viewer said, "If this goes on, we are going to end up with half the celebrities alive and still on telly instead of in hospital".

Said another, "When I saw that Davina completely uninjured I was so angry I kicked my plasma screen and broke my toe.

"I would go to Casualty, but I expect it's empty because they are all on reality shows."

Channel 4 defended itself, saying, "The Jump is groundbreaking and indeed leg-breaking television and we have to take risks. If, by some unfortunate accident, one of the celebrities does not come to any harm, we can only apologise."

Tweets All / No replies

Tim Peake @astro_timpeake   Dec 14 2015
Looking forward to tomorrow's space launch. Should be literally indescribable!

Tim Peake @astro_timpeake   Dec 14 2015
Wondering what song to hum to myself during space launch tomorrow. Wow! So many to choose from!

Tim Peake @astro_timpeake   Dec 14 2015
Currently favouring something truly catchy by Eurovision winners the great Brotherhood of Man.

Tim Peake @astro_timpeake   Dec 15 2015
Setting off in 9 minutes. Has to be Save Your Kisses for Me.

Tim Peake @astro_timpeake   Dec 15 2015
Successful launch 15 mins ago. As exhilarating as putting your foot on accelerator of really really fast car. Fantastic feeling. ☺

Tim Peake @astro_timpeake   Dec 15 2015
Up in space now. Amazing. Can't get Bee Gees Night Fever out of my head. Great song.

Tim Peake @astro_timpeake   Dec 15 2015
RIP Maurice and Robin Gibb. ☹ Glad you're still with us, Barry. ☺

Tim Peake @astro_timpeake   Dec 15 2015
Have to pinch myself to remind myself I'm still in space! So dark out there! Unbelievable!

Tim Peake @astro_timpeake   Dec 16 2015
Just completed 24 hours in space! Keeping busy! Just brushed my teeth!

Tim Peake @astro_timpeake   Dec 17 2015
Taking a "Peake" out of spacecraft window. Forgive terrible pun! ie "Peake" = "Peek". Sorry, guys!! ☺

Tim Peake @astro_timpeake   Dec 18 2015
Still very dark out there. But nevertheless literally amazing, indescribable.

Tim Peake @astro_timpeake   Dec 18 2015
Suppose if you had to compare it to anything you'd say it was like an exceptionally dark tunnel.

Tim Peake @astro_timpeake   Dec 18 2015
But TBH even darker than that.

Tim Peake @astro_timpeake   Dec 19 2015
Very sorry to hear of the death of Jimmy Hill.

☹ Tremendous contribution to "the beautiful game" ie football.

Tim Peake @astro_timpeake   Dec 20 2015
Just passed Great Wall of China. Only one word for it. Great.

Tim Peake @astro_timpeake   Dec 21 2015
Done bit of emergency repair work on twitter feed. Otherwise nothing much happening.

Tim Peake @astro_timpeake   Dec 22 2015
Took selfie.

Tim Peake @astro_timpeake   Dec 23 2015
Looking forward to Xmas in space! Two days to go. Different from Xmas at home but still great.

Tim Peake @astro_timpeake   Dec 24 2015
Just saw Rockies from space. Funny – they look very small from this distance! Must be the perspective. One more day to go.

Tim Peake @astro_timpeake   Dec 25 2015
Merry Xmas to all on Planet Earth! Sorry to miss Queen's speech.

Tim Peake @astro_timpeake   Dec 25 2015
But will make sure to catch up with it on my return.

Tim Peake @astro_timpeake   Dec 25 2016
Have had Slade's Merry Christmas Everybody in my head all day. Great song.

Tim Peake @astro_timpeake   Dec 27 2015
Privileged to perform space somersault for Good Morning Britain breakfast show. Big fan of Susanna Reid.

Tim Peake @astro_timpeake   Dec 28 2015
Monday. My day to do the bins, worse luck! ☹

Tim Peake @astro_timpeake   Dec 31 2015
New Year's Eve today. Which can mean only one thing. New Year's Day tomorrow. Great!

Tim Peake @astro_timpeake   Jan 1 2016
Wishing all on Planet Earth a Happy New Year. Sorry to be missing 1st of new series of The Voice but wish best of luck to all involved.

Tim Peake @astro_timpeake   Jan 2 2016
Hovering over Paris. Once had very pleasant weekend there, went all way up Eiffel Tower, pleasant lunch too, but forget name of restaurant.

Tim Peake @astro_timpeake   Jan 3 2016
Brasserie Something, I think. But that's probably not much help. Hoping it'll come to me later.

Tim Peake @astro_timpeake   Jan 4 2016
Name of that Paris restaurant still bugging me.

Tim Peake @astro_timpeake   Jan 5 2016
Just had tweet from fantastic Gary Barlow!!

Thank you! Always been a big fan, Gary. ☺

Tim Peake @astro_timpeake   Jan 5 2016
Fave Take That song of all time? No question. Relight My Fire. Or possibly Could It Be Magic. Hard to choose, really.

Tim Peake @astro_timpeake   Jan 6 2016
Took selfie.

Tim Peake @astro_timpeake   Jan 7 2016
Took another selfie.

Tim Peake @astro_timpeake   Jan 10 2016
Starry, starry night. Great song by Don Maclean.

Tim Peake @astro_timpeake   Jan 11 2016
Whoops – should have spelt it Don McLean! Even astronauts make mistakes! ☺

Tim Peake @astro_timpeake   Jan 12 2016
Performed space somersault for BBC One Show. Big fan of Alex and Matt.

Tim Peake @astro_timpeake   Jan 13 2016
Glad to hear Michael Douglas and Catherine Zeta-Jones back together after brief marriage split.

Tim Peake @astro_timpeake   Jan 13 2016
Romancing The Stone definitely one of my top ten films of all time.

Tim Peake @astro_timpeake   Jan 14 2016
Looking forward to spacewalk tomorrow. Hoping it will be totally indescribable.

Tim Peake @astro_timpeake   Jan 15 2016
Just back from spacewalk. Indescribable.

Tim Peake @astro_timpeake   Jan 15 2016
Closest I can come to describing it is by saying it's a bit like you always imagined floating in space would be.

Tim Peake @astro_timpeake   Jan 16 2016
Took selfie of self performing space somersault. One for the photo album!

Tim Peake @astro_timpeake   Jan 17 2016
Looking down on USA from space. Unforgettable.

Tim Peake @astro_timpeake   Jan 18 2016
Took selfie of self looking down on USA. Huge country.

Tim Peake @astro_timpeake   Jan 19 2016
Return to Planet Earth scheduled for 5 June 2016. Only 137 days to go!

Tim Peake @astro_timpeake   Jan 21 2016
Took selfie. Posted this tweet. ☺

As tweeted to
CRAIG BROWN

"Yeah, I like these, I'll take them"

"No, dear, I'm sure LGBT are not our energy suppliers"

"He's entirely self-taught"

WARNER

CAMERON TO SEND SON TO ELITE PREP SCHOOL

by Our Education Staff **Fee Glover**

The Prime Minister has taken the controversial decision of sending his son to Cakelet Court, the feeder school for the famous Public School, St Cakes (Motto: *"Quis Paget Entrat"*)

The Prime Minister has refused to comment on this apparent U-turn in his commitment to state education, though insiders say he is not guilty of hypocrisy.

Said one, "As Prime Minister, he has always been a supporter of state education, but obviously when he stops being Prime Minister he won't give a toss."

The headmaster of Cakelet Court, Mr Kipling Junior, son of the legendary St Cakes Headmaster Mr R.J. Kipling Senior, told reporters:

"Cakelet Court looks forward to welcoming the Prime Minister's sum, sorry, son. We are delighted that Mr Cameron has chosen to entrust his money, I mean offspring, with our bank, that is, school."

Mr Kipling continued, "Cakelet Court accepts children from all backgrounds, from the rich to the very, very rich.

"We boast a number of famous alumni here, including George Osborne, Eddie Redmayne and Mr Gropetrouser, the former Head of Classics who had to take a ten-year sabbatical in Wandsworth."

Mr Cameron's decision was said to be influenced by his wife's strong views on baking. Said Mrs Cameron, "Mr Kipling makes exceedingly good schools".

It is, however, a departure from the Camerons' previous decision on education for their daughter Nancy. She was sent to the local pub and was schooled by Barry the Barman.

Elwen Cameron, by contrast, will enter Cakelet Court in Bonus Term 2016 (formerly Michaelmas) and will join one of the three classes (Upper, Upper-Middle and Business Traveller). It is not yet clear which will be his house, but it looks as if the young Cameron will join either Mao Zedongs or Gazproms.

Cakelet Court is known for the high standard of its drama and this term it is putting on a production of *Oliver!* with an amusing twist, as the Head of the Orphanage, Mr Bumble, asks Oliver: "Please, sir, may I have some more money?"

Brexits will be on Feb 31st.

COLLECTIVE NOUNS
A Guide for Prime Ministers

Grapes *Bunch* ✔

Bananas *Bunch* ✔

Flowers *Bunch* ✔

Migrants *Bunch* ✘

Idiots *Bunch* ✔

Bill Gates
Desert Island Discs Highlights

THE Sun SAYS

Google off!

IT'S AN absolute disgrace – an International Media Company using its influence with politicians in order to minimise its tax liability and maximise its profits.

Can anyone imagine anything more devious and underhand?

How would readers of this newspaper react if they found out that its proprietor invited the British Prime Minister to his parties and, even worse, the Prime Minister accepted?

And wouldn't they be appalled if they discovered that the PM had regular meetings with our Chief Executive, shared intimate texts with her and even rode around on her horse in Chipping Norton?

Surely they would think this was a very unsavoury operation, run by deeply suspect people who should be brought to account and sent to... *(You're fired! Rupe.)*

 Dave Snooty AND HIS MINORITY PALS

IT'S A LANGUAGE CLASS TO STOP MINORITIES GETTING ISOLATED – AND TO HELP THEM INTEGRATE WITH THE REST OF SOCIETY...

WHAT A CAPITAL IDEA!

...SO AFTER ME, YOUNG SIR...

Pint of your best ale Squire
Sad about that Wogan chap, what?
See Corrie last night?
My missus has a tattoo, dontchaknow

I SUPPORT WEST ASTON HAM VILLA, ME!

YOU'RE PRACTICALLY FLUENT!

NORTH KOREA ANNOUNCES NUCLEAR BOMB

We've given it the code name 'Fat Man'

U.S. RESPONDS TO KOREAN ANNOUNCEMENT

We can't have a raving lunatic in charge of nuclear weapons!

FRUIT & VEGETABLES

"Easy Peelers? What the hell happened to aspiration and ambition?"

BOYCE

Parliament Debates 'Banning Trump'

by Our Westminster Staff
Tim E. Waster

THERE was widespread support today in the House of Commons for a motion calling for Donald Trump to be banned from entering Britain.

"We need to show Donald Trump that his plan to ban Muslims or anyone else from entering America displays staggering intolerance," said one MP, "and the only way to do that is by banning Trump from entering our country."

"People say debating banning Trump from the UK is nothing but a cheap publicity stunt for publicity-hungry MPs, and that's why we're so delighted it's taking place," tweeted all MPs.

One MP did point out that allowing Trump into Britain wouldn't be nearly as bad as laying on a lavish welcome for the President of China, a man who has actually committed some of the most heinous human rights abuses, as opposed to Trump who has only talked about it.

Thankfully, he was drowned out by the scores of publicity-hungry MPs hoping that taking a few cheap shots at Trump might get them an interview with Jon Snow on *Channel 4 News*.

SCANDAL HITS BRITISH TENNIS

by **Sir John Betjeman**

THE genteel world of lawn tennis was rocked by allegations of match fixing in an Aldershot tournament when a young subaltern deliberately threw the game against English hopeful, Miss Joan Hunter Dunn.

The sequence of scores from love-all to love-forty aroused suspicions at the time, which have subsequently been confirmed by the engagement announced in the car park between Ms Hunter Dunn and the subaltern (who cannot be named, for legal reasons).

The subaltern denied any impropriety, claiming that the singles match was "strenuous", but that he had been unable to defeat his opponent because she had "the speed of a swallow and the grace of a boy", and consequently won with "carefullest carelessness".

He did admit to feeling "weak from her loveliness" and conceded that he was "mad", "sad" and "glad" that she won.

The enquiry continues, during which time Ms J. Hunter Dunn has been suspended from the Aldershot Tennis & Golf Club.

SIR TERRY WOGAN RIP

by All Hacks Still Recovering From Writing Last Week's 94-page Tributes

He was in many ways the soundtrack to our lives, the star man who never reinvented himself and who always wore the same clothes and had the same wife and who inspired ordinary people to believe that it was OK not to be different and alien and chameleon-like, but to be normal and pleasant and *(You're fired. Ed.)*

Radio 2 Highlights

(Solemn, easy-listening music is played to denote death of great broadcaster)

Jeremy Vain *(for it is he)*: Well, I will novor forgot tho time when Terry met me... there I was, having run into work, when Terry met me in the Broadcasting House lift.

With seconds to go before his show, I wondered what Terry would talk about.

Me, of course! Completely unflustered, he described meeting me in the lift and it will be a memory for ever etched on Terry's mind – an encounter with a colossus of broadcasting.

Terry's advice was always "Don't make it about yourself, make it about the listener". And how right he was that memorable day when he met me.

(Puts on more solemn music, possibly Michael Bublé singing Mozart's Requiem or Jamie Cullum playing Chopin's Funeral March)

LORD KINNOCK SPEAKS OUT ON CORBYN

INTERVIEWER: So Mr Kinnock...

KINNOCK: All I'm saying is that Jeremy Corbyn needs to take a long, hard, hard and long look at himself in the mirror and decide if he's unelectable and if he concludes that he is, he should not go on and on and on like some of his deluded, hectoring and balding Welsh predecessors but, and I would add only this, if he wants to lead Labour back into power he needs to totally and utterly and utterly and totally learn the lessons of the past and connect with the voters in a succinct, brief, concise and in no way long-winded or loquacious, nay verbally-obtuse and over-embroidered, manner and if Mr Corbyn can heed, understand, accept and follow my advice based on

years of leading the Labour party to failure then he'll be alriiiiiiiiiight!!! Furthermore... *(cont. p94 onwards)*

31

Different fruit from the one we wrote about last time is apparently the secret to a long and healthy life

HAVING previously stated that blueberries/goji berries/cranberries/cherries/pomegranates (delete as applicable) are the secret to a long life, scientists now say that pomegranates/cranberries/blueberries/goji berries/cherries (delete as applicable) are actually the secret to a long and healthy life.

If you were eating blueberries/goji berries/cranberries/cherries/pomegranates (delete as applicable), you are therefore strongly advised to instead start eating pomegranates/cranberries/blueberries/goji berries/cherries (delete as applicable).

Other scientists, however, disputed the findings, saying the actual secret to a long and healthy life is just enjoying yourself and not reading articles about which food is the secret to a long and healthy life.

Fury at outrageous corporate tax deals

by Our Tax Staff
A. Void and E. Vade

THERE was such widespread fury amongst ordinary taxpayers today at Google's sweetheart tax deal, that millions of people briefly considered using another search engine.

"I was so angry at Google, I was all fired up to do it," said Roger Edwards from Deptford.

"But Google is the default browser on my laptop and at the end of the day it is very convenient to use and Google Maps is brilliant."

"It was just like when I briefly considered no longer using iPhones after hearing how Apple pays virtually no UK tax," tweeted Erica Roberts from Hull on her new iPhone 6. "But at the end of the day they're just so easy to use and I love the design."

"I felt exactly the same towards Starbucks and their disgraceful tax affairs," said Jennifer Salson from Hemel Hempstead, sipping her favourite frappuccino in Starbucks.

"I was all ready to boycott them, but the baristas here all know me and make my coffee exactly how I like it."

The Alternative Rocky Horror Service Book

No.94 A Service of Prayer for the Comfort of Sick Atheists at Their Hour of Need

President: We are gathered together to remember in our prayers our brother Dawkins who has been sadly struck down by an affliction.

All: Ha ha ha ha ha.

President: Let us now bow our heads, get out our phones and remember him in our tweets.

All: LOL!

(There shall now be a reading in a sarcastic voice from the Gospel according to St Richard, Chapter Ten – probably one of the bits about a malicious deity inflicting vengeance on non-believers.)

All: Ha ha ha ha ha.

(The congregation will now sing Hymn Number 94, "The Dawkins Thou Gavest Lord Is Over (Or Very Nearly)")

THE DISMISSAL

President: O Lord, we dismiss these accusations that there is anything ironic about these, our heartfelt and sincere prayers for the swift recovery of a Godless Heretic.

All: Indeed, we do!

President: There is a God!

Dawkins (for it is still he): No, there isn't!

© of E

Ceasefire Threatened by Continued War

by Our Military Staff
Donna Airstrike

THE fragile Syrian ceasefire agreed in Munich earlier this week was hanging by a thread, following the refusal of all the main parties to have a ceasefire.

As shells, bombs and missiles continued to rain down on the civilians of the main Syrian cities, there were serious questions raised about the nature of a ceasefire that allowed all the major parties to carry on firing as before.

So severe has the conflict been since the so-called "Munich" declaration that the people of Syria have begun to call for "an end to the ceasefire", in the hope of a return to peace.

President Putin, however, declared that he was delighted with the progress of the ceasefire:

"It has been extremely effective indeed. It has been almost as successful as the ceasefire in the Ukraine – where the other side ceased and we fired."

Facebook founder's amazing philanthropic pledge

by Our Social Media Staff
Sonia Harris, 15
(aka **Doug Faggs**, 58)

This week Facebook founder Mark Zuckerberg celebrated the birth of his daughter Max by making a historic promise for future generations.

"Having a baby changes your perspective on life. It enables you to see what really matters. And for that reason, from this point forward, I guarantee that Facebook will pay 99 percent no tax."

Zuckerberg, reckoned by one financial expert to be worth "literally squillions", said his promise would have a profound effect on the children of the world.

Thanks to him, public services will be driven into the ground, there will be no money for roads, schools or hospitals and people will have no alternative but to stay at home and put pictures of themselves pretending to be happy on Facebook.

When asked why he'd called his daughter Max, the gazillionaire tax dodger and personal data thief replied, "It's short for Maximum Avoidance."

EYE'S ENTERTAINMENT ROUND UP

TV

The Bridge

Scandi Noir Thriller in which a body is found on the Bridge between Denmark and Sweden.

It gets complicated when the body is found to be alive and belonging to an immigrant. Which of the countries is going to have to take him in and save his life?

Watch out for the scene when all his possessions (wallet, watch, trainers) are removed by the Danish authorities.

Eye rating: *British viewers will welcome this foreign import into their homes, unlike the migrant from the bridge*

The Giant Attenbaurus

An incredibly old presenter is discovered wandering around looking at dinosaurs.

Dating back millions of years, the Attenbaurus was a giant of natural history films and walked the earth well before the start of the Colour Age.

Amazing scenes as we piece together the long, long life of the Attenbaurus and his relatives, including the now extinct Dickieluwisaurus who was last seen roaming around Jurassic Park being chased by a Velociraptor.

Eye rating: *Absolutely massive*

FILM

Jihad's Army

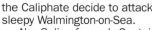

Yet another remake of the popular classic *Jihad's Army*, in which the amateur soldiers of the Caliphate decide to attack sleepy Walmington-on-Sea.

Abu Salim, formerly Captain Mainwaring, is the newly-radicalised convert bank manager, who leads his motley crew of butchers, butchers and butchers, in a holy war against 72 vergers *(Is this right? Ed.)*

Don't miss the wonderful theme tune *Who do you think we are killing, Mr Cameron?* and the classic scene when Jihadi John Le Mesurier asks "What do we put this head on?", and Abu responds "Don't tell him, Spike".

Eye rating: *We're all doomed*

NET FLIX

Making a Murderer

This gripping new show exposes the method to get someone unjustly banged up for murder:

1 Start talking about how you've been watching *Making A Murderer*
2 Keep telling all friends and family about how great *Making A Murderer* is
3 Don't stop, even when they ask you politely
4 Keep telling them, even as their eyelids start twitching
5 Tell them once more for good measure about how brilliant it is and how they should definitely watch it

Eye rating: *Murder*

NEW DWORKIN THURSDAY

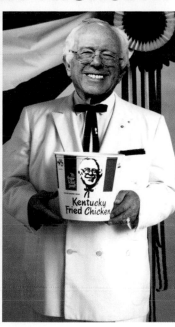

Presidential Race Hots Up

by Our Election Staff **Emily Clueless**

THE surprise winner of the New Dworkin Primary was none other than late entrant Ronald McDonald.

The larger-than-life head of a multi-million-dollar corporation had been written off as a colourful clown with ridiculous hair, famous only for appearances on television with his catchphrase "You're fried!".

But now Mr Ronald McDonald Trump is being taken seriously as the front-runner Republican candidate for the office of President of the United States. His adversary on the Democratic side is Colonel Sanders, who has been written off by some as being too old to be a serious contender, even though he's tipped to win the Kentucky primary.

Ronald McDonald Trump went on the attack, saying, "Bernie, you're no spring chicken. I'm going to eat you for breakfast, but only after my McMuffin. You're in for a battering!" Sanders replied, "I'm not scared of Ronald McDonald, he's no great shakes." *(That really is enough. Ed.)*

Both the leading candidates have the advantage of coming from outside the traditional political establishment and have no ties with the Washington elite. In their own ways, they both speak to ordinary 23-stone Americans in a language they understand (ie slowly and simply with jingles where possible).

Still in the race are Republican hopefuls Dr Pepper and Wendy Burger. And for the Democrats, Duncan Donuts and joke candidate, Hillary Clintstone, wife of Fred, former resident of the White Cave *(I said that's enough of this!)*

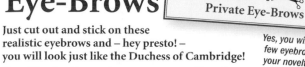

"Our customers prefer their fish to be irresponsibly sourced"

HOW BRITAIN WILL LOOK AFTER BREXIT

Mr Cameron did warn you this might happen

Glory Days Of Austerity 'Could Be Over'

THERE was a growing consensus in the City today that the recovery in the British economy that has led to Britons enjoying a prolonged period of upbeat austerity could be about to come to an abrupt end.

"The global share price meltdown means the glory days of austerity the British people have enjoyed during the past few years are simply no longer affordable," said one senior City analyst. "George Osborne will now instead have to impose harsh new austerity measures to balance the books.

"Enjoy the current period of happy-go-lucky austerity while you can, because many years of grim, backbreaking austerity appear to be just around the corner."

Pope in New Scandal

by Our Religious Staff
J.B. Priestley and Sir Trevor Nun

The Catholic Church was reeling yesterday after the shocking revelation that their former Supreme Pontiff the late John Paul II had been involved in a relationship with a woman.

A senior Catholic source was outraged: "This suggestion that the Pope was conducting a friendship with an adult member of the opposite sex is an affront to all the traditions of the Catholic Church".

He continued, "We do not expect to find our senior priestly figures writing gentle letters to platonic female friends. The Pope has abused his position rather than any altar boys and it will be very difficult for the church to recover any moral authority after this appalling lapse."

Daily Mail

EUROPE: WHAT DO DEAD PEOPLE THINK?

MAIL EXCLUSIVE on how the deceased will be voting in the forthcoming referendum.

Margaret Thatcher	**OUT**
Adolf Hitler	**IN**
Boadicea	**OUT**
Julius Caesar	**IN**
King Harold	**OUT**
William the Conqueror	**IN**
Napoleon	**IN**
Duke of Wellington	**OUT**
Lord Hokey of Cokey	**IN, OUT, IN, OUT, SHAKE IT ALL ABOUT**

"It's Adele – she says she's called a thousand times"

Spotlight wins best picture

by Our Academy Award Correspondent **Holly Wood**

THERE was widespread delight tonight as Spotlight unexpectedly picked up the "Best Picture" Oscar.

"This is an important movie, because we set out to document practices which were once considered acceptable, even commonplace, but would never be allowed to happen today," said the Spotlight producer.

"It was a strange time, long ago, when newspapers employed investigative journalists to dig up difficult stories," said a clearly overjoyed Spotlight producer.

"Had these journalists been employed today they'd be writing '17 Alpacas who look like Leonardo DiCaprio' lists for Buzzfeed or articles about Amanda Holden's side boob pics for Mail Online, rather than exposing paedophilia in the Catholic Church.

"Never again will there be a time when newspaper proprietors simply turn a blind eye to issuing large pay cheques to investigative journalists, when they could employ half a dozen data journalists in Korea for the same money to churn out lowest denominator clickbait."

 Dave Snooty AND HIS FAMILY FRIENDS

IT'S TEA TIME AT SNOOTY'S...

SPIFFING SPREAD, DAVE! SHALL I BE MOTHER?

GO AHEAD OLD BEAN!

STOP THE CUTS! YOU'RE RUINING THE COUNTRY YOU STUPID BOY!

I WISH I'D ASKED HIM TO **KEEP MUM**!

CLONK!

OLD MA CAM

NO TO CUTTING THE CAKE!!!

Cut out 'n' keep
THAT HISTORIC CAMERON DEAL IN FULL

1. The UK will keep the pound sterling.
2. Traffic will drive on the left of the road at least until 2029.
3. The UK will continue to be an island surrounded by water.
4. Other details will be decided later, after the above conditions have been agreed by the European parliament.
5. Er... That's it.

THOSE OTHER NON-BREXIT EXITS IN FULL...

Mexit Donald Trump's expulsion of immigrants, back over the Texan border

Sexit resignation of MP after texting photos of own genitals

Multiplexit rush to leave cinema after five minutes of *Zoolander 2*

Chexit transaction on departure from dinner/ball hosted by Prime Minister

Fexit departure from living room, due to TV showing another repeat of *Mrs Brown's Boys*

T.Rexit departure from planet due to over-large body and too-small arms

Ukrexit what Russia aren't going to do out of Ukraine

StarTrexit death of unnamed *Enterprise* crew member, shortly after landing on planet with Kirk and Spock

PoshnBexit celebrity departure from club/PR launch

AntandDexit switching off Brit Awards as Adele blubs through yet another acceptance speech

Wessexit giving up on Thomas Hardy novel after finding it a bit slower than the latest film version

Earlyexit what to do at a dinner party, when everyone is boring on about the EU

CAMERON REPORTS PROGRESS

I've negotiated some enormous concessions from Europe

"If we make them welcome, they'll respect our culture and boost our economy"

HUNTER

NORTH TO BE MOVED SOUTH

by Our Northern England Correspondent **E. Bah. Gum**

THE Government today has announced that the North of England is to be moved South, in a major restructuring of the country.

"The fact that everything is to be moved South, just shows our commitment to the North," said a spokesman, yesterday.

"By this move we are demonstrating that the North is so important to us that we are moving it down South so we can keep a really good eye on it.

"Several of our studies show that the North is situated in an inconvenient, out-of-the-way place which is badly positioned to take advantage of the benefits of the UK economic miracle, which is comprised mainly of breakfast cereal cafes, vegan delicatessens and pop-up t-shirt emporiums," he continued.

"So I think it's best for everyone if the North was down here, where we have the infrastructure, money and Ascot."

Report gives new names for world's oceans and seas by 2050

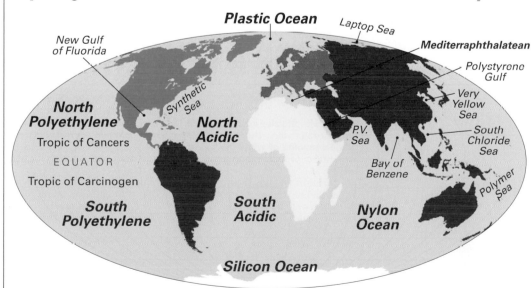

ASSANGE ARBITRARILY DETAINED

I demand to be released... and I won't take no for an answer

Whoops!

35

Nursery Times

Friday, Once-upon-a-time

PALACE DENIES PRINCE IS LAZY

By Our Royal Correspondent **Idle Jack**

FOLLOWING accusations in the Nurseryland Press that Prince Charming has become "a lazy part-timer", Palace officials have leapt frog-like to the Prince's defence.

Said a spokesman, "Although he has only been charming twice this year, the Prince remains committed to carrying out his royal duties of being charming, including smiling, waving and asking his subjects 'What do you do?'"

When asked by one of his subjects recently "Well, what do *you* do?", the Prince replied, "Er... I am jolly busy flying my helicopter, rescuing people and, er, looking after my children."

Critics, however, claim that he has effectively given over his charming duties to his lovely wife, Princess Snow White Teeth, who has a lovely smile and is more than happy to go around Nurseryland asking people if they have come far because she certainly has, all the way from the lower middle-class to the upper echelons of the Royal Family.

Seasoned Royal watchers now fear that if this goes on, Charming could end up like his father, Prince Charmless, who spends his days writing Incy Wincy Spider letters to Nurseryland ministers and feeling resentful that he was never as popular as his late wife Princess Cin-di-rella.

The Eye's Controversial New Columnist

He doesn't suffer fools or cuddly toys gladly

This week, I am very angry about this government scheme to give £3,000 to mothers so they can choose to have their babies at home. Speaking as a baby myself *(see photo)*, I view this as the nanny state gone mad!

There is no need for such social engineering. Mothers already have a clear choice whether or not to have their babies at home, without the need for costly, wasteful schemes that sound like they have been cobbled together by Brussels bureaucrats and Labour Corbynistas!

I am pleased to say that with ambulances growing ever more scarce, our government is providing a clear alternative for parents, ie instead of going to hospital to have your baby, you can have it at home while you're on the telephone to the 999 service, listening to Greensleeves and wondering why they take so long to (*cont. p94*)

SCAB! PUSTULE! OEDEMA! POLYP! HAEMORRHOID!

NHS TRUST H○

Junior Doctors' Strike

Sturgeon 'backing the EU'

Scotland First Minister Nicola Sturgeon today pledged to work tirelessly to make the case for Britain remaining a part of the European Union.

"You would have to be out of your tiny mind to think there was any sort of a future for Britain outside a union that has offered it stability, safety and jobs," the First Minister told reporters in Glasgow.

"Were we to leave the union it would be a dangerous leap into an uncertain future where there would be a clear and present danger of economic turmoil.

"This is not a risk worth taking simply to accommodate outdated notions of national sovereignty."

Historic day for rail travel

There were scenes of jubilation from train spotters from all over Britain today when a train arrived at its destination.

The Flying Scotsman travelled from York to Scarborough, taking ten years and costing £4.2m.

Said commuters, "It's a bargain and so quick. I wish Virgin was equally reliable and efficient."

Should Tony have been sacked?

by Our BBC Staff
Pete O'Phile

FOLLOWING the dismissal of Tony Blackburn as an attempt to distract attention from the failures of BBC management, the question remains: Should Tony Hall have been sacked instead?

Tony Hall was quick to defend himself. He told BBC news, "Don't make me the scapegoat just because I'm in charge. I am merely a lowly DJ (*surely "DG"? Ed*) and I have no memory of why I mishandled this situation so badly."

Tony Blackburn is 94.

TV HIGHLIGHTS

Jan'll Fix It

BBC classic in which Dame Janet Smith of the Savile Inquiry makes people's wishes come true!

This week, members of the BBC management write to Jan asking if she can fix it for them not to be blamed for ignoring Jimmy Savile's crimes over the previous 40 years.

Jan comes up with a super treat for all the senior executives and makes their dream come true by exonerating them in full and giving them Tony Blackburn's head on a plate!

Eye Verdict: *Heartwarming family viewing.*

MOST IMPORTANT SCIENTIFIC DISCOVERY FOR A GENERATION

by **Phil Space**

A HUGE black hole opened yesterday in the public's understanding of what the latest scientific breakthrough was all about.

No light was shed at all by a huge dense mass of newsprint which collapsed in on itself as it attempted to explain the importance of gravitational waves.

The amount that the public understood about the subject was so microscopically small that at first instruments could not detect it, but after refinement the comprehension level measured less than a billionth of an atom.

Said one hurt astrophysicist, "This could be the most significant lack of understanding since the last thing the public didn't understand."

However, a member of the public was quick to congratulate the scientific community: "Look, we're very happy that they are happy and I'm sure the whole gravitational wave warp factor thing will help us defeat the Klingons and destroy the Death Star... or is that the other one?... anyway, that was a good bit."

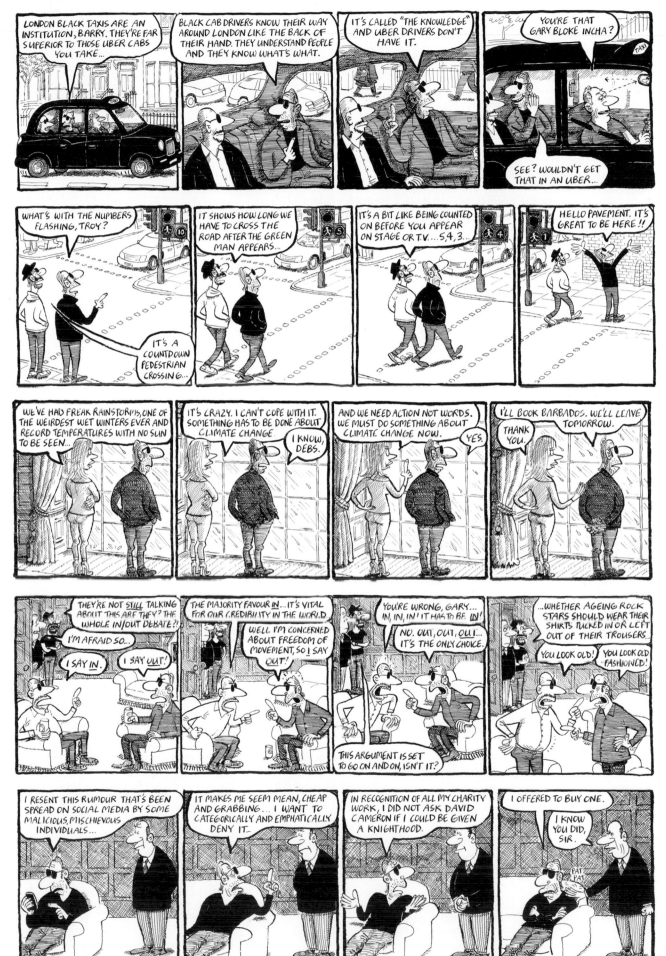

Letters to the Editor

British business and the EU

Sir, We the undersigned are very important business persons and, as such, have been asked by the prime minister to write this letter to the Times expressing our objective and wholly independent view that he is completely right in wanting Britain to remain in the European Union.

We are all immensely successful and very rich captains of industry who have first-hand experience of being given large amounts of money by this excellent organisation, which has also allowed us to ensure that our companies pay very little tax (by the way, when Number Ten sent us the draft of this letter, they forgot to put this bit in!).

We represent a huge range of British industries, many of them owned by foreigners, covering every type of activity from the immensely successful banking sector to pioneers of the dot.com revolution and the manufacturing of world-beating sex toys.

We are therefore in a very good position to tell the rest of you which way to vote on 23 June. We can assure you that if the British people are foolish enough to leave the EU, there will soon be no British industry left and you will be unemployed, starving and begging our friends in Brussels to let you back in.

SIGNED BY 198 business leaders including:

SIR JOHN BAILOUT, formerly chairman of the Royal Bankrupt of Scotland,
DIESEL VAN DER PUMP, chairman of Royal Duchy Original Oil Co.,
RUTH ROGERS MBE, proprietor of the Spud-U-Like River Cafe,
VITTORI OVER-THE-TAXMAN, CEO of Vodaphoney plc (Luxembourg and Grand Cayman),
SIR MIKE RAKEITIN, chairman of British Telecom Group,
DAME JACQUELINE GOLDMINE, CEO of the Ann Summers-Like-It-Hot chain
(*Letter coordinated on behalf of Number Ten by Sir Roland Ratt, head of Ratt Public Relations.*)

SPOT THE DIFFERENCE

1 Stupid hair
2 Spouts nonsense
3 Known philanderer
4 Inexplicably popular
5 Famous for cheap TV show
6 National Joke
7 May get top job
8 Terrifying prospect
9 Not even vaguely funny anymore
10 Help!

1 Stupid hair
2 Spouts nonsense
3 Known philanderer
4 Inexplicably popular
5 Famous for cheap TV show
6 National Joke
7 May get top job
8 Terrifying prospect
9 Not even vaguely funny anymore
10 Help!

Letters to the Editor

Military security and the EU

SIR – We the undersigned are very important former service chiefs and, as such, have been asked by the prime minister to write this letter to the Daily Telegraph, expressing our objective and wholly independent view that he is completely right in saying that it would be utterly disastrous for Britain to leave the European Union.

We have all had unrivalled experience in organising the hugely successful military interventions in such places as Iraq, Afghanistan, Libya and Syria and therefore know what we are talking about when it comes to keeping Britain secure and respected throughout the world.

As we look around the world, it is clear that Europe is facing a series of challenges quite unprecedented in human history. The rise of the dictator Putin, the threat of Isil, the uncontrolled flood of refugees from such places as Iraq, Afghanistan, Libya and Syria, call for a robust response from a united and determined international alliance, such as Nato (Number Ten did ask us to say "the EU" here, but of course we know what we are talking about!). That is why it would be an act of supreme folly for Britain to leave the EU and, were the British people silly enough to vote for such an option, we can assure them that the Armed Forces would be quite incapable of coping with our immediate invasion by millions of fanatical Jihadist terrorist refugees led by President Putin.

Unless Europe was ready to come to our aid, the UK military would be wholly powerless to resist such a threat, due to the crippling cuts imposed on them in recent years by Mr Cameron. (We didn't show this bit to Number Ten!)

General Lord Brasshat, Air Vice-Marshal Sir Jock Strap, Admiral Lord Lifebuoy, General Sir Michael Jackson and five other members of the celebrated Jackson family (*surely nine other senior service chiefs?*)

NUCLEAR POWER
THOSE CHEAPER ALTERNATIVES TO HINKLEY POINT IN FULL

1. Burn £16.9bn in tenners instead
2. Use natural gas provided by EDF excecutives telling you what a good rate this is
3. Take all civil servants who signed off on the plan and set fire to them
4. Burn oil used to grease wheels of the incredibly bad deal

5. Harness tide of public opinion rapidly turning against such a stupid project (*That's enough silly nuclear power jokes. Ed.*)

I'M WORRIED ABOUT ONLINE SURVEILLANCE

I KNOW

K.J.Lamb

WORLD EXCLUSIVE
Sarah Vain
It's not about EU – it's about ME!

My husband's months of torture

AS someone who is now married to one of the three most famous politicians in the country – and don't mean Mr Cameron or Boris(!) – only *I* know the real story behind my hubby's sensational intervention in the whole of this EU debate.

For months, I've had to keep mum about it, even with my nearest and dearest readers of the Daily Mail.

But I can tell you that it has been absolute torture for me, watching this principled, upright, decent man wrestling with his conscience over one of the most important political decisions of our time.

Should he betray one of his (and our) very closest friends, David Cameron, who came to our wedding, as you can see on the video, along with lots of other famous people?

Or should my wonderful, thoughtful, honest hubby do the right thing and fight for the future of his country?

Whether we were at our smart home in west London or on holiday in the wilds of Norfolk, every night Michael would come to bed with five or six huge tomes on the history of the European Union.

Even my charms were no match for *An Analysis of the Pooled Sovereignty Concept* by Professor Conrad J. Snoozeburger, holder of the Chair of European Political Science at the University of New Dworkin!

Typically, it all came to a head over half-term. Michael was, as usual, doing his stuff as a hands-on dad, taking the kids to their violin and Taekwondo lessons, while yours truly dashed off a quick newspaper column on the big question of the day: "Gwynnie's new bottom – yes or no?"

Anyway, we were invited over to dinner that night by none other than Boris Johnson, and his lovely and incredibly intelligent top-lawyer wife, Marina Someone-or-other.

As soon as we were shown into the Johnsons' delightfully dishevelled drawing room (how different from what we are used to chez Gove Towers!), it was obvious that this would be one of those evenings that would be pored over by historians for generations to come.

BORIS came out with it straightaway. He too had wrestled with his conscience for what seemed like quite a few minutes, he told us, but he had now come to an absolutely firm conclusion.

"Michael," he told my hubby, as he sprawled on his rather tatty sofa, "I'm going to stab Dave in the back – are you on for it?"

Obviously, their discussion had got into such deep political and philosophical waters that I signalled to Marina that it was time for us girls (including a charming young Russian called Mr Lebedev, who was a fellow guest) to beat a tactful retreat to the kitchen to check on how the shoulder of lamb was doing in the microwave.

By the time we returned, the boys had sorted it all out. Michael would go first, to make big news on the Saturday. Then Boris would follow it up with his announcement, in time to catch the evening news on Sunday.

It would be a double-whammy, which would totally transform the future of British politics for decades to come.

Only one question remained to be settled. Who on earth could write the definitive, exclusive account of the most historic political meeting since Churchill met Stalin and Roosevelt at Yalta in 1945 (Boris said he knew all about this because he'd written about it in his amazing book!).

We all decided that there was only one person who could do justice to the excitement and the significance of the Gove-Johnson summit.

Me, Sarah Vain. In the front row of history!

RUSSIAN SUPERSTAR CAUGHT USING BANNED SUBSTANCES
by Our Drugs Staff **Mel Donium**

THERE was shock this week when one of the most famous Russians on the world stage was discovered to have used a substance banned by all international bodies.

That substance was polonium, which is a radioactive isotope guaranteed to affect your physical performance in a very extreme way, ie by killing you.

Big-hitting Vladimir Putin is alleged to have used polonium to beat his rival Alexander Litvinenko in what was described as a grudge match in a tea room in London.

Putin denies that he has done anything wrong and claims he's been using polonium for years for health reasons, to keep himself strong.

He defended himself, saying, "In the last ten years, nobody's ever objected, largely because they're all dead."

However, Putin stands to lose no money whatsoever as a result of these revelations. Some of the biggest names in corporate sponsorship, including McDonalds, Coca-Cola and Nike have decided to punish the Russian SuperTsar by doing nothing at all and keeping their businesses firmly in Russia.

Putin is perhaps better known for his work as a model, and is often pictured topless riding horses, wrestling with tigers and invading Ukraine.

Sharapova 'praised'

by Our Tennis Correspondent **Grunt Chapps**

MARIA Sharapova was praised last night by newspaper editors across Britain for remaining gorgeous in the wake of her failing a drugs test.

"For too long we've had to put up with pug-ugly German shot putters and hairy, female Russian weight lifters with thighs like tree trunks failing drugs tests," said one delighted newspaper editor.

"But full credit to Sharapova for putting the 'Phwoar' back into Per-Phwoar-mance-enhancing drugs.

"We look forward to Maria being stripped of her titles and of her clothes in our 19-page 'Sharapova Supplement' featuring all our favourite bikini pictures of the tennis beauty."

Nike confirmed last night that it has immediately cancelled its multi-million pound sponsorship deal with Sharapova.

"Just do it, but don't be stupid enough to get caught doing it," said a Nike spokesman.

"You're overthinking it"

SOMETHING OLD, SOMETHING OLDER...

A new love story by Dame Sylvie Krin, author of
Heir of Sorrows and *Duchess of Hearts*

THE STORY SO FAR: After a whirlwind romance, octogenarian billionaire media mogul Rupert Murdoch is marrying the beautiful ex-supermodel, Leggy Hall. Now read on...

A LIGHT drizzle shrouded the historic church of St Young Brides in Fleet Street, as the limousine conveying the world's most powerful man drew up outside.

Rupert Murdoch, accompanied by his sons Jimbo and Lachlustre, stepped out onto the ancient cobbles.

"Nervous, dad?" inquired Lachlustre, as Rupert walked shakily past the line of armed police. "No, I don't think they're going to arrest me this time!" quipped Rupert, as they ran the gauntlet of the vast crowd of paparazzi covering what was already billed as the wedding of the century.

"Fourth time lucky, eh, sir?" ventured Jimbo nervously, always worried nowadays about saying the wrong thing.

His indulgent father laughed happily. Nothing could dampen his triumphant mood. Here he was, a jaunty jackaroo in a bonzer blue suit, with a sharp crease in his strides and the smartest pair of brown shoes this side of Digger's Bum Creek, made from the finest Dundee Crocodile.

"Excellent choice of footwear, sir." It was Witherspoon, the editor of the London Times of London, helping his boss into the nave of the famous "journalists' church" where, in days of yore, so many practitioners of that noble profession had gone to pray before being sacked or arrested.

"Nearly as leathery as your face, you dirty old bastard," joked a familiar antipodean voice. It was Barry McKenzie, Rupert's irreverent old mate from the Land of Oz.

"Didn't recognise you there, Barry, because you've not dressed up as a sheila, you pommie poof!" retorted Rupert, with the sort of quickfire repartee that had dazzled the world's boardrooms for over a century.

As he walked down the aisle, he nodded to the dazzling array of the great, the good and Alan Yentob, packed into the pews. "Jeez!" thought Rupert. "You'd have though little Yentob could have changed out of his pyjamas for the occasion. I paid him enough money for hacking his phone to afford best bib and bloody tucker!" Still, everybody else had dressed in their finest finery to pay their respects on his big day.

There was the crème de la crème of British society – Sir Alfie Caine with his young wife Shangrila, Sir Andrew Lloyds-Bank and his young wife Evita, Billy Wyoyman with his even younger wife Lolita... strewth, talk about class!

As he took his seat in the front row, he could hear the roar of the paparazzi, as his beautiful bride from the Land of the BBQ-Bean-Burrito-To-Go arrived.

"This way, Leggy! Over here, Leggy! In the middle, Leggy!..."

"Y'all have a nice day now, y'hear?" drawled the sultry southern belle with the seven-foot legs, as she sashayed in her elegant, viagra-blue designer Vivienne Sweatshop wedding dress towards the church, accompanied by her stunningly attractive bridesmaid daughters, Sulky and Pouty, the fruit of her legally unbinding union with Sir Mick Jiggy.

The congregation listened to the excited cries of the photographers wafting down the chancel... "Show us some more leg, Leggy! Flash us your knickers. Go on, take your top off, love!!"

Rupert frowned. He would have to have a word with the editors of his newspapers

for this lack of deference at what were, after all, his sacred nuptials. But, before he could fire anyone, the organ struck up with the processional music, Vivaldi's *Gloria Hunniford*...

T HE vicar, Reverend Canon Dawn Dibley, had reached the most important part of the ceremony – the plighting of the troth. Rupert looked meaningfully at his son Jimbo.

"Did you remember the ring?" he asked him.

"I have no memory of the ring. I cannot recall any mention of a ring. I cannot attest to any recollection of a ring."

"I emailed you, you idiot boy."

"I didn't read my emails on that occasion."

This was beginning to get embarrassing – the globe's mightiest media mogul standing at the altar, looking lost. Fortunately, his daughter Lizzie, the former Mrs Matthew Fraud, and always the brightest of the bunch, came to the rescue, discreetly approaching the altar rail.

"Have my old one, Daddy. I brought it just in case the boys made a balls-up, as per!"

Relieved, Rupert turned back to Vicar Dibley to concentrate on the vows.

"I, Rupert Dirtswell Diggeridoo Murdoch, take thee, Rebekah... I mean, Wendi... I mean, Leggy... er..."

The polished prelate of St Young Brides moved swiftly through the ceremony.

"Now, Leggy," she asked, "are you going to obey Rupert?"

"No," interrupted Murdoch. "She's not the bloody prime minister."

The congregation roared with laughter at Rupert's ripper riposte and no one was laughing louder than Her Majesty's Secretary of State for Justice, Mr Michael Gofer, accompanied by his stylish wife, Sarah Vain, dressed in a gold lamé poncho with matching flares.

"Ha ha ha ha ha," laughed Michael, thinking of the wonderful wedding present he was going to give Rupert, in the shape of a hush-hush Royal scoop about the EU...

Vicar Dibley decided to move things on apace. "I now pronounce you billionaire and wife..."

T HE themed reception in the upstairs snug of the Ex-Printers' Arms in Riot Street, Wapping, was buzzing. Even his old rival, Paul Swearer, from the Daily Blackmail had come to pay his respects.

"Are you going to put me and Leggy on yer front page?" enquired Rupert, jovially.

"Too f***ing right I am, you old f***ing c***! Under the headline 'Money For Old Rupe!' Let's hope Leggy has a Pre-*Nap*! Ha ha ha!" Thank heavens Mr Swearer was out of earshot of the younger bridesmaids from his former marriage, Wendolina and Rupertella.

Rupert tapped his champagne flute to call the room to order. "Charge your glasses with amber nectar, folks, I'm serving vintage Castlemaine XXXX Wife Special Brew."

The editors of Newscorps titles hurried around the room, topping up the thirsty guests' glasses from chilled tinnies.

"There's gonna be no best man's speech," continued Rupert, "because I'm the best man in the room and I'll fight any jumped-up jackaroo who says otherwise."

The assembled worthies cheered approvingly, as Leggy looked adoringly at her gerontocratic groom.

"Instead, I'm going to read the telegrams." Rupert put on his designer Giorgio Clooni reading glasses.

"This one's from the Queen..."

A cheer went up from the clearly impressed coterie of celebrities and colleagues.

"Dear Mr Murdoch, Congratulations on reaching 100 years old... Bloody hell..." Rupert hastily crumpled up the official missive from Buckingham Palace and began another...

"Dear Rupert, I'm sorry I can't be with you, but my fee for attendance at weddings is $50,000, payable to the Tony Blair Foundation in Grand... Strewth!" Rupert was getting flustered now and flung the message to the floor. Surely there was a genuine expression of goodwill amongst the apologies for absence.

This one looked promising...

"Good ruck, Reggy and Lupert. You're gonna need it, gurrible glandad and gleedy fortune cookie hunter!"

Outside, the rain fell steadily, as the sky darkened...

(To be continued)

THE Sun

Friday, March 18, 2016

GOD BACKS BREXIT

By Our Political Staff
SAINT ANTHONY OF GALLAGHER

IN AN amazing new twist, God, who traditionally doesn't comment on political matters, has come off the cloud and declared himself a supporter of the Leave Campaign in the forthcoming European Referendum.

Following the Queen's surprise declaration last week, God is now the most high profile figure to join this newspaper in its campaign to do whatever Mr Murdoch says. *(Surely "to leave the European Union for social and economic reasons"? Ed.)*

This is a massive blow to Satan and his "Project Fear", which the Sun has long exposed as little short of pure evil.

However, sources close to God deny the story, saying that the Supreme Being cannot recall any conversation in which he suggested that staying in Europe was the equivalent of "going to hell in a handcart".

But one Brexit supporter said, "That's God all over – he moves in mysterious ways, and now he's intervened in human affairs for the first time since he supported the so-called Paradexit, when Adam and Eve freely voted to leave Eden."

The supporter continued, "You will remember that the serpent told them this was a leap in the dark, but they never looked back and went on to a life of suffering, childbirth, back-breaking toil, murder and… hang on!"

SAYS

This newspaper stands by our Almighty scoop

We have impeccable sources, namely Michelangelo, who painted God quite clearly telling Adam to "Get Out!" *(see above for uncropped picture)*, and a large number of cherubs who overheard the conversation clearly and leaked it to our reporter, who had voices in his head after ten pints down the "The Wapping Lyre".

"Has anyone seen my anti-depressants?"

ME AND MY SPOON

THIS WEEK

KRISTIN SCOTT THOMAS

Do you have a favourite spoon?

Yes, I love French spoons. They are so chic and stylish... unlike British spoons, which are ghastly, unattractive and vulgar.

So you don't like British spoons?

No, they are so obvious and so common, flaunting themselves around the kitchen without any sense of embarrassment, when they really should stay in the cutlery drawer.

What type of spoon do you prefer?

Well, the typical French *cuillère* is elegant, thin and refined, whereas your average English spoon is far too heavy and is usually a fake orange colour. Urghhh!!!

Spoonwise, this is a bit unfair, isn't it?

No. These crude spoons spend all their time dipped in drink and end up falling onto the floor.

That can't be true of all British spoons...?

No, there are very rare exceptions when an English spoon looks like a French spoon and is cool, slim, subtle, beautiful and sexy. In fact, there was one in the marvellous film "Four Forks and a Spoon".

Has anything amusing ever happened to you in connection with a spoon?

Non.

NEXT WEEK: *Tom Bower, "Me and My Bower".*

WELCOME TO
MACEDONIA
NO MIGRANTS WILL BE KEPT
IN THIS COUNTRY OVERNIGHT

41

'Lazy Prince' Row Grows

by Our Royal Staff
Phil Royal Pages

BUCKINGHAM PALACE was once again on the defensive last night following a series of attacks by this newspaper on work-shy royals.

Our latest 94-page exposé yesterday revealed the astonishing fact that the Prince, who is third in line to the throne, does ALMOST NOTHING the whole time.

We can reveal that this idle prince not only goes on expensive skiing holidays, but when he **is** in the UK, he spends his day:

● lying around asleep
● watching CBBC on TV
● playing in the garden
● hanging out with friends.

Prince George has performed no royal duties whatsoever and does not even have a full-time job as an excuse for his laziness.

As our editorial puts it frankly, *"It's time to grow up, Your*

Highness. Act your age and pull your Postman Pat socks up", otherwise this newspaper will recommend that you are passed over and we give the throne instead to your sister, Charlotte.

Late News

● Charlotte "even lazier than George" shock. Fourth in line to throne can't even be bothered to sit up, walk or use potty.

THE ALTERNATIVE VOICE

DAVE SPART (Co-Chairperson of the Gary-Rhodes-Must-Fall Return-The-Benin-Cockerel To Athens No-Platform-For-Germain-Greer Pro-Anti-Tory Momentum Alliance)

Once again, we are confronted with the totally sickening spectacle of the Neo-Conservative establishment in full cry, supporting the euro-capitalist Remain conspiracy that merely serves the vested financial interests of the American-Franco-German industrial military complex by co-opting the support of closet quasi-socialist lickspittles and running dogs of the proto-fascist hegemony, ie members of the pro-EU so-called "Labour Party", who have, in fact, totally, utterly and sickeningly betrayed the euro-workers' solidarity movement and sold out to the Brussels bankers and Frankfurt financiers in a grotesque display of utter hypocrisy and total class treason and who are currently led by none other than the biggest turncoat and people's traitor in living political history, ie that Tory scum, Jeremy Corbyn, and his so-called comrade, John "Judas" McDonnell, whose utter, total and sickening support for Tory austerity is even more sickening than the sickening sight of Comrade Corbyn getting into bed with the Old Etonian mafia of David Cameron and Boris Johnson, er... er...

*"Do you have to put on a face mask **every** night?"*

Jonesy

The Secret DIARY OF SIR JOHN MAJOR KG aged 77¾

Monday

I was reading the morning paper while enjoying my regular bowl of Ready Brexit, when I could not help but notice the growing tide of malcontents in favour of leaving the European Union.

"This will never do, oh yes!" I remarked to Norman, as she made our favourite breakfast beverage, namely tea in the teapot. "It's like those bastards all those years ago, who made my life a not inconsiderable misery."

"What do you mean, John?" asked Norman inquisitively.

"Flirting with leaving seems to me to be very dangerous," I said. "Oh yes. It is sheer folly, verging on the reckless," I continued. "The broken relationship is more likely to be poisonous than harmonious. Resentment will be deep. Negotiations with an irate ex-partner could be very difficult, oh yes."

It came to my attention that Norman had been somewhat quiet during my informed peroration.

"You seem somewhat quiet, my dear," I observed observantly.

At this, she broke her silence. "Talking of bastards," she said, "flirting and broken relationships..." She paused mysteriously before concluding, "...resentment would indeed be deep!" And with that she began to pour the tea, missing my cup entirely.

I felt a not inconsiderable burning sensation in the groin area of my striped Winceyette pyjamas, causing me to say, quite loudly, "Ow!!".

THE TIMES | Friday 18 March 2016

Letters to the Editor

A very important person writes

Sir, As a very important and wholly independent Governor of the Bank of England, I have been asked by the prime minister, Mr David Cameron, to make it clear to the British people that if they were to vote to leave the European Union, this would immediately trigger the greatest run on the pound in history.

Hundreds of foreign banks and businesses would immediately make plans to leave Britain; the City of London and the entire UK economy would collapse and bodies would remain unburied in the streets being gnawed by giant rats.

I am Mr Cameron's obedient servant,

MARK CARNEY,
Governor of the
Bank of England.

GUIDE TO STATE PENSION CHANGES

AGED 55 – 65
You will retire in your 60s with a generous state pension that will allow you to enjoy a decent standard of living.

AGED 45 – 55
You will retire in your 70s with a reduced state pension that will allow you to enjoy years of worrying whether you can afford to turn the heating on.

AGED 35 – 45
You will retire in your 80s with a miserly state pension that will allow you to enjoy dog food and hypothermia.

AGED 25 – 35
You will retire in your 90s with a state pension so minuscule that it will allow you to make just the one phone call to Dignitas.

THE INTERVIEW THAT FINALLY SET THE GREAT EU DEBATE ON FIRE

ANDREW MARR (*for it is he*): Boris Johnson, you've belatedly jumped on the Brexit bandwagon in quite a cynical way, haven't you?

BORIS: Well, cripes, that's a bit of a low blow. You see, the important thing is…

MARR (*interrupting*): But that's not what British business thinks, is it?

BORIS: …the EU is like a prison, you see, and the jailer chap has for once left the door open, so…

MARR: The trouble with your side is that you haven't got a remotely coherent exit plan, so…

BORIS: Hang on, Marr, let me finish my metaphor about this prison thingie, and out of the door we can see this wonderful sunlit future for the jolly old UK…

MARR: So you don't think much of the Prime Minister's deal, which surely gives us all that we could…

BORIS: Just a minute, I haven't finished with the sunlit vista bit yet… So everyone's saying, "Oh, no, we are too frightened to go out through the door in case something ghastly happens" and…

MARR (*talking over Boris*): But that's not what you used to say. We never heard much of all that sunlit upland stuff in the old days…

BORIS (*talking over Marr*): …and out there in the sunshine are all these happy chaps and chapesses, who couldn't be more chuffed to have escaped from the shackles of the Brussels prison…

MARR (*still talking over Boris*): I really can't let you get away with this, this is not the Boris Johnson Show, it's the Andrew Marr Show – and the viewers want to know my opinions on Brexit, not yours.

BORIS (*still talking over Marr*): …so that's why I think the future couldn't be rosier.

MARR (*now shouting over Boris*): Let's face it, the only future that interests you is the thought of getting David Cameron's job, isn't it? Everyone realises that's the reason why you're…

BORIS (*now shouting over Marr*): …that's just a pyramid of piffle, a whiff-whaff of waffle, a typical BBC gigabyte of garbage…

MARR: Well, that's all we've got time for, thank goodness. And now, we've got the German Europe minister, Frau Eva Klöser-Union to tell us how important it is for Britain to remain in the EU and how, if we don't, we face disaster on a scale which no one has yet dared to imagine.

TURKEY READY TO JOIN EU

by Our Diplomatic Staff **Des Potism**

PRESIDENT Erdogan of Turkey last week gave what he called a "practical demonstration" of the way in which his country is meeting the EU's high standards of human rights.

The president announced that he had "overnight" turned one of Turkey's most popular newspapers, Zaman, from an "irresponsible scandal sheet" into a "responsible, independent, quality journal of record".

Up until 3 March, Zaman had run stories about the president, suggesting that it could be argued that he had authoritarian tendencies and that there might be questions to be answered about Turkey buying oil and selling arms to Islamist groups in Syria.

On 4 March, Zaman appeared under a new name, "The Daily Erdograph", and took a slightly different editorial stance. It led with a full front-page photograph of President Erdogan beneath the headline, "Turkish people united in admiration for Glorious Leader Erdogan except for the appalling Kurds who don't count because they are not really Turkish anyway and who our gallant president is quite rightly locking up and bombing as part of his Islamist Reform Programme which is rapidly taking Turkey into the EU" (*surely "fifteenth century"? Ed.*) Said the president, "The freedom of the press is very important to me and I will make sure that they are free to write whatever I want". He added that the new Daily Erdograph would now be a first-class newspaper with positive stories about Turkey, but no stories about Elton John and absolutely no women's pages.

Late News

● President Erdogan pledges to continue the fight against journalism for ever.

THE BIG BUMPER PRESIDENT ERDOGAN JOKE BOOK

NO. 37

"Knock knock"

"Who's there?"

"The secret police."

NO. 94

What do you call a satirist in Turkey?

An ambulance.

UN-PC WORLD

Shadbolt

CUT-OUT-AND-KEEP GUIDE FOR AMERICAN VOTERS

THINGS IN WHICH DONALD TRUMP SHOULD BE PRESIDENT

★ An episode of The Simpsons where Homer runs for public office

★ A low budget Hunger Games spoof starring Lindsay Lohan

★ A bad dream you have after eating a whole baked camembert

★ Legoland

THINGS IN WHICH DONALD TRUMP SHOULD NOT BE PRESIDENT

★ Real life

43

Lookalikes

Old rocker   **Off rocker**

Sir,

I wonder if your readers have noticed the striking resemblance between Germaine Greer, well-known female eunuch and trans-gender challenger, and Noddy Holder, Black Country rocker, who makes a fortune every year by asking us if we are hanging up our stockings on the wall?

MICHAEL WOODS,

Via email.

Sir,

I woke up this morning wondering how long Douglas Carswell, UKIP's MP for Clacton, will hang on after the election?

NEIL PATTERSON,

Kintbury.

Angela Merkel   **Elton John**

Sir,

For your consideration of your Lookalike section. Do Mutti Merkel and ageing rock legend Elton John share the same stylist?

LORRAINE CARROLL,

Beckenham, Kent.

Penfold   **Michael Gove**

Sir,

I was watching an episode of Danger Mouse. I couldn't help noticing the cowardly bespectacled hamster and Danger Mouse's reluctant assistant, Penfold, had a remarkable resemblance to a certain other bespectacled assistant, Michael Gove. "Oh carrots, Danger Mouse!!"

PAUL FALCONE,

Via email.

Green   **Maxwell**

Sir,

Has anyone noticed the similarity of the deceased multi-millionaire luxury yacht owner and plunderer of Mirror Group pension funds, Robert Maxwell, and multi-millionaire luxury yacht owner Sir Philip Green? Could they be related?

IAN BALDWIN,

Hingham, Norfolk.

Steptoe   **Vardy**

Sir,

With all due respect to the wonderful, dearly-departed Wilfrid Brambell, I feel that Steptoe's real son is alive and (literally) kicking, somewhere up in Leicester.

ALLASTAIR MCGILLIVRAY,

Sydney, Australia.

Peperami Man   **James Delingpole**

Sir,

Uncanny!

CHRISTINE SYERS,

Via email.

Angela Eagle   **Brienne of Tarth**

Sir,

Has anyone else noticed the resemblance between Brienne of Tarth off Game of Thrones and Angela Eagle? Are they by any chance related?

TIM HANNAH,

Via email.

Evil Scientist   **Rupert Murdoch**

Sir,

Don't hold back the truth, we depend on your Private Eye to lay it out as it is: Is the Evil Scientist from "A Nightmare Before Christmas" now married to Jerry Hall? Well? Is SHE?

Yours in fear and loathing of Rupert MurkyCock,

R. STUNALEY,

Via email.

Enver Hoxha   **Jonathan Ross**

Sir,

Your readers may be interested to note the striking resemblance between the two famous figures shown in the attached photographs – Mr Enver Hoxha, the late Albanian dictator and guru of Jeremy Corbyn, pictured taking a well-earned break from the stresses of the class struggle, and Mr Jonathan Ross, the popular entertainer, somewhat surprisingly clad in military uniform.

ROGER DAVIS,

Peterborough.

Cook   **O'Grady**

Sir,

Has Paul O'Grady now taken over as CEO at Apple? Can we now look forward to Lily Savage launching a future model of the iPad? I think we should be told, etc...

MATTHEW JONES,

Via email.

Potter   **Backbencher**

Sir,

Now that Harriet Harman has retired from front-bench politics, will she just potter around on the back benches?

P.F. GOURD,

Via email.

Turin Shroud   **Jeremy Corbyn**

Sir,
    Is this J.C.?
            ENA B. LEVER,
Via email.

Peston   **Sergei**

Sir,
    The fact that these two must be related is much easier to spot now that they are appearing on the same channel... What would weekends be without "Sergei on Sunday"? Simples;-)!
            HORST KOPLECK,
    Glasgow.

Philip May   **Arthur Askey**

Sir,
    Before your very eyes! An old friend of Private Eye is back.
            Ay-Thang-Yaw,
            ANDREW CULTON,
Via email.

Owl   **Nicky Morgan**

Sir,
    Nicky Morgan looks like an owl.
            ROB TILSLEY,
Via email.

Woman in burqa   **City of London**

Sir,
    Has the City of London been radicalised? I think we should be told.
            Yours sincerely,
            MARK SIMS,
Via email.

Kim Jong-un   **Ruth Davidson**

Sir,
    May I be the umpteenth reader to remark on the similarity between Ruth Davidson, the leader of the Tory party in Scotland, and another world leader with perhaps more immediately recognisable features. Perhaps they're related. I think we should be told.
            JOHN CAYLEY,
Isle of Skye.

Rowley Birkin QC   **Lord Sumption QC**

Sir,
    I wonder if readers have noticed the striking similarity between some of our leading lawyers?
            MS B. HALF,
Via email.

Trump   **Mussolini**

Sir,
    Has anyone noticed, as I have, the extraordinary similarity between the political leaders Donald Trump and Benito Mussolini?
    Are they by any chance related?
            STEVE LEVERETT,
Via email.

Caligula   **Osborne**

Sir,
    Lest these statesmen be confused, allow me to distinguish them for the benefit of your readers. One is a notoriously deranged and sadistic despot. The other is the Roman emperor Caligula (painted version of Caligula bust in Ny Carlsberg Glyptotek, Copenhagen).
            F. MCGHEE,
Via email.

Timmy   **Tim**

Sir,
    I can't be the only one to be delighted to see that Timmy from South Park has become leader of the Liberal Democrats, surely?
            A. PSEUDONYM,
Via email.

Vader   **Abbott**

Sir,
    Has anyone noticed the remarkable similarity between Diane Abbott and Darth Vader? One lives in a completely different world from the rest of us...
            NEIL JAMIESON,
Salford.

Comedy   **Tragedy**

Sir,
    In Naples, we found a mosaic of a Roman tragedian which reminded us, for some reason, of a Celtic comedian.
            MIKE AND POLLY,
Via email.

Cowardly Lion   **Julian Assange**

Sir,
    Cowardly Lion – Assange.
            DOUGLAS MCCARTHY,
Via email.

Rock Giant   **Big Friendly Giant**

Sir,
    Separated at birth?
            SIMON GOSDEN,
Via email.

Fears that violence will descend into Trump rally

by Our US Staff **Biff Protestors**

There was mounting concern across America last night, from New Dworkin to Pig's Knuckle, Arkansas, that routine violence on the streets was turning into pro-Trump rallies.

The police said they couldn't be expected to control the rising tide of inflammatory rhetoric and pointless stupidity which was now infecting even the most ordinary punch-up.

A police spokesman, Officer Dibble, said, "Even a standard bar-room brawl is turning into a bad tempered debate about immigration, Muslims and America's place in the world.

"Even minor domestic incidents are turning into loud-mouth, ill-informed attacks on Mexicans, anti-gun lobby liberals and Hillary Clinton. We simply can't cope!"

He concluded, "Hopefully the next president will sort this all out, and take the senseless politics out of US violence."

From The Archives

THE ☙ TIMES
27TH MARCH 1912

Competition To Name New Ship Sails Into Trouble

THERE was a certain amount of disquiet in nautical circles when a public competition to name a new ocean liner was hijacked by a number of mischief-makers, leading to a selection of rather silly names being suggested. These include:

Shippy McShipface

Sinky McSinkship

Floaty McLifeboat

Freezy McFrozen

Icy McIceberg

Ratty McJumpship

Said a spokesman for the White Star Line, "We are disappointed by the public's immature response.

"We don't want our massive ship to be given an inappropriate name that will make us a laughing stock for generations to come, so instead we're going to call it 'The Titanic'."

BIBLICAL TIMES
4,000 BC

Competition to name new ship sails into trouble

BY OUR SCRIBE

The famous meteorologist, zoologist and ship-builder Noah was unhappy last night at the result of a nationwide poll to name his recently finished 300 x 50 x 30 cubits wooden vessel.

Said Noah, "I regret asking the public for their suggestions as to what to call my new craft. We have ended up with the name *Arky McArkface*."

Nursery Times

YET ANOTHER MAGICAL TRICK FROM THE WIZARD

By **Little Boy Blew It All**

FOR a day or two last week, it looked as though the Wizard of Ozborne had at last been exposed as a total fraud and was facing the gravest crisis of his career.

Furious Munchkins surrounded the Palace of Ozminster to call for the Wizard's abdication, after he had been caught out refusing to provide any more assistance to the Emerald City's Disabled Community, ie providing the Tin Man with a new heart and the Scarecrow with a prosthetic brain.

The Wizard had said he needed the money to give tax breaks to the Wicked Witch *(surely "Wicked Rich"? Ed)* and also for his favourite infrastructure project, the new high-speed YBR2, which will cut five minutes' travelling time along the Yellow Brick Road which connects the capital city to what the Wizard calls "my Northern Magic Powerhouse".

Everyone in the kingdom was in agreement, yet again, that it was the end for the Wizard, and for several days he vanished totally from view behind his famous curtain.

But then, suddenly, he popped out and explained that everyone had got it wrong. He wasn't going to take any money from the poor at all. In fact, he was going to pour out more money than ever before, for everyone.

And the Munchkins cried, "But, Wizard, how are you going to pull off the incredible trick of finding the money to pay for it all, when you told us there wasn't any left?"

"Simple," said the Wizard. "I'm going to borrow it!"

And all the Tory Munchkins were filled with admiration at what a brilliantly clever magician he was, and shouted with one accord, "Hurrah for the Wizard of Ozterity!".

---

gloop *EXCLUSIVE*

Gwyneth Paltrow's 2016 beauty tips

Being stung by bees

Allowing yourself to be stung repeatedly by angry bees is a PHENOMENAL way to reduce inflammation and scarring.

Stabbing yourself with scissors

Repeatedly stabbing yourself with scissors is the BEST way I know to rebalance your karma by increasing blood flow to specific regions of your body.

Being hit in face with a sock full of wet cement

This is AMAZING for tightening the facial muscles and removing crow's feet and occasionally one of your eye sockets.

Contracting ebola

Contracting ebola is my HOT HOT tip for rapid weight loss if you have a special size zero party outfit that you just have to fit into! Both Beyonce and Adele SWEAR by it.

HAPPILY EVER AFTER...

A new love story by Dame Sylvie Krin, author of *Heir of Sorrows* and *Never Too Old*

THE STORY SO FAR: Blissful newlyweds Rupert Murdoch and Leggy Hall are honeymooning in the South of France. Now read on...

THE spring Provençale sunlight streamed through the shutters of the luxurious Loon de Miel Suite in the 6-Star Hotel Splendide on the famous Côte d'Argent.

"Jeez," thought Rupert, lying on the antique Louis the Roux phwoar-poster bed. He hadn't felt such pure, unbounded joy since the day he had shut down the old printing presses on Fleet Street, smashed the unions and put thousands of pommy bastards out of work!

The aroma of Texan rosehip-scented bath oil signalled the arrival of Leggy from the ensuite bathroom, elegantly draped in a designer His and Hermes silk towelling robe.

"Happy, darling?" drawled the 6'9" southern belle from the Land of Bucket-of-BBQ-Wings-To-Go.

"I'm as happy as a dingo who's discovered he can lick his own boll..."

"Yes, thank you, darling... I thought perhaps we could go out later and look at the Matisses in the Musée de St Paul de Gascoigne?" interrupted Leggy, keen to savour the cultural highlights of the Cap de Benefit region.

Strewth! thought the billionaire tycoon and proprietor of the Sky Arts and Elbow Channel... not more pictures of weird-looking blue Sheilas prancing around in the all together!

But out of his mouth came only the tender words, "Whatever you say, my bonzer blushing bride."

Leggy flopped onto the bed beside him and began flicking through the album of wedding photos which had been specially couriered out to the hotel in Nice Mais d'Ime by Rupert's loyal manservant Witherspoon, the editor of the *London Times of London* in London.

"What a perfect day that was," cooed Leggy, as she turned over page after page of golden memories from the previous week. And Rupert, with his amazing post-Leveson recovery, could remember it all perfectly!

And what a wedding party that had been! There was Cabinet Minister Michael Gofer doing the twist with renowned playwright Sir Tom Stoppit. And there was pop star Sir Bob Fuckoff leading the conga around the room, followed by top artist Tracey Paper,

popular actor Richard E. Cant and the BBC's Alan Botney, all dancing along to the Abbo tribute band "Super Rupert", who had done such a great job belting out all the classic numbers, including *Mama Murdoch*, *Brexit Queen* and *Thank you for the Money*...

A KNOCK on the door interrupted their enraptured reverie. "Room service, Monsieur."

"Come in, you froggy bastard," replied the global media baron charmingly, his irrepressible antipodean good humour overflowing from every pore.

The waiter brought in a trolley laden with silver salvers which he lifted dramatically to reveal the various energy drinks, protein shakes and male wellness vitamin supplements that constituted a power breakfast for the young-at-heart octogenarian who still had a bit of puff in his didgeridoo.

"Why, thank you, young garçon,"

breathed Leggy breathily. "You have a nice day now, y'hear?"

The waiter blushed and exited the room hastily, only just remembering to present a selection of the day's papers and magazines for the languid lovebirds to enjoy with their leisurely repast.

But what was this on the cover of *Le Fugaro*? A photograph of none other than Rupert's ex-wife, Wendi, the dragon lady of the Deng Dynasty.

Rupert was aghast, but Leggy too had seen the picture and began to read out the headline in her supermodel French... "La Romance de La Century, Wendi et Putin fait le Legover".

"Sacré bloody bluey!" Rupert exclaimed. "Pardon my french, Leggy."

But there on the front of *Paris Macho* the story was repeated, accompanied by photographs of a topless Vladimir Putin astride a huge stallion and a sizzling Wendi in a Suzy Wong designer bikini, sitting on the super-yacht belonging to Russian cellist billionaire Oleg "Olly" Garkovich (*The Polonium*, registered in Panama).

Rupert turned the pages of the French periodical frantically and he and Leggy read the dreadful news in stark, uncompromising black and white...

Wendi Deng, le gorgeous former squeeze du très vieux tycoon Rupert Murdoch, maintenant cherche le happiness dans les manly arms du plus riche et powerful homme dans le world. Oui, c'est vrai! Vlad et Wend sont un item! Elle a les looks. Il a les tanks... C'est le plus exciting liaison dans l'histoire du monde!

Dit Wendi: *J'ai traded up! Dans les mots de Boney M, Vlad est comme Lasputin! He est un Russian ruv machine! God! Son torso est lipped! Il est même plus buff que Tony Brair!"*

Sur des autres pages
● Rupert et Leggy – qui cares? **94**

"Can this be true, Rupee?" asked Leggy in a small voice.

"Well, it's not in any of my newspapers, so it probably is," replied the muted global press magnate.

Rupert felt a strange chill descend on the Honeymoonover Suite, and outside the window dark clouds scuttled across the previously azure sky...

(To be continued...)

"Well, that's good. You haven't got dementia. You're just a stupid old git"

WE MUST NOT GIVE IN TO TERROR BY OVER-REACTING

ON OTHER PAGES

PANIC! 1 FEAR! 2 HORROR! 3 DEATH! 4 SLAUGHTER! 5 APOCALYPSE! 6 ARMAGEDDON! 7 HELP! 8 WE ARE ALL GOING TO DIE! 94

GREAT *Trivial Pursuit* QUESTIONS REVISITED

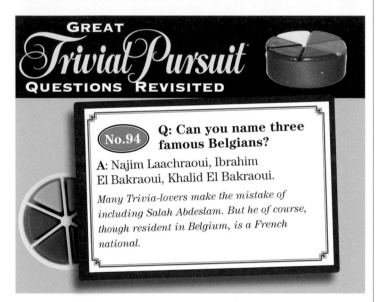

No.94 **Q: Can you name three famous Belgians?**

A: Najim Laachraoui, Ibrahim El Bakraoui, Khalid El Bakraoui.

Many Trivia-lovers make the mistake of including Salah Abdeslam. But he of course, though resident in Belgium, is a French national.

What You Missed

The Today Programme
Radio 4

John Humphrys *(for it is he)*: And news just coming in from Brussels that there have been explosions at the airport. Obviously we will keep you informed throughout the rest of the programme.

Mishal Husain: And we've got on the line from the airport an eyewitness who can give us a first-hand account of what's happening. Claire Thair, tell us what you saw...

Thair: Well, I really haven't a clue what's going on here. I was just having my breakfast when there were these two very loud bangs and then there was dust everywhere, but at the moment I can't really...

Husain: Yes, but what we really want to know is, have you seen any dead bodies or horrendous injuries?

The ghost of Sue McGhastly *(for it is she)*: Hang on, young lady, that's the kind of thing I used to ask...

Humphrys: That's quite enough from you, Sue. It's time for the weather *(continued 94khz)*

"Take that ISIS!... and that!... and that!"

GRAEME KEYES

BRUSSELS LATEST

Confusion grows on Facebook

■ There is growing concern amongst Facebook users regarding the effectiveness of changing one's Facebook profile pic to the city where the latest terrorist atrocity has taken place.

"I'm quite disappointed ISIS didn't get the message that enough was enough after I changed my profile pic to an image of the Arc de Triomphe in the wake of the attack on the Bataclan concert hall," said one Facebook user.

"It's almost as if ISIS just ignored that, plus the sad poem I retweeted on Twitter about terrorism being bad... and simply continued with their barbaric ways."

"I don't even know any Belgium landmarks," complained another. "Can't I just use the Eiffel tower again? I've already photoshopped that one."

The Facebook users, however, said they hadn't fully given up hope that social media updates could change the world.

"I'm going to post this picture of TinTin crying, because if that doesn't melt the hearts of the Jihadists and have them renouncing violence and immediately handing themselves into the authorities, I don't know what will."

World leaders hurriedly meet

■ World leaders met today in an emergency summit called in the wake of the Brussels terror attack to agree on the best empty slogan for them to use.

Some leaders, including Britain's David Cameron, favoured the tried and tested "Je Suis Bruxelles", whilst other leaders, including President Obama, were pushing for a more radical approach, suggesting such trite empty slogans as "Je Suis Frites" or "Je Suis Poirot".

All leaders agreed it was vital that the world unite behind the one empty slogan rather than actually formulating an effective plan to stop ISIS.

TV Film Highlights Easter Special

Good Easter Friday Eve
They Didn't Fly to Bruges
BBC1 9pm

Remake of the classic 1940s black-and-white wartime thriller updated to the modern day. This time, no one flies to Bruges because they've shut the airport and everybody is far too scared to go to Belgium.

Good Bank Easter Holiday Saturday
Murder on the Brussels Express
BBC2 2pm

Top Belgian investigator, the legendary Hercule Poirot, misses all the clues and fails to round up any suspects, despite them being known to the authorities and living in a suburb right under his nose.

Bank Holiday Maundy Sunday
Double Impact
ITV3 2am

Two bombs explode in an airport and there is no fantasy Belgian paramilitary action hero called "The Muscles from Brussels" (played by Jean-Claude van Damme) to do anything about it.

(That's enough films. Ed.)

DIARY

BRUCE ANDERSON: THE PLEASURES OF THE TABLE

It was a Bâtard-Montrachet, a very drinkable mid-to-early morning wine with a hint of smoked vole about it and more than a suspicion of unsoaped flannel. For those of us who like a wine that is flirtatious yet seemly, with an embonpoint that is neither too hidden nor to overt, it proved an ideal libation.

Whensoe'er I sup upon Bâtard-Montrachet, I find my mind drawn ineluctably to the hay stacks of yore, filled, as they were, with buxom wenches happy to bring joy to the weary traveller to an accompaniment of trumpet or ukelele.

The perfect companion to a fried breakfast of haddock, gammon, guinea-fowl, barn-owl, haggis, goat and a dozen eggs daintily scrambled in lard by a pert female skivvy, that nimble bottle proved a far from unwelcome adornment to our conversation.

To the distant sound of china and eating-irons being scrubbed clean by womanly hands rendered less enticing by the years, the talk among the gentlemen turned to Europe. We were in broad agreement that the frogs are a sluggardly race, energetic only in the hoisting of the white flag. But what of the Kraut? Has he finally brushed himself down after the hammering we gave him in the last skirmish, or is he still smarting from readiness to hit back? My suggestion that we settle the matter over a couple of fine bottles of 1980 Caillerets (not a special year, but perfectly willing to please) was eagerly received.

A short while later, the ladies were anxious to kick us out of the kitchen in order to prepare our luncheon. Gentlemen all, we were prepared to make such a sacrifice, and exited with barely a show of discontent. I then seized the opportunity to repair to the smallest room, armed only with a modest pair of lamb cutlets, successfully purloined from the frigidaire, along with a bracing tumbler of Bulgarian plonk as *une aide à l'evacuation*.

There are, I would argue, few pleasures in life greater than the voiding of one's bowels after an agreeable repast, particularly when the sublime activity is not undertaken hither and thither, but in a room expressly designed for that purpose. But what is the wine best suited to act as its handmaiden? Yes, my Bulgarian plonk would do, but in an ideal world one would opt for the push and thrust of a bold young Burgundy, or the astringent swagger of a Petit Chablis, but only from a reputable supplier.

Ablutions undergone, elevenses beckoned. Every time one door closes, another opens, as the Bard might have put it. Why, I wonder, does this most magnificent of morning meals suffer such neglect in these barren times? Unaccountably, my hosts had decided simply to by-pass it, blind to the demands of peckishness in that perilous half-hour between a late second breakfast and an early pre-luncheon "snack".

Finding the dutiful ladies buried deep in their gossip and chitter-chatter o'er the mixing-bowl and saucepan, I stole past them into the larder, where a voluptuous cake of cream and chocolate sat longingly beneath some netting.

No race is won by the timid. In the absence of a knife (is it not a sign of our mean-spirited times that hosts provide no cutlery in their larders?) I fell back on my hands, cutting a slice with my right forefinger, before scooping it into my opened mouth using my left palm as a makeshift shovel. I then repeated the process four or five times, cutting myself a further slice for storage in my jacket pocket in case of emergency, and wiping my hands on the dishcloth conveniently placed over a large jelly, from which I also took a modest scoop.

Back in the drawing-room, I felt that I should be doing my fair share of the donkey-work, so applied the corkscrew with due haste to a couple of bottles of Leoville Barton, a little young, perhaps, but with all the polish and sophistication of a senior statesman, such as my dear friend Peter Carrington, who is, incidentally, a dear friend.

The second bottle was an improvement on the first, and I was entertaining high hopes for the third when my fellow guests entered the room, all eager for sustenance. "This needs to breathe a little" I observed, placing the Leoville Barton to one side, and offering a serviceable Rosé to the others.

After pouring them their glasses of Rosé, I glanced at my watch. "It must have breathed enough by now," I said, and helped myself to a goblet of the Leoville Barton. If civilisation is to endure, it will owe its biggest debt to those who have had the fortitude and patience to hold out for the finer wines.

The wine flowed over lunch, quite literally so, as midway through an amusing anecdotal I managed to knock a bottle of semi-decent Saint-Estèphe over the roast potatoes, much to the consternation of my hostess, who then spent many minutes interrupting the flow of my opinions with her sordid array of cloths, sponges and suchlike. Nor did she bother to thank me for working so hard to keep the conversation afloat through all these distractions, but then the "fairer" sex, for all its many attractions, is blessed with little or no knowledge of the convivial arts. It may be unfair, but, then again, life is unfair. There is nothing we can do about it, other than make sure that it is unfair for others, too.

Cheersh! Your doughy draughty doughty scrivener scrivens these final paragraphinations at tea-time, tea for two and two for totty, a restorationalitive flagon of squiffable squaffable quaffable Cognac at his elbow diddly with a nimble yet buxom 2001 Château d'Yquem on hand knees and boomps a daisy to accompany it on its sway down the proverbial hatch. The 2001 is a serious wine that demands attention all shipping, dogger, fisher, German bite, he will bite if you let him, the Hun may look like us but he's a different kettle of fish plenty more fish in the sea the sea change, loose change, all change, this train is stopping here, stop, top, society improve from the top up did someone just offer a top up well thank you very much I wouldn't say no.

As told to
CRAIG BROWN

Fallen angels

"Always lovely to see passion for the job, but before we 'start giving our patients a better quality of life' could we look at filling out 456/C through to 789/DG!"

"Good news... social services have found somewhere for you to go!"

"This year, they are having to go further afield to get the agency staff"

"The GOOD news is that we've got a date for your operation, the BAD news is that you'll be dead before then"

"If there's a massive queue, you have to prioritise... start with the people who have most followers on Twitter"

"And if you get peckish, there's a food bank at the end of the street!"

PANAMA TAX SCANDAL
CAMERON HITS BACK

I wasn't evading the question...

...I was avoiding it

Hats off to Pa'n'ma!

EU-phemisms

"Juncker is the man to deal with tax havens"

E.U. TO CRACK DOWN ON TAX HAVENS

RGJ

He ran one as prime minister of Luxembourg

Notes & queries

What is Mossack Fonseca?

● The Reverend Hiddlestone is quite wrong to suggest that Mossack Fonseca is a little-known Italian character actor last seen in Fellini's classic *La Dolce Latte* (1963). It is of course a dry, sparkling wine from the Fonseca region of Northern Panama, fermented from a grape grown on the mossy slopes of Mount Mossack. The wine is an acquired taste and is very rich, very opaque and almost impossible to find.
Major "Corky" Hollander, Mallorca.

● Major Corky Hollander has been drinking too much sparkling wine, but certainly not Mossack Fonseca! The Mossack Fonseca is, as everyone knows, a classic sports car, designed in 1957 by the Croatian automotive engineer, Tomasz Mossack. The Fonseca was a gull-winged, rear-wheel drive sports coupé with a three-litre V2 rocket engine and a galvanised clutch, which finished a creditable ninth in the 1958 Mille Miglia, driven by legendary British duo Sterling Mossack (no relation) at the wheel, with Tom "Tom" Satnav navigating.
Lady Olivia Colman, Broadchurch.

● Oh really! One doesn't mind lady amateurs, until they intrude on one's own patch of special knowledge. Sterling Mossack and Tom "Tom" Satnav did indeed drive the Mossack Fonseca in the 1958 Mille Miglia, but I can assure Lady Olivia that they came in eighth, NOT ninth, after stewards disqualified the American car driven by Richard "Dick" D'Astardly for having on board his pet dog, Muttley, which contravened the Italian regulations, much to Muttley's amusement.
Professor Hugh Laurie Roper, St Stephen's College, Cambridge.

● Enough! For the record, the Mossack Fonseca is in fact a Russian dance, originally performed by Muscovite Cossacks (known as Mossacks) and most famously set to music by Rimsky-Korkykov (1898-2015), as an interlude in his opera *Borisnot Goodunov*. In the Fonseca, the Mossacks down a glass of vodka, smash the glass and then throw money at the waiter, as they run out the door, pursued by the police.
George ☺, The Circus.

Answers please:

Is Sigmundur Gunnlaugsson the star of a new Nordic police drama on BBC4 or is he the hero of an 11th Century Norse saga?

Daily Mail

COMMENT

The politics of envy and why inheritance tax is immoral

ENOUGH is enough! It is time we stopped persecuting the Prime Minister for having innocently inherited a small amount of money from his father, and instead began to attack the mean-spirited jealousy which would try to stop the perfectly normal human desire to pass on one's newspaper and non-dom tax status to your children.

Who hasn't wanted to leave their hard-earned Daily Mail newspaper to their young heir and give him the best start in life a multi-millionaire could hope for in terms of financial status and political influence?

For heaven's sake, let's have no more hypocritical talk about the immorality of inheritance when we all know that it is motivated solely by self-interest.

©*Lord Rothermere, son of the late Lord Rothermere, and father of the future Lord Rothermere, proprietors of the Daily Male Primogeniture, 2016.*

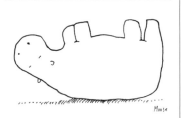

Hippoposthumous

Those Tax Havens in full...

🌴 **Treasure Island** – tropical home of fiscal lawyers Long, John and Silver, ideal for turning your pieces of eight into pieces of 94.

🌴 **Neverland** – tropical home of Peter Panama, where people never die, thus avoiding inheritance tax.

🌴 **Tracy Island** – tropical home of International Rescue, an offshore family business, committed to saving money (*surely lives?*). No strings attached. Investors include top aristocrat Lady Penelope and global terrorist, the Hood.

🌴 **Craggy Island** – Irish offshore domicile fronted by Catholic priests, including Father Ted, Father Dougal and Father Cameron.

🌴 **Islands in the Stream** – offshore Country & Western islands run by financial experts Parton Rogers, where you can sail away to another world, rely on each other and avoid making any useful contribution to the society you live in, ah-ha.

🌴 **Desert Disc Island** – where your records will be safely kept and if anyone asks to look at the books, they are told that they include Shakespeare, the Bible and the Mossack Fonseca Guide to Optimising Your Wealth Management.

OFFSHORE MILLIONS – A GUIDE FOR CONSERVATIVES

The good kind

The bad kind

TAX ADVISOR HITS BACK

by Our Specialist Staff **E. Vashun and A. Voydance**

A SENIOR tax specialist with the accountancy firm of Dodgy, Splv & Crooke has defended wealthy individuals opening offshore accounts in Panama, insisting there are many perfectly reasonable explanations as to why someone would want to set up highly secretive accounts in a tax haven. These include:

● They simply didn't have time to pop down to the High Street to open a bank account.

● They wanted to open a bank account for their children, but didn't want a free CD.

● They're doing it to win a bet.

● They're worried about their money catching flu, so they send it to a more tropical climate.

● They want their money to travel and see the world.

● They desperately want to give the one legged blind man living in a shack on the beach the chance to better himself by being appointed as the local managing director of the firm.

"Annabel's totes devastated – her Daddy wasn't named in the Panama Papers leak"

Lives of the Saints and Martyrs No.94
St Iain of Chingford
Taken from Liam Fox's Book of Martyrs

AND THERE was in those days an ambitious young former soldier who aspired to become the ruler of the land. But just when it seemed that worldly power might be within his grasp, Iain developed a terrible affliction, which his enemies said was divine punishment for his overweening pride.

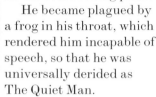

He became plagued by a frog in his throat, which rendered him incapable of speech, so that he was universally derided as The Quiet Man.

So unpopular did the hapless Iain become that he retreated into the wilderness where, for many years, he gave his life to the study of the poor, the halt and the lame.

After much prayer and contemplation, he concluded that the answer to all their problems was, in his own words, to "get off your beds and work".

Word of his saintliness soon spread across the land, until it reached the ears of the man who had become ruler of the land instead of him – one David of Cameron.

This great and powerful man sent for the saintly recluse and said, "I have a holy task for you, Brother Iain, which will allow you to fulfill your mission on this earth.

"I will give you supreme charge of all the poor, halt and lame persons in the realm, so that you can cut their benefits."

"Don't you mean 'provide them with all the assistance they need to help themselves out of poverty'? Iain respectfully asked.

"Of course," laughed the young ruler. "That is the story we shall tell, and your holy work will be celebrated for generations to come."

And lo, all went well for several years, as St Iain went about his Godly work with a will, devising every kind of ingenious scheme for removing alms from the poor and even, in some cases, their bedrooms.

But then came the moment when the scales fell from his eyes, and he realised that David and his friend George were only using him to rob the poor to give money to the rich.

"This is jolly unfair," he told the entire nation in his *Letter to the Cameronians*, and he then went on to be very unsaintly about George in particular, but in quite a clever way, so that he couldn't be accused of being openly disloyal.

And the cry went up from the people, "Lo, we were right... Iain is truly a saint after all, even though he took all that money from the poor. And now he is a martyr as well."

Nursery Times

Friday, Once-upon-a-time

FIRST SIEVELOAD OF JUMBLIES SENT BACK

By Our Migration Staff **Les Bos**

THERE were pitiful scenes last night, as after months of fraught negotiations, the first sieveload of Jumblies were deported from the Torrible Zone and the hills of the Chankly Bore.

After risking their lives, travelling from the Lands where the Jumblies live (far and few, far and few), the migrant Jumblies had nearly drowned in the stormy seas in a leaky sieve sold to them by unscrupulous Jumbly traffickers.

They were, understandably, devastated to find that they were immediately being shipped back to Turkey (the country, not the one who married the Owl and the Pussycat in the Land where the Bong Trees grow).

The Jumblies had arrived, hoping to find a better life, where they could buy an owl and a useful cart and a pound of rice and a cranberry tart. But they found instead they were discriminated against.

Said one Jumbly, "We expected to be welcomed, but found that the authorities in the Torrible Zone do not want any more people with green heads and blue hands. They want us to go back to where we came from, in order for them to be able to ship over some other Jumblies who haven't made the long voyage in a sieve. There's no rhyme or reason, it's all nonsense."

NURSERYLAND AGHAST AT FARMER'S WIFE KNIFE FRENZY

By Our Radio Correspondents **Jack and Gillian Reynolds**

THE Nurseryland Broadcasting Corporation was today mired in controversy, following the shocking transmission of a story of domestic abuse and violence between a farmer's wife and three blind mice.

For months, listeners had heard the farmer's wife being psychologically tormented by the blind mice running around, bumping into things and running up clocks just before they're about to strike one. But last night, it all got too much for the farmer's wife and she lashed out with a carving knife in one of the most graphic scenes ever heard.

Fans of the popular agricultural nursery rhyme could not believe their ears and at first thought that the mice had been stabbed to death, but it later transpired that they had just had their tails cut off.

Critics complained that they'd never seen such a thing in their life, but the producer defended the explicit violence on the radio *Fortywinks* programme, saying, "I'm sorry if it upsets people, but it is important for nursery rhymes to address topical issues, such as mental cruelty and rodent disability".

On other pages

● Old woman who lives in shoe has IVF triplets. "I don't know what she'll do," says one of her other children **2** ● Three little pigs in "buy to let" scramble, but gazumped by big bad wolf **3** ● Crooked man buys crooked house with crooked sixpence, via Panamanian holding company **94**

"I'd like Rover chipped, please"

52

The Charles Moore Jeremy Kyle Show

THIS WEEK: Who's the Real Father?

Charles Moore: On the show today is Justin, an archbishop, who's worried that his mum hasn't told him the truth about his dad!!

Audience: Boo! Scum!

Charles Moore: So what's the story, Archbish?

His Grace the Archbishop of Canterbury: Well, I have been having concerns about my paternity and it does seem possible that my mother had a liaison with Anthony Montague Browne shortly before she married Gavin Welby...

Audience: Boo! Slut!! Slag!!!

Charles Moore (*very excited*): Let's get this straight... your mum was a tramp who had it off with any old private secretary to Winston Churchill she fancied. Was she on the piss?

Archbishop: She did have an alcohol problem, but I'm very proud of the way she overcame it...

Charles Moore: Ok, so she was blotto all the time and, by all accounts, so was the sucker she fooled into raising you as his son!!

Audience: Boo! String him up!!

Archbishop: Well, if we consider the example of Joseph, who raised Our Lord despite not being technically his real father, who was in heaven at the time...

Charles Moore: Shut it! Let's bring on your scheming mum and see what she's got to say for herself...

(Enter charming old lady)

Audience: Boo!! Hiss!

Lady Williams: I'm very proud of my son, Justin...

Charles Moore: You should have taken precautions... and not spoken to me!!

Lady Williams: I did and...

Charles Moore: But we've got the DNA results!!!

(Audience go wild with baying hysteria and start casting first stones)

Charles Moore (*reads out medical certificate*): Yes! It's 100 percent certain – you are the son of nobby shagger Anthony Montague Browne and NOT dipso whiskey salesman Gavin Wellpissed!!

Audience: Boo! Boo! Booze!

(Audience begin to erect wooden cross, ready to crucify everyone involved in highly important justifiable story about inter-personal relationships)

Charles Moore: Fantastic! Let's bash the bishop!

(Audience laugh hysterically and throw pews at each other in delirium. Archbishop recites Lord's Prayer in attempt to console his mother...)

Welby: Our Father, who art in the Telegraph, whatever be thy name...

Charles Moore: Join us after the break when I pillory sleazebag journalists who stop at nothing to flog copies of their tawdry rags...

Audience: Boo! Scum! Filth!

(Cont. Channel 94)

From The Message Boards

Members of the online community respond to the major issues of the day...

Sunday roast dropped from menu

Guys, I see Wetherspoons has announced that it will no longer serve traditional Sunday roasts in its pubs, preferring more 'fashionable' Mexican and Indian dishes instead. Although I've never set foot in a Wetherspoons, this saddens me. The Roast Beef of Old England is a national institution, and the Britishness Audit found that it beat the BBC and fish and chips as the thing we most associate with our country. Not for nothing do the French call us Les Rosbifs! – *Bogbrush*

y they call us that – *colin*

It's French for roast beef, which we eat, you idiot. – *Jon*

not bein funny but that dont make sense? we call them frog's but they dont eat frog's – *Hayley 321*

they do eat frogs to be fair – *hatfield gooner*

wtf 😮 so there not calld frog's cos there ugly? – *Hayley 321*

sad there dropping traditional food, chinese bin dropped as well 🙁 probly ofend's muslim's and they never even go to the pub, they must drink cheap can's at home or in there mosk's – *Hunny pot*

when i was a kid the hole famly went to nans for sunday dinner pizza chickin nugget's potatoe wedge's crisp's and all the trimming's but these day's the lazy scrote's cant be arsed to micrawave a proper meal – *Darling Deneyze*

wetherspoon's aint bad as it go's the beers cheap and sundays always's special i get there early cos theres always soap and paper towl's in the toilet's and i strip down for a proper wash save's putting the hot water on at home then a few pint's and a roast few more pint's and a good shit with posh toilet paper 😊 sorted – *the beerhunter*

if i wanted to eat a shit roast surrounded by pissed up looser's id go to my mums 😊 lolz – *Danny Daz*

My husband and I are in our sixties and have many hobbies, including real ale, non-league football, swinging and dogging. We have a regular 'Sunday Roast' at our house to raise money for charity – four of us girls and about fifty blokes. It's a great way to work up an appetite, and we go to a local carvery afterwards for beef and Yorkshires. – *Gilfy Gracie*

Can't wait to hear what the satirical comedians come up with! Toby or not Toby (meaning Toby carvery)? UKIP are so stupid they think the EU has banned Sunday Roast? Anyway it's bound to be brilliant! *Jeremy*

Great stuff guys! – *Bogbrush*

"OMG! Standards must be slipping! That's a Garrick Club t-shirt!"

HEATH

GAME OF HEIR-TO-THE-THRONES

It's terrible. No one ever dies

2012 OLYMPICS 'SABOTAGED'

You've tested positive for gin and Dubonnet

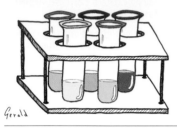

Gerald

DRUGS IN SPORT
Latest scandal

by Our Sports Staff
Anna Bolic-Steroid

AN in-depth investigation has uncovered evidence of a shocking use of drugs throughout the world of sport.

According to a whistleblower, today's top-performing sports pages have become totally dependent on drugs to improve their performance.

"It's very sad," said one seasoned sports reporter. "There was a time when sports journalism was all about describing people running, jumping, and playing entertaining matches. But now, unless the story is boosted by banned substances, editors just don't want to know."

However, one editor was suspiciously quick to fend the practice, saying, "Everyone's doing it. If we don't, we just won't be able to compete with the big boys. It pumps up the circulation and gives us all extra energy."

UKAD, the UK Anti-Doping agency, has been criticised for failing to stop the recent injection of drug stories into the back pages.

Said one critic, "As a body, UKAD is just too weak, it needs to up its game and it really should do something to beef itself up." He continued, "One thing's for sure, this drug story will run and run and run and run and..."

(cont. p94)

Sarah Vain

The column that speaks for me!

The cover of fashion bible "Vogue" used to be reserved for really beautiful women who were fashion icons. So how depressing to see the 100th-anniversary issue adorned by the dull, frumpy and, let's face it, totally boring Duchess of Cambridge. Forgive me, but y-a-a-a-wn!!

This woman has no fashion sense, nothing to say of any interest about anything and, dare I say it, isn't even very attractive to look at.

Let's face it – if it wasn't for the fact that she is married to a famous man, no one would take a blind bit of notice of her – let alone give her a huge column in the Daily Mail. *(Surely you mean "give her the front page of Vogue"? Ed.)*

I can think of at least one woman who would be much more suited to that coveted slot – and who isn't too thin or too boring – and whose husband got where he is in the Cabinet on merit and not just because he was born into a posh family!!

NEW OLD PROVERBS

"Two's company, three's an injunction"

Unaccompanied Refugee Children 'Could Fall Prey To Abuse'

by Our Child Welfare Staff **Clare Holmes**

THERE were concerns expressed today by Amnesty over the latest government U-turn which means unaccompanied Syrian refugee children who've reached Europe will be allowed into Britain.

"How do we know that these children's safety won't be compromised by them ending up in the care of Bradford Children's Services?" said an Amnesty spokesman.

"Obviously the refugee children's safety will be our number one priority," said a Downing Street spokesman, "but sadly we can't give cast iron guarantees that some of these vulnerable youngsters won't end up in care homes in Bradford.

"The last thing we want is for children escaping the threat of trafficking and abuse to end up in a far more nightmarish world of trafficking and abuse."

CUSTOMERS REPORT 'SATISFACTION' AT NEW ROLLING STONES EXHIBITION

by Our Music Staff
Ruby Tuesday

A new exhibition at the Saatchi Gallery traces the history of one of the world's most rebellious, anti-establishment and yet very rich rock bands.

From the early days when they sang "Satisfaction", right up to 2016 when they wow fans with "Satisfaction", the Stones have delighted audiences with their greatest hits, including "Satisfaction".

The exhibition captures the spirit of the iconic rock 'n' rollers, as it threatens to go on and on and on and on forever. But the highlight of the show, as with so many galleries, is the gift shop, where fans can stock up on some authentically overpriced Stones memorabilia, including...

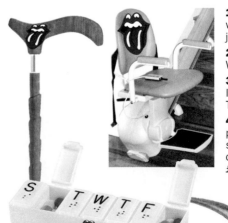

1 The Jagger Stairlift – for when Jack Flash tires of jumpin', £1,963.99

2 The Ronnie Wood Walking Stick, £12.99

3 The Charlie "Watts that, I can't hear you?" Ear Trumpet, £249.99

4 The "Keef" Drug Kit – pills for every rock 'n' roll situation, from angina to constipation. Street value: £50,000 a kilo.

ALSO AVAILABLE: The "Let's Spend The Night Together" Bed Pan, £200 for five. The "Start Me Up" Pacemaker, £75,000. The "It's All Over Now" Funeral Plan, 99p. *Hurry now, while Stones last! (Warning: You can't always get what you want)*

OBAMA'S SCARY BEDTIME STORY

> And then your little country left the EU and was never heard of again

---

A letter from ZAC GOLDSMITH

Hi everyone! Zac Goldsmith here, standing for Mayor of London. Now, I've been fighting a good, positive election campaign in the hope that you'll elect me. But I think it's only fair to let you know a few things about my rival for the post, Mr Sadiq Khan. For one thing, he's RADICAL in his policies. He is a RADICAL. His views, and quite possibly some of his family, are RADICAL. Now, that's completely irrelevant, and the fact that KHAN is a RADICAL doesn't necessarily mean anything at all. But I do want to leave that point there, for you to mull over. Think about it. Funny name, Khan, isn't it?

Now, as I said, I want you to vote (for me!) in a friendly, positive way and I want London's future to be a bright and cheerful one. But here are some things I think you ought to know about KHAN:
1. KHAN used to be a HUMAN RIGHTS LAWYER. Do you know what sort? A RADICAL one. I think that speaks volumes.
2. KHAN's favourite vegetables are RADISHES.
3. KHAN is an anagram of RADICAL. *(Amanda, can you check this one, please? I can't get it to work.)*

That's it from me – now, enough, I have lots of positive, friendly campaigning to get on with!

Bye!

Winner of the Sunday Times Short Short Story Competition 2016

HEIR OF SORROWS

by Dame Sylvie Krin, author of
Duchess of Hearts & You're Never Too Old

CHARLES relaxed and sank back into the soapy waters of his 19th century cast iron baignoire, made by the celebrated Victorian bathmakers Furnish & Elton. The model of the royal barge *Gloriana* floated gaily around his royal knees, as he mused that his mother really should have bowed to public opinion and opted for the name Bargey McBargeface.

She was getting on a bit now and losing touch with the sort of Zeitgeist thingy. Still, he mustn't dwell on his long apprenticeship for the throne whilst in the bath, as it had led to too many previous misunderstandings.

His reverie was interrupted by the steward of the sovereign soap, Sir Alan Fitztightly, who was retrieving a bar of Crown Imperial Leather from the vicinity of the plughole.

"I'm trying to get hold if it, but it's very slippery – as Backstairs Billy used to say to the Underfootmen in the days of your dear old Gan Gan..."

"Yes, thank you very much, Sir Alan," interrupted the unamused Monarch-in-Waiting. "I don't think we need to hear all that again."

There was a brief pause before Sir Alan broke the awkward silence with an attempt at conversation.

"Sad news, my liege..." he began, "...the artist formerly known as Prince is dead."

"Am I?" Charles sat bolt upright, as if he had been subjected to an electric shock.

"Prince?" "Dead?" "Artist?" The words swirled around his confused, uncrowned head until they reassembled themselves with what seemed like a terrible clarity.

It had finally happened. His worst nightmare. The Queen was alive and he had died. Or had he...?

In one bound, he had leapt out of the bath, showering Sir Alan in Royal Duchy Bard 'n' Swan Stratford Bath Oil and creating a mini tidal wave that sent the model *Gloriana* to a watery grave.

"But, sire..." remonstrated Sir Alan, but it was, as usual, too late... and he could only watch as Charles sprinted naked down the corridor to find his beloved consort, Camilla, who was at that moment in the Edward the Eagle Morning Room, entertaining the members of the Windsor Transgender Muslim Women's/Men's Non-Binary Institute. She could tell him the answer he needed to know...

"To be or not to be be, that is the question," shouted Charles, as he burst through the doors...

(To be continued...)

 ## *Dave Snooty* AND HIS OLD SCHOOL PALS

HE'S THE FUTURE OF THE PARTY ... HE'S AN OLD ETONIAN, A LONDONER, PART OF A FAMOUS FAMILY - AND CAN'T BE TRUSTED WITH THE LADIES ...

ANOINTED ONE

NOT YOU, BORIS ...

ZAC !

BACK ZAC AND SACK BOJO !

THE VAROUFAKIS GUIDE TO AVOIDING AUSTERITY

1. Become Finance Minister in anti-austerity government
2. Ruin negotiations with impossible demands
3. Fall out with everyone, including your Prime Minister
4. Get fired
5. Write best-selling book about how brilliant you are
6. No more austerity for you!

POETRY CORNER

Lines on the achievement of Leicester City Football Club in winning the Premier League competition

So. Congratulations
Then Leicester City.

You have pulled off
An impossible feat,
Overcoming odds
Of 5,000 to one.

Keith says this
Miracle can only
Be explained by
Divine intervention.

Apparently, your owners
Flew in a team of
Buddhist monks before
Every match to pray
For your victory.

Sometimes they chanted
"OM"
And sometimes
"AWAY".

Sri J. Thribbaddhanaprabha
(17½ points clear)

FOOTBALL TEAM WIN FOOTBALL COMPETITION

On other pages: Shame On You Ma'am! Why Won't the Out-Of-Touch Queen Fly the Leicester Flag Over Buckingham Palace and Give Ranieri a Knighthood Now?! p 2-94

Premiership Miracle Gnomemart

Blue Red Leicester Cheese!

Commemorate the historic triumph of Leicester FC with this football-themed commemorative cheese made by the master fromagiers of Oadby. Live every moment of the 2015/16 Premiership as you savour a slice of delicious Blue Red Leicester Cheese.

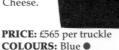

PRICE: £565 per truckle
COLOURS: Blue ●

Warning: Novelty blue paint may be unsuitable for human consumption

THE VARDY PERENNIAL
PLANT LOVERS

Celebrate the top Leicester goal-scorer with this unique blue climbing plant. Just get it in the box and watch it blossom! Be the envy of all your footie-loving friends, as the Vardy Perennial scores over all their feeble plant challengers.

Price: £9 (Packet of 100 seeds)
Colours:
■ Blue

WARNING: The Vardy Perennial may appear to have fallen over and look dead, but it is actually perfectly healthy

Richard III Statuette

CELEBRATE the greatest year in Leicester's history with this fabulous Richard III deformed skeleton football statuette. Cheer on the greatest team you hadn't heard of this time last year with the Foxes' number one fan, rendered in finest redcardium by master soccer sculptor Roger 'Offside' Law.

PRICE: Kingdom or a horse.

The Ranieri Trouser Press

Now your creases will go all the way from the bottom to the very top! At last you can be confident that the Ranieri Trouser Press will expertly manage your trousers and leave them looking like they are in a league of their own!

♪ Plays theme tune to BBC Radio 5 Live Sports Extra ♪

Peston on Sunday Show sets agenda for the week's news

Yes! Everyone is talking about it and make no mistake – the new ITV flagship political cultural magazine talk show has got the nation standing by their watercoolers earnestly discussing the key issue of the day.

1 Peston's haircut – Yes or No?

2 Should Peston wear a tie? No or Yes?

3 In or Out? Should Allegra Stratton's hands be 'in' or 'out' of her pockets?

4 Are tweets from the public on a big screen just a desperate way to fill up airtime between ads? Yes or Yes?

5 Peston or Marr? New poll says 95 percent prefer IKEA

6 Watercoolers – is the conversation around them overrated?

7 Do you think we should go back to work now?

8 Yes.

9 Er...

10 That's it.

WHAT NEWS OF LEICESTER, LORD BURLEIGH?

STILL PURSUED BY THE HOTSPURS, YOUR MAJESTY

London Mayoral Election In Full

Private Eye looks at the highlights of the most exciting political campaign since the Gwent Police and Crime Commissioner Election

Zac Goldsmith (Tory)
"Sadiq Khan is a terrorist"

Sadiq Khan (Labour)
"My dad was a bus driver"

Zac Goldsmith
"Er..."

Sadiq Khan
"That's it"

JOHN WHITTINGDALE 'DEFENDS STRIP CLUB VISIT'

I behaved at all times with Restraint and Propriety...

...who were two of the lap dancers

WHITTINGDALE CONFIRMS 'QUESTIONABLE RELATIONSHIP'

by Our Political Staff **Dominatrix Lawson**

THE embittered Culture Secretary, John Whittingdale, admitted yesterday that he had been involved in a long-term relationship with a partner some commentators might find "unsuitable".

"It's true," said Mr Unwhittingdale, "that this person enjoys exercising power over others and has been involved in a very sleazy industry. But at the time I had no idea what Mr Murdoch did for a living."

He continued, "When I first started seeing Rupert, it was just mutual attraction between people of similar interests.

"But now I understand the full nature of his unsavoury working practices, I am even keener to get into bed with him."

Learn To Speak Obvsborne

"Yo guys! Get yourself some Downing Street-cred, and learn to talk suburban slang with ur bro, The Chancellor of the Excheq!"

Obvs = obviously "obviously", as in "the economy's f***ed, obvs".

Awks = awkward, as in "whatever he does, George Osborne looks awks".

LOL = lots of lolly, as in George's dividends from Osborne & Little.

Hoe = friend of Mr Whittingdale.

WTF = what Mr Whittingdale does with his "hoe".

Homie = somebody who lives in your street. Namely, Downing. Namely, Dave.

Second Homie = somebody who also owns a property in Notting Hill, but rents it out. Namely, Dave. WTF!

FYI = depressing new era of transparency regarding George 'n' Dave's tax returns. Awks.

OMG = the size of our national deficit.

IMF = who's going to bail us out in a couple of years. Obvs.

The TIMES

Saturday 23 April 1616

ANOTHER CELEBRITY DIES
HOW MANY MORE WILL WE LOSE?

by Our Showbiz Staff **The 3am girls (played by boys)**

THE nation was in deep mourning again, as the tragic news was read out on every street corner in Old London Town that one of the nation's favourite comedy writers and a much-loved National Treasure had passed away.

William Shakespeare joins a long line of top celebrities who have been taken from us in recent times. We've lost such greats as Christopher Marlowe, Edmund Spencer, Thomas Kyd and Francis Beaumont. They were all far too young (Thomas was just a kid) and they all had so much more to give. But no celebrity passing has hit us so hard as that of the author of such great hits as 'Sonnet Number 18', 'As You Like It' and 'Dinnerladies', later renamed 'The Merry Wives of Windsor'.

Will, as he was known to fans, famous for his long-running hit comedy shows, and later forays into more serious drama, had disappeared from public view of late, making only occasional showbiz appearances, as he found entertainment executives harder and harder to deal with.

Top actor Richard Burbage, famous for complaining about members of the audience sending each other carrier pigeons in the middle of a performance, led the tributes from the world of showbiz, saying, "He was quite good, but I was the one who brought his plays to life."

Fellow playwrights were quick to join in, including Ben Jonson, who said, "But for him I would never have become a writer, and the world would have been deprived of my masterpieces such as 'Volpone', 'Tamburlaine The Great', and of course the brilliant 'Sejanus'." However, everyone agreed that the name of Shakespeare would be remembered for years to come, possibly even a hundred, though this may be just understandable sentimentality in a moment of national grief.

LATE NEWS

🐾 The world of music has been equally shocked by the devastating news that Giovanni Gabrieli has joined a growing list of great musicians who have recently suffered an early demise. First, Giovanni da Palestrina, then William Byrd, and now *(cont. p94)*

LATE LATE NEWS

🐾 A production of Christopher Marlowe's play 'Dr Faustus' has been cancelled due to the strike action taken by the actor playing Junior Doctor Faustus. He quoth, "I will not work weekends and evenings! This is no task for a gentleman!" The part of Junior Doctor Faustus will now be played by the distinguished apothecary Mistress Sue Perdrug.

PAUL DANIELS TRIBUTES POUR IN

"I liked him... not a lot, but I liked him"

57

The Daily Telegraph

Spy chiefs' Brexit warning prompts swift rebuttal

by Our Referendum Correspondent
Clare Monger

IN what's being seen as a key intervention to the Brexit security debate, 100 highly respected Bond villains have today sensationally backed leaving the EU in an open letter to The Telegraph:

We, the undersigned, reject the assertion made by former heads of MI6, such as Sir John Sawyer, that leaving the European Union would be catastrophic for Britain's security.

We refute the alarmist stories about the UK's vulnerablity to attacks. We are certain that outside the EU, Britain would be perfectly able to defend itself from any security threat, such as huge laser cannons hidden in secret underground island bases somewhere in the Pacific.

We firmly believe Britain's security could actually be bolstered by entering instead into a loose alliance with smaller, vulnerable Commonwealth countries that have no access to laser cannons or anything like that.

The explosive letter, signed by such evil luminaries as Goldfinger, Ernst Stavros Blofeld, Dr No, Francisco Scaramanga and Le Chiffre, all highly successful businessmen employing thousands of employees in yellow jumpsuits, is being seen as a major boost for the Brexit campaign.

However, speaking from a table to which he'd been strapped inside one of the villain's secret lairs, 007 James Bond urged caution in accepting the villain's arguments about international security .

"Yes, we've been expecting Bond to say that," tweeted Blofeld disparagingly.

There was some embarrassment, however, for the Brexiters when it emerged that two of the signatories to the letter, The Barclay Brothers, were not in fact Bond villains.

"They live in total secrecy on an island fiefdom where the locals live in complete fear of them. It was an easy mistake to make," insisted a Telegraph hack.

BRITAIN'S BORDER PATROL: NEW PICS

"We've rebranded the referendum to appeal to the social-media generation"

JUNE 23 IS... VOTEY McVOTEFACE

PROJECT FEAR BREXIT GOES NUCLEAR

There could be a World War!

Or even worse, house prices might fall!

GLENDA SLAGG

Fleet Street's Unmanned Drone!!? Geddit???!

■ **SIR TIM RICE?!!!!? Don't-chaluvhim??!?? I say hats off to the musical maestro who is going to be a daddy again at the age of 72???!!!! Jesus Christ Superstud?!?? Good to see there's still lead in the pencil that you write the lyrics with!?? (Geddit???!??) And cricket-loving Sir Tim is still bowling the maidens over with his old balls!!!!?**

■ SIR TIM RICE?!!? What a disgrace!!? Can't you tie a knot in it, you lyrical lothario??!?? Who do you think you are – the Lion King??!?? Geddit!!?!? Urgh!!!! Sounds like One Knight in Bangkok too many to me?!!? You may have lead in your pencil, grandad, but take a tip from Auntie Glenda – use a rubber!!!!?? (Geddit??!?!)

■ **RUSSELL BRAND??!? Russell B-randy more like??!?? Now the loquacious, lecherous leftie has got his partner up the duff!!! Just think of it!!!! All that whinin' and a-whingein', attention seeking, tantrums and infantile behaviour that poor Baby Brand is going to have to put up with??!? Geddit?!!?!?**

■ RUSSELL BRAND?!!? All together now – aaaah!!!?! At long last, Romeo Russell is becoming a doting daddy??! From now on, it's a different type of babe he'll be cuddling??!? And if the little 'un won't go to sleep, he can always start telling the nipper about the paradigm shift in political ontology that ushers in a post-capitalist utopia... zzzzzzzzzz!!!! (Geddit???)

■ *HERE THEY ARE – Glenda's May Bank Holiday Hunks?!?!*

● **Sir David Attenborough!??!?!!** Ok, so he's 90, but TV's Mr Wildlife keeps going on and on and on!!??!?! That's how to keep a gal, tiger!!!

● **Ruth Davidson MSP!?!!** She's the lovable laughing lesbian who has turned Scotland blue!???!? Well, you're certainly "turning" this gal, Ruthy – I'm Scots **Nuts** over you!!!!?!

● **President Recep Tayyip Erdogan!?!!** Crazy name, crazy – and frankly despotic – guy!?!!

Byeee!!

As the great Referendum Campaign approaches its climax, Private Eye has invited the lead spokesman for each side to sum up the essence of why they think Britain should Remain or Leave

REMAIN
The Rt. Hon. David Cameron

Let me be clear about this. No one in the world would be keener to see Britain leave the European Union than Abu Bakr al-Baghdadi, the Leader of the so-called Islamic State Terrorist Organisation.

As Prime Minister, I know this to be true and it has been confirmed to me by the head of all our Intelligence and Security Services, MI5, MI6 and the top secret M25. They have made it absolutely clear to me that if Britain leaves the EU, Abu Boris al-Bigdaddy will be ordering hundreds of suicide bombers to mount a full-scale assault on Britain's cities; leading to the setting up of a new caliphate based in Dewsbury.

ISIS will change its name to IDS in honour of the most treacherous figure in British political history.

A Leave vote would swiftly transform Britain into a smouldering ruin.

And I promise you can trust everything I say because I am David Cameron, your prime minister, and I would never mislead you in any way.

LEAVE
Boris Johnson MP and former Mayor of London

Cripes. This EU that everyone's going on about. Do you know who it reminds me of? Adolf Hitler, that's who. They both had only one ambition. To take the whole of Europe and put it under German rule. Just like that fellow Napoleon. And Louis XIV. And of course the jolly old Romans, which I know all about because, unlike my friend Dave, I read all the classics at Oxford rather than lounging about reading a feeble little non-subject like PPE!

Veni, Vidi, Vici. That's what the Roman dictator Julius Caesar said when he absorbed Britain into his version of the European Union. Hitler would have said just the same thing but in German, ein Volk, ein Reich, ein Europe.

And today the EU is exactly the same in every detail, except that it doesn't have an army (yet!), the Commissioners carefully don't wear jackboots and the only people they've put in camps are poor old refugees from the Middle East.

A Remain vote would swiftly transform Britain into just a small vassal state in the Greater European Reich, ruled over by the ghastly dictator Frau Merkel and her sinister drunken lieutenant Herr Jean-Claude Junkers, which us historians remember was the name of those terrifying Nazi dive-bombers in all those brilliant black and white films. What we need now to win the war is a few "Dave" bombers to hurl back the invading European hordes!

And I promise you can trust everything I say because I am Boris, your former Mayor of London and your future Prime Minister, and I would never mislead you in any way.

TV STARS COME OUT FOR REMAIN

Letter from Leading Actors Has Dramatic Impact on Referendum Vote

by Our Thespian Staff **Mimi Mee**

An extraordinary intervention into the EU Debate by Britain's leading actors, urging the nation to remain in the European Union, caused a huge surge in the polls for the Leave campaign.

In a letter to the Daily Terrorgraph, the actors had argued that British film, television and theatre could not flourish without EU support and many of them had taken time off from filming in Los Angeles to add their names to the petition.

The letter read:

*"We, the undersigned and very important people, believe passionately in **Remaining** in the public eye and not **Leaving** centre stage. And we are utterly dedicated to being IN rather than OUT of work.*

We urge people to vote Remain on June 23, unless they've got a voiceover in Hollywood or a recall for a big part on Broadway. Bless!"

The Remain campaign, who had organised the letter, praised the actors concerned for their bravery in speaking out, which prompted the actors to write another letter saying:

"Are you sure? You're not just saying that? You really liked it? Thank you... thank you... thank you..."

Late News

World of Luvviedom Thrown Into Chaos by Ken Loach Pro-Brexit Speech

Hundreds of actors today reacted with panic at the news that someone left-wing and in the media had supported the Leave campaign.

Said one, "Oh no! It's too much. We all love Ken Loach! How can I cope with the stress? Will I be **in** his next film? Or will I be out in the cold for ever? It's so complicated. Maybe I should say other people's lines..."

HOW BORIS THINKS HE LOOKS WHEN HE EVOKES HITLER

HOW BORIS ACTUALLY LOOKS

"Nice to see a man without tattoos for once"

DUMB BRITAIN

Real contestants, real quiz shows, real answers, real dumb!

Tipping Point, ITV

Ben Shephard: In Christianity, Calvary is the location where which Biblical figure was believed to have been crucified?
Contestant: Joan of Arc.

Shephard: Members of which religion are banned from being King or Queen of the United Kingdom?
Contestant: I should know this, because I'm a Roman Catholic. I'm going to say Mormon.

Shephard: In 1955, which British Prime Minister resigned and was replaced by Anthony Eden?
Contestant: John Major.

Shephard: Grenadiers were traditionally named after what weapon that they threw?
Contestant: Spears.

Shephard: Which famous vet wrote *It Shouldn't Happen To A Vet?*
Contestant: Dr Doolittle.

Shephard: Which world leader did the CIA make over 600 attempts at assassinating, including one with an exploding cigar?
Contestant: It must be an American. I'll say Bill Clinton.

Shephard: Which Northern Ireland politician led the Democratic Unionist Party from its foundation in 1971 until 2008?
Contestant: I know this one so I'm going to play it. It's Gerry Adams.

Shephard: The trading town of Timbuktu is located on what continent?
Contestant: Ireland.

Shephard: Which Italian scientist broadcast the first radio signals in the late 1890s?
Contestant: Galileo.

Radio Ulster

Presenter: What European capital city is named after the Greek goddess Athena?
Caller: Er... Rome?

Celebrity Mastermind, BBC1

John Humphrys: In the medical specialism ENT, E stands for ear, N stands for nose. What does T stand for?
Contestant: Testosterone.

Sam FM, Bristol

Presenter: Which brothers made the first powered flight?
Caller: The Everly brothers.

BBC Radio 2

Zoe Ball: Name a James Bond theme tune sung by Shirley Bassey.
Caller: Er... Dr Pussy.

Metro Radio, Newcastle

Presenter: In which country would you find the Sphinx?
Caller: Germany.

Fifteen-to-One, C4

Sandi Toksvig: Which German word meaning "health" is an equivalent of the English expression "Bless you" and is commonly said to a person who has just sneezed?
Contestant: *Achtung!*

Toksvig: Which 1924 novel by EM Forster is largely set in the fictional city of Chandrapore, and includes the characters Adele Quested, Mrs Moore and Dr Aziz?
Contestant: Midsomer Murders.

Toksvig: In which 1879 Gilbert and Sullivan operetta does a character known as Frederic, who has spent much of his childhood at sea, land in Cornwall and fall in love with Mabel, the daughter of a major general?
Contestant: *Oklahoma!*

Toksvig: Gorky Park and the Pushkin State Museum of Fine Arts are visitor attractions in which city?
Contestant: Liverpool.

Toksvig: Which biographer and critic, a member of the Bloomsbury Group, wrote the influential 1918 work *Eminent Victorians*?
Contestant: Gyles Brandreth.

The Chase, ITV

Bradley Walsh: What name links a ship on which a famous mutiny took place, and a chocolate bar?
Contestant: Cadbury's.

Walsh: What national November holiday was first proclaimed by Abraham Lincoln?
Contestant: Movember.

Walsh: Which famous ship began construction in 1510?
Contestant: The Titanic.

Walsh: Which former Labour party leader is the father of Stephen Kinnock, the MP for Aberavon?
Contestant: Tony Blair.

Walsh: Asteroid 4238 Audrey is named after which Hollywood actress?
Contestant: Kim Basinger.

Walsh: Which prime minister did Geri Halliwell call the first Spice Girl?
Contestant: John Major.

Walsh: When was the United Nations Charter signed?
Contestant: 1066.

Pointless, BBC1

Alexander Armstrong: We're looking for an Old Etonian, initials GO, who wrote the 1945 novel *Animal Farm*.
Contestant: George Osborne.

Pressure Pad, BBC1

John Barrowman: Which king, who came to the throne in 1485, was the first Tudor monarch?
Contestant: Oliver Cromwell

Heart Wales Radio

Jason Harrold: Roughly how long does it take for the Earth to complete one full orbit around the Sun?
Caller: Um... 25 years?

For What It's Worth, BBC1

Fern Britton: Which Roman road stretches from Rome to Brindisi in southern Italy?
Contestant: I don't know. Is it the A5?

Britton: *The War Requiem* and the opera *Peter Grimes* are works by which British composer?
Contestant: I know this, but it isn't coming to me. Lennon and McCartney.

Britton: In which 2015 TV drama did Mark Rylance play Thomas Cromwell?
Contestant: Downton Abbey.

Britton: Shakespeare is often referred to as the Bard of... what?
Contestant: Er... Yorkshire.

In It To Win It, BBC1

Dale Winton: What is the name of a herb which is also a word that mean wise or clever? Is it sage, basil or tarragon?
Contestant: I've absolutely no idea at all. This probably sounds really stupid but I think there's a character called Basil Brush. I think I've heard of that. I've got no other inkling, so I'm going to go with basil.

Two Tribes, BBC2

Richard Osman: Which famous figure became queen of Egypt on the death of her father in 51 BC?
Contestant: Queen Elizabeth I.

Decimate, BBC1

Shane Richie: Judi Dench made her stage debut playing which character in Hamlet?
Contestant: Lady Macbeth.

Richie: The manager of the England football team between 1994 and 1996 was Terry who?
Contestant: Pratchett.

Radio Lancashire

Ted Robbins: What did St Patrick drive out of Ireland?
Caller: A motor car. No, there wouldn't have been motor cars in his day. A horse and cart.

BBC WM

Sunny Grewal: Which fabric is made by worms?
Caller: Leather.

Radio Clyde

Presenter: Before the introduction of the Euro, what was the Dutch currency?
Caller: The Deutschmark.

DJ: Which singer is the film Amy about?
Caller: Adele.

Premier Christian Radio, Breakfast Show

John Pantry: Name a character in the Bible beginning with G.
Caller: Gandalf.

Think Tank, BBC1

Bill Turnbull: Which politician won his sixth Parliamentary Beard of the Year award in 2015?
Panellist: Diane Abbott.

Nursery Times

Friday, Once-upon-a-time

MR ▮▮▮▮▮▮▮ MUST REMAIN ANONYMOUS

by Our Injunction Staff **Ann Onymous**

THE Supreme Court of Nurseryland has upheld an injunction by the celebrity dwarf that he must not be named by any of Nurseryland's newspapers and particularly not by any publications owned by Rupert the Bear-All, including the *Sun-Has-Got-His-Hat-On* and the *Sun-Has-Got-His-Hat-On on Sunday*.

The injunction also covers titles such as *Mirror-Mirror-On-The-Wall* and the *Daily* and *Sunday Fairygraphs*, owned by the Barclay Brothers Grimm.

Said the judge, "No one must try and guess the name of the dwarf, even if all the birds in the trees are busy tweeting it to each other and the whole of Nurseryland has looked it up on Wikidwitchipedia.

"The *Nursery Times* is obliged to obey the injunction and we are not allowed to give the name of the mystery dwarf. Though in unrelated news, one mystery dwarf was overheard singing to himself in the forest:

"Merrily I'll dance and sing,
The lawyers will all go kerr-ching
While the courts conceal
my fame,
For Rumpypumpystiltskin,
is my name."

OUTCRY AS RECIPES TAKEN OFFLINE

FOOD LOVERS throughout Nurseryland were in uproar last night as the NBC (Nurseryland Broadcasting Corporation) removed all its popular recipes from its website.

Gone were household favourites such as: Four-and-Twenty Blackbirds Pie, Roast Hansel & Gretel, Curds and Whey, "Just Right" Porridge, Gingerbread House, and the three little pigs' recipe for Lightly-poached Wolf. Said Little Jack Horner, "It's terrible, not only am I starving hungry but I've got nowhere to put in my thumb and pull out a plum," adding, "what a very annoyed boy am I!"

Pundits have suggested that the NBC's announcement that it was wielding the woodcutter's axe to its recipe pages, was just a ploy to gain public sympathy in response to the Wicked Witchingdale's Snow White paper which decreed that the NBC's licence fee should be cut from five magic beans to three and should not live happily ever after. The End.

On other pages

● Toad poop-poops notion of driverless cars **3**

● Experts say GM Beanstalk perfectly safe **7**

● New hope for hare as Russian tortoise's urine sample to be retested **94**

LEAVE WARNS OF 'DANGEROUS TURKS'

by Our Scare Staff
Lunchtime O'Boo

THE Leave campaign issued its official poster last night in which it warns of the dangers of letting Turkish immigrants into Britain.

The warning focuses on the possibility of disreputable Turks entering the UK through the back door and then terrorising the country.

Said a spokesman, "Make no mistake. A renegade Turk, let's call him Boris, could easily end up getting access to Downing Street and then attempt to destroy the country.

"We are not being racist, but the Turks and their descendants just can't be trusted and will stop at nothing until they have imposed their fanatical beliefs on the rest of the country."

Mr Boris Ali Kemal said, "Cripes! I haven't thought this one through! Blimey!"

YOU LAST HAD SEX 147 DAYS AGO

Memory Foam Mattress

Tipping

Your Questions Answered

Q I am a married actor about to pay an escort girl £195 for her services. What is the etiquette vis-à-vis tipping?

A *Dear Married Actor, this is a very simple case. Though you may be under the impression that some kind of "service" has already been included, it is always best to leave a generous percentage on top of the original fee. In this case, £150,000 payable to your lawyer should do it. And here's another tip – don't sleep with prostitutes.*

Q I am a well-known multi-billionaire upmarket newspaper proprietor who is trying to engage the services of an escort girl to spill the bloody beans on what a lousy shag the married actor is. How much should I offer the ghastly slapper on top of the normal fee? And bloody hurry up with your answer!

A *Dear Mr Murdoch, I suggest you don't offer her anything at all and then reprint it from the National Enquirer once the legal dust has settled.*

Q I have just bought a famous High Street retail company for one pound. The seller seems very generous – should I offer him a little bit more, say 10 percent?

A *No, Sir Philip has had quite enough money already. Don't give him any more.*

Jeremy Corbyn WRITES

Hello! It's me again.

I guess you've all heard the big news! I've been taking advice from Ed Miliband about how to become Prime Minister! Why Ed? Well, he's the obvious choice, really. I think it is very important to get the best advice from people who've really been there and done it.

Not people who've been Prime Minister, obviously! They're not really my kind of person. They're ambitious and start horrible wars and ignore noble, bearded backbenchers who make principled stands on all manner of subjects! I think having meetings with those kinds of people would be quite uncomfortable for me.

So who's left, if you want someone who's really been there and done it, but hasn't been tainted by the whole "being a Prime Minister" thing? Why Ed, of course! (Well there is Neil Kinnock, but Ken doesn't like him much. So Ed it is!)

And thank heavens! Ed's been a great help over the last couple of months because, would you believe it, everything he's advised me to do… is stuff I've done already! Distance myself from the previous Labour government? Check! Move the party to the left? Check! Avoid talking to a hostile press? Check! Obsess myself with internal Labour party politics? Check! Pick a different issue every week to get mad about and hope for the best? Check, check and mate! So I'm ahead of the game!

And who knows? Come 2020, with Ed's help, it may well be me who'll be the next ex-Labour leader, walking away from the rubble of a disastrous election result, having the honour of advising my successor how to try to win in 2025!

One can only dream!

Cheerio!

JOHN WHITTINGDALE 'BBC WARNING'

by Our Media Staff
Lord Wreath

CULTURE Secretary John Whittingdale has lashed out at the sheer arrogance of the BBC for scheduling hit shows such as *Poldark* on Sunday night at 9pm when ITV is trying to attract an audience for its less popular shows.

"The BBC seems to have forgotten that its remit is to produce shows which are so dreary and amateurish that viewers have no alternative but to switch over to the far more superior product on the commercial stations," said a clearly angry Culture Secretary.

"The arrogance in thinking BBC1 is a better channel than Rupert Murdoch's Sky 1, simply because BBC1 produces British dramas of the quality of *War and Peace*, *The Night Manager* and *Happy Valley*, rather than filling its schedules with stuff like *Supergirl* and *The Flash*, is breathtaking.

"The BBC must immediately move *Poldark* from Sunday to one of the nights of the week when Sky 1 and ITV aren't showing anything at 9pm.

"The Corporation really should have thought about this when they stupidly scheduled that story about me and a sex worker on the ten o'clock news."

PUBLIC TO DECIDE NAME OF SIR PHILIP GREEN'S NEW YACHT

1. Booty McBootyface
2. Fishy McFishface
3. Greedy McGreedface
4. Fatty McFatface
5. Shamey McShameface
6. The Lady Ghislaine

(That's enough. Ed.)

Robby Buller

"These people traffickers are getting more and more daring..."

SNP SEX SCANDAL 1: STEWART HOSIE

I have always wanted independence

Good... I'm chucking you out

SNP SEX SCANDAL 2: ANGUS MACNEIL

I'm for Remain

No, you're going to Leave

Reproduced by kind permission of the Gnomey McGnome Book of Caledonian Verse and Song

Scots Wahay!

With apologies to Robert Burns (and to those members of the SNP who haven't slept with Serena Cowdy at time of going to press)

Scots, wha hae wi' Salmond bled,
Scots, wham Sturgeon has aften led;
Welcome to your expenses-paid London Hotel bed,
　　And on to Cowdy!

Now's the day, and now's the hour;
See the tabloids wield their power;
See the Scot Nat MPs cower;
　　Chains and slavery!
　　　　(Is Mr Whittingdale involved as well?!)

Lay the fruity hackette low!
Both of you – though not at one go!
Here comes the wife, she doesn't know!—
　　Oh no, we're going to die!

Donald, Where's Your Troosers?

I've just come down
From The News on Skye
The story's big and I'm awful shy
'Cos the lassies shout when I go by
Angus, where's your troosers?

CHORUS

Let the wind blow high
Let the wind blow low
Through the streets
In my pants, I'll go
All the lassies say hello
Stewart, where's your troosers?

Lines written on the discovery of the Scottish political love triangle scandal by William McGonagall

'Twas in the year of our Lord
　　two thousand and sixteen,
That a lassie by name Serena compared
SNP politicians to the Mujahideen,
Brave, fearless, champions,
　　marching under a rebel flag,
Off to the four star Park Plaza Hotel
　　for a wee, crafty shag.

(That's enough of this filth – you're fired. Ed.)

HEIR OF SORROWS

by Dame Sylvie Krin, author of *Duchess of Hearts* & *You're Never Too Old*

THE STORY SO FAR: The Queen has been enjoying a day of equine pageantry in honour of her 90th birthday. Now read on...

"AND at four score years and ten, Her Royal Majestyness remains a supremely enduring symbol of glorious regalitude..."

The voice of Alan Titchmarsh boomed out its eloquent eulogy from the old-fashioned black and white Major Ferguson television set in the corner of the Queen's withdrawing room in the North East turret of Windsor Castle.

"What a toad-eating arse creeper that chap is," exclaimed the Duke of Edinburgh to the assembled company who had all gathered, at the Queen's insistence, to view the TV highlights of the day's events.

But Her Majesty was having none of her husband's salty sea-dog scorn.

"Do be quiet, Philip – and offer the Emir of Bahsthaad a glass of non-alcoholic whisky."

As the Duke moved to the Victorian novelty drinks cabinet, a globe where all the British colonies were coloured in pink, Princess Anne kicked one of the corgis, Witchell, off the Louis Van Gaal chaise longue and flopped down to watch the television.

"Quite right, mater. This is top-notch TV. Horses. More Horses. And then more horses with extra horse thrown in."

The flickering television showed the Canadian Mounted Traffic Police riding in the formation of a giant moose followed by the men of the 7th/11th Mounted Bombardoons charging with their drawn sabres reflecting the beams of the laser son-et-lumière narrated by the deferential duo of Ant and Dec...

"SycophAnt and Dec more like..." interjected the Queen's consort, grumpily.

"Pater's right, Mummy," agreed Charles. "We *have* just sat through hours of this bally clip-cloppery... do we have to endure the whole thing again? Can't we watch something else? How about a nice documentary about Palladian architecture?"

"Put a sock in it, Charlie," countered his sister, the Olympic horsewoman and 1971 Sports Personality of the Year.

"It's mater's big day, so don't spoil it by sulking, as per!"

On the television, the Royal spectacular continued to delight the nation...

"And now, entering the arena is the Queen's 22nd godchild, the Honourable Zara Tara Boom-dee-ay, riding a miniature Shetland Pony called McFlurry. A delightful counterpoint to the frightening bareback warrior women of Poshanbekistan whom we saw..."

Charles remained unimpressed. "It really is... I don't know..."

"Appalling?" chorused his entire family, as well as the guest of honour, the princely potentate of the Palms, who raised his glass of Glen Halal Whisky (made in Bradford) in mock tribute.

"If you don't like it, you can naff off!" barked his sister Anne, ending the debate about the evening of Royal viewing.

"Alright, I'm going to go and have a bath before dinner. Sir Alan...!" shouted Charles at his Equerry-as-Folk. "Get me my organic loofah and miniature Sir David Attenborough research vessel... you know, Thingy McThingface..."

AS the last of the famed Spanish dancing horses from Tio Pepe pranced and pirouetted out of the arena to the strains of world-renowned soprano Katherine Jenkins singing *Viva España*, the Queen wiped away a tear from her wise old eyes.

"Do you think they'll have it on BBC as well?" she asked, punching the keys of the remote control to change channel.

Prince Philip groaned. However, the screen filled not with horses, but sad-looking commoners from the East End of London.

"Leave it out! Shut it, you muppet!" shouted one of the men with a bald head at another man with a bald head, who retorted, "Not on my manor."

The continuity announcer then explained that the next episode of the popular BBC TV programme EastEnders would be unmissable, due to the sad death of the leading character, the matriarchal "Queen of the Vic", played by Barbara Windsor herself.

Camilla took a drag on her e-fag, exhaled the vapour wearily and idly mused to herself, "I do hope Chazza isn't half-watching the TV in the bath and hearing a garbled version of this, with the words 'Windsor', 'Queen', 'matriach' and 'dead'..."

At that very moment, the door burst open to reveal the heir to the throne, stark naked in the doorway, covered in bath foam and clutching only a red miniature research vessel to protect his modesty, shouting "Carolus Rex! Vivat myself! The Elizabethan age is over. The Carolingian age has begun!"

There was a hushed silence as the Queen slowly got up and then quietly closed the door on her son and heir, leaving him alone in the corridor with his hopes and dreams...

(cont. p94)

The Simon Cowell Children's Book

Once upon a time, in a village called TVtown, there was a fat cat called Simon. He made a popular show where other cats sang for him, and Simon made them cry by being rude.

You're useless! I could do better than that! Get off!

One day, Simon's kitten, called Eric, asked him to read a bedtime story. Simon didn't like books, but he agreed anyway. He wasn't impressed.

This is useless! I could do better than that!

So Simon went away and wrote a book. It took him all day.

What do you think?

It's useless! I could do better than that!

Simon's eyes filled with tears.

Then a big smile spread across Simon's face.

I'm so proud! I knew you'd end up just like me! you're going to be a star!

William Sutcliffe/Henry Davies

Huge Tory election fraud exposed

by Channel 4's **Michael Crook** and **Jon Snowjob**

POLICE forces in 29 counties have been redeployed from investigating historic sexual abuse cases to a huge new scandal arising from the conduct of the Tory party during the 2015 general election.

We have now uncovered detailed evidence to show that the winning candidate, a Mr David Cameron, committed wholesale fraud when he was last year touring the country in his battlebus canvassing for a Tory victory.

We can reveal that no less than 218 pledges made by Mr Cameron during the campaign were entirely fraudulent and that he never had any intention of carrying them out.

● Cameron repeatedly promised that, if he became prime minister, he would reduce immigration to "the tens of thousands". Instead of which he has increased it to 10 billion *(is this right? – I hope it is! Ed.)*

● He promised that he would cut the deficit to bring Britain's borrowing "under control". Instead of which he increased the national debt to an all-time high of £10 trillion *(is this right? If so, it's rather alarming! Ed.)*

● He promised that he would slash disability benefits to force the disabled back to work. Instead of which, Iain Duncan Smith resigned, saying that the Conservatives were "the party of the rich" *(but surely they are, aren't they? Ed.)*

● He promised to build hundreds of thousands of new homes to house Britain's booming immigrant population, to be built by skilled Bulgarian workers. Instead, he built no houses at all so that house prices would continue to rise and the Daily Mail would be happy *(good idea! Ed.)*

● He promised to launch a "real crackdown on tax avoidance" which would save the Treasury billions of pounds a year. Instead, he benefited from the tax arrangement made by his father in Panama and concluded that there was nothing wrong with tax avoidance after all.

Among the 213 other promises broken by Mr Cameron in flagrant breach of the Telling The Truth At Elections Act 1832 was his pledge that he would build a new railway to cut travelling times between London and Birmingham by six minutes, when not an inch of track has been laid.

He also gave a solemn guarantee that Heathrow would be given a third runway, that he would not further reduce Britain's armed forces, that the NHS would not be reorganised again, and that he would never say anything to the electorate that wasn't true.

On every single count the evidence we have unearthed suggests that Mr Cameron is guilty of one of the greatest frauds in Britain's electoral history.

But will the police have the courage to arrest the prime minister and put him behind bars so that we can rerun the general election and put Ed Miliband in Number Ten as the man who was robbed of office by the greatest electoral fraud in *(You've said all this. Ed. – but not Miliband.)*

ENGLAND BACKS BREXIT

We'll be out of Europe in no time!

The Eye's Controversial New Columnist

The columnist whose first words were "Brussels Bureaucrats"

This week I am very angry about criticism of Michael Gove saying "people in this country have had enough of experts". Mr Gove, as usual, is quite correct. It is always so-called "experts" that get us into messes, and top columnists like myself and Mr Gove that get us out of them. You think of any problem that we used to suffer from in the past, such as babies falling from tree tops, London Bridge falling down, and weasels going pop, and you will discover it is "experts" that chose to put babies in such precarious positions, it is "experts" that constructed London bridge in such a shoddy way and it is "experts" that chose to experiment on weasels by force-feeding them with treacle. It is only by my single-minded highlighting of these terrible states of affairs in my top column, week after endless week, that these problems are now not an issue anymore. So take heed of columnists, for it is only by truly shedding oneself of preconceptions, assumptions and facts that one can make a proper decision about Brexit. I myself am for Remain, unless I get a bit cross and sleepy in the afternoon, and then I am for Leaving without further *(cont. p94)*

'CAVEAT EMPTOR'

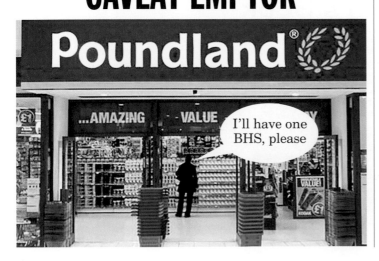

I'll have one BHS, please

THE THREE BREXITEERS

"All for out, and out for ourselves!"

DIARY

KIRSTY WARK MEETS DAMIEN HIRST AND JEFF KOONS

KIRSTY WARK: They were once the *enfants terribles* – the terrible children – of the art world. Their work caused SHOCK and OUTRAGE as well as other really important things too.

These days, Jeff Koons and Damien Hirst are GIANTS of modern art whose work sells for SO MUCH MONEY literally MILLIONS AND MILLIONS OF POUNDS.

Welcome, then, to a ONCE IN A LIFETIME opportunity to see the first show of Jeff Koons' work in this country in ALMOST SIX MONTHS.

From the childlike to the frankly SEXUAL and PORNOGRAPHIC, it's a veritable feast for the eyes. It comes from Damien Hirst's own BRILLIANT and AMAZING private collection of 36 MAJOR ICONIC and EXTREMELY IMPORTANT works by Jeff Koons – and Jeff Koons is about to see it for THE VERY FIRST TIME.

JEFF KOONS: Wow! Oh, wow! Oh, wowy-wow! Damien, this looks really amazing, so amazing, oh, it's amazing. Let me give you a hug! Wow!

DAMIEN HIRST: It's like er me who should be y'know thanking er you or whatever and stuff.

KIRSTY WARK: It must be truly wonderful, Jeff, seeing all your wonderful art here in this brilliant gallery of Damien's for the very first time. And, let's face it, it's worth literally MILLIONS! What's this one, for instance? Tell me about it!

JEFF KOONS: This is one of my Christmas Cracker pieces. I just fell in love with the whole concept of Christmas Crackers, so I went out and purchased twenty boxes of Christmas Crackers, then I took special care not to do anything with them except placing them in these lovely perspex boxes. I think they say something very profound and beautiful about Christmas. And about Crackers. And above all, about Christmas Crackers.

KIRSTY WARK: And, believe me, they're worth MILLIONS!

DAMIEN HIRST: When I like saw that cracker for the first time it must of been like 1986 1987 I just thought yeah like that's like a cracker but it's not just a cracker it's more than a cracker in some way like it's a cracker but it's not a cracker it's just amazing for me it's about death, like you can pull it if you want but if you pull it then it's like all over and it's not a cracker any more in one way but in another way it is and that's just amazing and stuff.

KIRSTY WARK: And I bet it would sell for a FORTUNE at auction! So it's officially brilliant! And what's this one, Jeff?

JEFF KOONS: It's one of my Doggy-Doo pieces.

KIRSTY WARK: AMAZING! To all intents and purposes, it looks exactly like a dog mess, but it's over two storeys high, and it's made of the most AMAZING stainless steel! So it's not a dog's mess at all! It's the most brilliant art! Tell me, Jeff, how important to you is it that it looks like a dog mess – only much, much bigger?

JEFF KOONS: Sure, it has a kind of Egyptian, Etruscan quality, almost a sub-Saharan quality, or a Matissean quality, there's something very Rembrandt about it, almost Caravaggio, so there's a discourse going on and that was very important to me. In one sense, it's very feminine, but in another sense it's very very masculine.

DAMIEN HIRST: I guess it's a metaphor for death like on one level it's just dog shit something that's like come out the arse of a dog an' that but on another level it's er it's er it's er it's somethin' else completely somethin' like a metaphor to me like it's all about death and not just death but life but mainly death.

KIRSTY WARK: And of course, at over 20 feet high, it's far too large to be, as it were, deposited on the street, or, indeed in a gallery, by any REAL dog without a very serious rupture. And that's what makes it so ICONIC and PROFOUND! And now we come to one of your most TRULY EXPENSIVE works!

JEFF KOONS: Wow! This is one of my rubber duck pieces.

KIRSTY WARK: Only it's a duck that's fifteen foot high, so it wouldn't fit in a real bath, would it? So was that your INTENTION, Jeff? Were you making the point that in some very important and radical way there was, as it were, a DISJOINT between the function of the duck, as PER SE a rubber duck, and the environment in which it found itself?

JEFF KOONS: Yes, I was hoping to reference rubber and ducks, and, through ducks, all wildlife, and water, too, and I was also discoursing with Velazquez and Bernini and enjoying an ongoing dialogue with international artists from the past. When I was about six or seven years old, I had this rubber duck in my bath and I remember thinking, wow! It's rubber! And it's a duck! And I thought it would be a great object to work with. It's a metaphor for how we can accept ourselves and accept other people and thus truly enrich our lives. You know what? Tomorrow is the first day of the rest of your life. And love is never having to say you're sorry. That's what art teaches us.

DAMIEN HIRST: And like let's not forget death to me it's a metaphor for death like you have this duck and it's not a livin' duck so it must be a dead duck and being dead it's like really dead so like it's like a metaphor for death and that's why I wanted to buy for as much money as I could so now when I look at it I think not just of death but of money too which is like profound and stuff.

KIRSTY WARK: And presumably a rubber duck that is not actually made of rubber but solid metal wouldn't have a chance of floating, so it would literally SINK. And there's something DEEPLY DISTURBING about that, wouldn't you say? No wonder it's worth MILLIONS AND MILLIONS! Amazing! Well done! And how would you describe this one, Damien? From the outside, it looks like a great pile of coins and notes, reaching all the way up to the sky.

DAMIEN HIRST: It's like my favourite of all Jeff's work and stuff I've like always thought of money as something profound like love or death and stuff like something you need to respect and like coming to terms with money has been a major part in my life so when I look at it now I just think of money and death and stuff and that's great.

KIRSTY WARK: Wonderful! You guys are so EXTRAORDINARY! And to think it's all worth COUNTLESS MILLIONS! And what does money mean to you, Jeff? What lesson has it taught you?

JEFF KOONS: Oh, wow, it's taught me so much. I'd like to build the world a home, and furnish it with love. Grow apple trees and honey bees and snow white turtle doves. And you know what? I'd like to teach the world to sing in perfect harmony.

DAMIEN HIRST: It's like a metaphor for death and stuff. And death. And stuff.

As told to

CRAIG BROWN

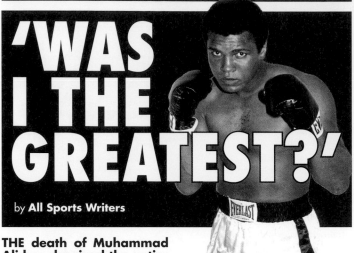

'WAS I THE GREATEST?'

by **All Sports Writers**

THE death of Muhammad Ali has deprived the entire world of the chance for me to write more classic pieces about his fights.

Still never mind, here are all the pieces I wrote before, proving without a shadow of doubt that not only was I a poet, a role model, and icon for future generations, I really was the Greatest of All Time.

On other pages

p1 An old piece we've been holding on to since 1987.

p2 An old piece we've been holding on to since 1978.

p94 Dozens more pieces and hundreds of pictures from the sixties that we've had ready to go for years.

Tragic Ali Suffered Parkinson's

THE former world heavyweight champion became a victim of Parkinson's disease in the 70s and 80s, being repeatedly interviewed on the BBC chat show.

It clearly had an effect on Ali, as Parkinson told him endless anecdotes about his greatest fight – against Emu, when heavyweight Parkinson was floored by the lightweight bird puppet. The so-called Thriller in Shepherd's Bush who (cont. p94)

EYE 94-PAGE TRIBUTE

Was he the finest boxer of all time?

PRIVATE EYE asks whether the late Jeremy Clarkson was the very best heavyweight fighter in history?

Clarkson was known as a great wordsmith as well as a great pugilist and no one will ever forget his catchphrase "Float like an elephant, hit you in the face when the food isn't hot".

"Can we talk?"

Hankin

An Apology by MR DAVID CAMERON

IN RECENT weeks the Prime Minister, Mr Cameron, may have given the impression that he considered Mr Sadiq Khan a dangerous Islamic extremist who was totally unfit to hold any responsible position in British political life.

Speeches made by Mr Cameron in the recent London mayoral election may have reinforced the idea that Mr Khan was little better than a terrorist whose only ambition was to allow his friends and close political associates from various extremist Islamicist organisations to blow up London's transport system and impose Sharia law on the entire area within the M25 before announcing that County Hall was now the headquarters of his Islamic State in London (Isil).

Mr Cameron now realises that there was not a jot or titter of truth in any of the above, and that Mr Khan is in fact a thoroughly responsible and far-sighted politician whose moderate Muslim beliefs do him huge credit and have led him to the very wise decision to vote on June 23 for Britain to remain in the European Union.

Mr Cameron would like to apologise for any confusion that his earlier misconstrued comments may have caused.

RADIO HIGHLIGHTS

Just a Minute

What you will hear, on Radio 4 Extra

Nicholas Parsons: So, Clement, I'd like you to talk for one minute on the subject of Celebrity Paedophiles.

Clement Freud *(for, unfortunately, it is he)*: Celebrity Paedophiles are not easy to spot…
(Buzzer)

Kenneth Williams: Deviation.

Parsons: Yes, Clement, legally that is "deviation".

Freud: Just as well I wasn't caught, then.

Parsons: Carry on, Clement.

Freud: I will!
(Buzzer)

Derek Nimmo: Repetition!

Parsons: Yes, you repeated the offence, didn't you, Clement?

Freud: I did.
(Buzzer)

Williams: Hesitation?

Freud: No, I didn't hesitate at all.

Parsons: Carry on with the subject, Clement.

Freud: I was grooming my dog, Henry, the other day, which made a change…
(Whistle goes)

Parsons: Oh, it's the police!

Policeman: Hello, Mr Freud. Can I get your autograph?

Parsons: You have no time inside to do, Clement. You are the winner. So, thank you, everyone – you've been listening to *Just a Minor*, with Clement Fraud and Knickerless Persons.

(That's enough appalling taste. Ed.)

"No, not that one – I'm not allowed to live near a school"

Man reads book at Hay shock

YESTERDAY a man at the Hay Festival sat and read a book quietly for half an hour.

The man did not watch Benedict Cumberbatch delivering an impassioned plea about arts funding, or witness a former head of MI5 being indiscreet about national security, nor did he witness Stephen Frears interviewing Simon Schama while Simon Schama interviews Russell T. Davies about the reasons Shakespeare is such a bloody snooze-fest these days and it's about time we spiced it up with some Daleks.

On discovering that the man had not been to an exciting interactive event and had, in fact, just been reading *The Mill on the Floss* for 28 minutes, festival organisers immediately had him removed and then apologised through the medium of an interactive debate on Big Data led by Patrick Stewart.

On Other Pages

● Hay, Hay, Hay, Hay, Hay **94**

New Visiting Professor At LSE – That Citation In Full

SALUTAMUS ANGELINAM JOLIEM UXOREM BRADI PITTI. THESPIANA CELEBRATA ET STELLA PULCHRITIDUNA HOLLYWOODENSIS FAMOSISSIMA UT LARA CROFTA IN "SEPULCHRUM RAPTOR" SED NON IN SEQUELLES REBOOTIENSES."SEPULCHRUM RAPTOR II" AUT "SEPULCHRUM RAPTOR III" AUT "SEPULCHRUM RAPTOR XCIV". MATRIARCH ET MATER SEXTI PUERI ET PUELLAE CUM NOMINE ABSURDO VIZ PAX MADDOX ZAHARA SHILO KNOX VIVIENNEQUE. NUNC ACADEMICA SERIOSA ET MAGISTER VISITANS IN "PACEM SECURITAM ET STUDIA FEMINA" IN SCHOLA LONDINIUM OECONOMICUM CUM CO-MAGISTER ET BONO AMICO SOLO WILLIAM HAGUEM QUONDAM DUX CONSERVATORUM SED IAM "HOMINEM YESTERHODIE". ANGELINA ET WILLIAMUS LABORANS IN TANDEM EDUCARE STUDENTES PAUPERES QUI PAGENT MMMMMMMMM LIBRA PER ANNUM PRO UNUM AUT DUUM LECTURI PISSPORI CELEBRITATI SED PRINCIPES PATHETICES DE SCHOLA LONDINIUM OECONOMICUM GAUDEANT ENORMITER CUM MULTAS PUBLICITAS ET SELFIES CUM FRUITISSIMA ANGELINA.   © LSE 2016-06-02

THAT CELEBRITY DIVORCE
Who Gets What?

AMBER HEARD	JOHNNY DEPP
Custody of dogs (Boo, Pistol)	Custody of turkeys (Lone Ranger, Mortdecai, The Tourist etc)
Black eye	Blackened name
Bad publicity	Worse publicity
Papped	Pissed
The money	The bill
	Er... that's it

Twitter user 'knows exactly what happened'

by Our Social Media Staff
Johnnie Stalker

LOS ANGELES police have confirmed they've suspended their investigation into allegations by Amber Heard of domestic abuse against her estranged husband Johnny Depp, after Twitter user LEXICON4356 revealed he knows exactly what happened.

"We were so relieved Thursday morning when LEXICON4356 tweeted to his 937 followers that he knows precisely what happened behind closed doors between the two stars," said LA police detective Andy Rosen.

"My partner and I could have had to spend months interviewing Amber and Johnny, investigating the alleged crime scene, taking forensic evidence, speaking to witnesses and eventually deciding whether to press charges, but LEXICON4356 has saved us all that legwork.

"The powers granted to Twitter users to see exactly what happens behind closed doors without any shadow of doubt is going to save us so much time in the future."

"Bad news, I'm afraid... your cat is completely unfunny"

JOHN HUMPHRYS WRITES:

'The awful background noise that ruins all our lives'

You know what it's like, you enter a room and there it is in the background. You can't ignore it, it goes on and on in that dull dreary way until you want to rip your ears off. Someone has left the radio on and there's the Today programme with the relentless drone of myself asking the same interminable question to some hapless politician who never gets to answer because I never stop blathering on and *(that's enough – Ed.)* No, let me finish, the listeners want an answer to *(No, we're going to turn you off)* no, I think that *(Click. Silence.)*

The next person who says I'm just trying to be Jeremy Clarkson gets a slap

---

THIS WEEK

CHRIS EVANS

Do you have a lot of spoons?

I've got millions of spoons. A lot more than Jeremy Clarkson.

But you said you wanted at least five million spoons and you're not close...

No. If you take a consolidated aggregate of the spoon figures, you will find that spoonwise I have more spoons than any other spoon enthusiast ever, particularly Jeremy Clarkson. FACT.

But just looking at your spoon collection, it's a bit disappointing, isn't it?

NO. FACT. My spoons are top-quality spoons and everybody loves them.

But they have had some lukewarm reviews in the press, haven't they?

No. My spoons are a hit. OFFICIALLY. That is a FACT, folks, and just because some critics are living in the past doesn't mean that compared to Jeremy Clarkson's spoons my cutlery collection is a flop. It is not. FACT.

So what about the headlines such as 'Flop Drawer', 'Evans is a spoonatic' and 'Clarkson's Grand Tureen will be much better'?

Newspapers have never been less relevant to what's happening in the real world of spoons. They are pathetic. FACT. OFFICIAL. OFFICIAL FACT.

I've got the latest figures on your spoon collection here and they seem very low indeed...

I am going to be sick. FACT.

Has anything amusing ever happened to Matt Le Blanc in connection with a spoon?

Nooooo. Eurgh....

NEXT WEEK: *Jenson Button, "Me and My Button".*

First Ever Edition

BOTANY BAY TIMES

PROPRIETOR: R MURDOCH

January 1788

AUSTRALIAN POINT SYSTEM 'NOT PERFECT' SHOCK

by Our Man in the Colonies **Sidney Harbour-Bridge**

THE immigration system that has been held up worldwide as a model may have some flaws, according to Aboriginal critics. The large numbers of economic migrants coming from Tilbury Docks in little convict ships have caused problems to the indigenous population.

"I'm not being racist," said one local, "but they are all white, they do bring a lot of diseases and many, if not all of them, are criminals. They're supposed to be useful to our society, but I'm not sure if we need all these highly skilled thieves, prostitutes and murderers."

However, the First Governor of Botany Bay defended the system, accusing local leaders of scaremongering, saying, "This is just Dingo whistle politics at its worst!"

How the system works:

1 point for being poor

2 points for stealing bread

3 points for knifing landlord in tavern brawl

4 points for being Irish

5 points for being a useful cricketer

The locals remain unconvinced. One man with a boomerang said, "They should go back to where they came from!"

FARAGE WANTS 'PINTS SYSTEM'

You have seven and start talking about rape and immigrants

DODGY OLIGARCH EMBARRASSED BY PRINCE ANDREW LINK

by Our Staff **Phil Boots**

THERE were calls last night for Kazakh billionaire Timur Kulibayev to stand down as a representative for Dodgy Oligarchism, following revelations of his business dealings with Prince Andrew.

A spokesman for international corruption said, "Mr Kulibayev's relationship with this tainted minor member of the British Royal Family is hugely embarrassing for him and for all of us involved in the Kickback, Backhander and Bribe Community.

"As a Kazakh oil tycoon with a dubious reputation to protect, he should have known better than to get involved with 'Air Miles' Andy, whose friendship with a known paedophile must surely put him beyond the pale."

When asked for a comment, the head of Prince Andrew's private office, Sir Foxton Winkworth, said, "How much is it worth? Do you want to buy Andrew's house? How about the asking price plus 4 million? Bargain."

"Regrets, I've had a few..."

THAT LEAVE CAMPAIGN IN FULL

Immigration

Immigration

Immigration

THAT REMAIN CAMPAIGN IN FULL

Intimidation

Intimidation

Intimidation

SAYS

We are about to make the biggest political decision of our lives.

Surely we are capable of standing on our own two feet, of making up our own minds – not being bullied into submission by faceless, unelected men, men with a long track record of embarrassing failures.

That's why today we here at The Sun say "no" to telling the British people to vote leave, just because we've been ordered to do so by our New York-based billionaire proprietor Rupert *(You're fired – Ed's boss)*

HELLO! It's me again. I must confess I'm a bit down in the dumps this week.

I did a speech about Europe, and unfortunately my clear and strong message about Sort Of Wanting To Stay In The EU If We Must At This Present Moment was completely overshadowed by Laura Kuenssberg being booed and hissed by my supporters as she tried to deliver a question.

I find this turn of events completely unacceptable. Why was Laura there to ask a question at all? She must have known that that would happen. And of course the right-wing press (I'm looking at you, BBC and the Guardian!) have to construct some disgusting subliminal nastiness, spinning the story so that a spontaneous and high-minded exercise of free speech in the form of democratic booing gets made into something which is perceived as 'negative' in some way.

That, in a nutshell, is why I avoid the right-wing media as much as possible. Unfortunately, there is quite a lot more of it than I first thought! A web production company called Vice cynically constructed some more subliminal nastiness against me by recording things I've said and done, and editing them together. So I'm sad to say, the internet is also part of the right-wing media too!

So, my endless quest to find a media outlet which isn't corrupted by right-wing bias against me continues and some of the young people who advise me may have the answer.

Apparently Grindr is a great way to get in touch with like-minded people…

Cheerio!

PS: I have discovered the identity of the Labour insider who is undermining the party at Prime Minister's Question Time – it's me!

'Once In A Lifetime Opportunity To Settle Nothing' Say All Sides

by Our EU Referendum Correspondent **E. Ternity**

Both sides in the EU Referendum debate have agreed that Thursday's historic vote is a never-to-be-repeated chance to solve no issues when it comes to Britain's fractious relationship with the EU.

"This momentous result will decide once and for all who will hate who when we start arguing about the result and what it means right after we get the result."

Both sides agreed that any truce in hostilities would last at most a few minutes after the result was announced, with normal service of vicious personal attacks and mud-slinging instantly resuming on Facebook and Twitter.

"Amid all this rancour, bile, name calling, and unsubstantiated claims of vote rigging, demands for a second referendum would grow ever louder and continue until the end of the recorded time," said both the Leave and the Remain camp.

EURO 2016

Anger as Football Disrupts Violence

by Our Man in Marseille
Andrew Marrseille

THE world of violence was rocked to its foundations, as an outbreak of football threatened to ruin the Euro 2016 Hooligan Championship.

Time after time, England hooligans had to put down their broken bottles and chairs, stop fighting and sit through 90 minutes of uninterrupted football.

Said one yob, "It was appalling – this is not what we came here for. We came here to drink too much, enjoy the fighting, and end up in jail. We did not expect the sickening sight of a one-all draw against a mediocre Russian football side."

Said another, "It's just a minority of people, just 22 to be precise, who want to play football. It's terrible when it all kicks off, and it spoils it for the majority, who want to enjoy a good punch-up."

The authorities believe they know the organiser of the football, a Mr Roy Hodgson, who has unashamedly been caught on camera, running up and down the touchline, orchestrating the horrific scenes of football.

"There is no place for this kind of sportsmanship in modern violence," said the organiser of the pressure group "Kick Heads Not Balls – Actually Kick Their Balls as Well".

● *LATE SCORE –*
SHOCK DRAW
England 8 (people in hospital)
Russia 8 (people deported)

CAMERON DENIES SCAREMONGERING

We at Remain have run a positive campaign based on the facts

Cordell

THE BREXIT PARTY – THOSE MANIFESTO PROMISES IN FULL

When the UK frees itself from the financial shackles of the unelected bureaucrats of Brussels, the new, unelected Brexit government will immediately receive the EU rebate of £700 billion trillion a week, which they will then spend on the following...

1. Brand new NHS, with new hospitals, millions of doctors and nurses from all over the world except Europe, and a brand new cure for cancer

2. Brand new transport system, with high-speed trains going everywhere at high speed except to Europe

3. Free money for poor people

4. Free money for rich people

5. Sunshine for everyone, guaranteed 24 hours a day, twelve months a year, including nights

6. Bluebirds over the white cliffs of Dover

7. A nightingale singing in Berkeley Square

8. Raindrops on roses, whiskers on kittens

9. Bright copper kettles and warm woollen mittens

10. Brown paper packages tied up with strings

11. Things as they used to be in the good old days.

© M. Gove (PM)

I'm feelin' really emotional

How come?

Well my great grandad fought in France then me grandad did...

and now I 'ave.

Aw, powerful mate, cheers

YOBS EURO 2016 SPECIAL by TONY HUSBAND

Letters to the Editor

An open letter from leading British idiots

SIR – We, the undersigned, are a group of idiots. In previous weeks the country's newspapers have seen letters from economists, soldiers, farmers, actors, scientists, businesspeople, and numerous other groups weighing in with their opinions on whether Britain should remain in the EU or leave it, and yet nobody has asked us, a substantial group in modern Britain (and one which contains a lot of economists, soldiers, farmers, actors etc), what we think. Today, that must end.

It is our considered opinion that nobody knows anything, particularly us, but also everyone else, and that anyone telling us what will happen after a Remain/Leave vote is almost certainly so wrong as not to be worth listening to. Furthermore, it is insulting to us that so many spurious facts have been bandied around, especially as we don't listen to facts anyway and base our reactions solely on whether we were once pickpocketed in Rome, or, alternatively, whether we like halloumi and think it will be banned if we vote Leave.

We intend to make up our minds in a vacuum of facts, depending on whether we think Boris is a bloody good laugh and sound fellow or a facile, deceitful prat.

Signed,
Sid Bonkers, Doris Bonkers and 395 other foremost idiots

"Wait... can't we use a bit of perspective?"

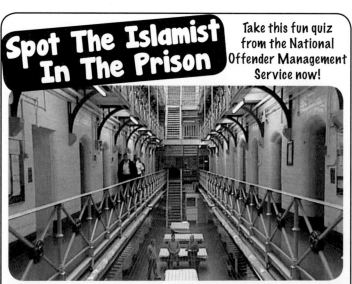

Spot The Islamist In The Prison

Take this fun quiz from the National Offender Management Service now!

QUESTION: Can you spot the Islamist in this picture of a prison?

ANSWER: There isn't one. There is no problem with radicalisation in prisons and there's nothing to see here.

The Eye's Controversial New Columnist

The columnist who exposed the scandal the newspapers dubbed 'Cowandgate'

This week I am inserting myself into the Referendum debate, because I want to talk about the EU. Speaking as a baby *(see photo)*, I know how frustrating it is to be ruled over by individuals who tell you what to wear, what to eat and how to behave. The two unelected minions who lord it over me create hundreds of directives every day that are just designed to bind me up in red tape. Don't eat the stuff in the cat's litter tray! Don't pull the dog's tail! Don't pour orange juice on the carpet! You must have a nap right now! Every day these directives pile up and up, and there is no sign of them slowing. I call these people "Brussels bureaucrats" because they even have a directive that forces me to eat my Brussels sprouts! Of course I try to appeal against their diktats, but the fact I don't speak their language makes me frustrated, so I just repeat myself in a louder manner, and then, conveniently, up pops another directive that forces me to have another nap! I'm sure I would do just fine without them, and envisage no disastrous outcome if I voted to be rid of them and was given the opportunity to fend for myself, so listen to me all of you! Take this from someone who has lived this terrible existence all his life and thought about the issue for several minutes. Vote leave and never *(cont. page 94)*

POETRY CORNER

In Memoriam Lord Parkinson, former Chairman of the Conservative Party

So. Farewell
Then Cecil Parkinson,
You were once
A high-flying
Tory Minister,
Tipped to become
Tory leader.

But you were best
Known for having
A love child with
Your secretary, so
You had to resign
In disgrace.

You should have
Known that you
Were only allowed
One mistress, ie
Mrs Thatcher.

E.J. Thribb (17½)

PS. I use the
Term "love child"
Rather than "bastard"
Because that really
Applies to you.

In Memoriam Ian Kilmister, Rock and Roll legend

So. Farewell
Then Lemmy
from Motörhead.

I didn't know
Many of your songs
Apart from
The Ace of Spades.

"That's the way I like it,
Baby, I don't wanna
Live forever."

Now, at least, you know
You won't have to.

E.J. Thribb
(17½ thousand decibels)

"I'll call you back... I'm just going into a tunnel"

LEAVE SPECIAL

CAMERON LEAVES MESS

GOVE LEAVES BORIS

MAY LEAVES NO ALTERNATIVE

FARAGE LEAVES UKIP

TORIES LEAVE GOVE

LABOUR LEAVES CORBYN

COUNTRY LEAVES SENSES

The Daily Turkeygraph

TURKEYS VOTE FOR CHRISTMAS IN REFERENDUM CLIFFHANGER

by Our Poultry Staff **Jeremy Paxo**

BY the narrowest of margins, the majority of Britain's turkeys voted in favour of Christmas. The decision, which will have a dramatic impact on the lives of millions of turkeys, came following months of argument about the pros and cons of leaving the farmyard.

The proponents of "Leave" argued that even though they weren't sure what would happen to turkeys when they left the farm in a truck on December 24th, it was well worth the risk to find out. Said one, "I'm happy to put my neck on the line if it means that we can take control of our own destiny."

The minority "Remain" turkeys had claimed that life outside the farmyard would be very, very much worse, but this was dismissed by their critics as "Project Fear" and described as "gobbledygook".

However, already there are signs that some turkeys are regretting the so-called Brexmas vote, as evidence is piling up that, come Christmas lunch, they will in fact have their heads cut off, their giblets put in a plastic bag and be well and truly stuffed.

Said one worried turkey, "When I voted for Christmas I didn't think it would actually happen, despite the evidence of the past 2,000 years. I was swayed by the promises that there would be a bright new dawn on Boxing Day.

"No one said that I wouldn't see it. And no one mentioned bread sauce, roast potatoes and, in particular, the much-loathed Brussels sprouts."

One thing is for sure, the heated nature of the debate (Gas Mark 6) shows no sign of cooling.

LEAVE VOTERS 'STUNNED TO HAVE LEFT THE EUROPEAN UNION'

by Our Referendum Correspondent **Lee Verr**

LEAVE voters who voted to leave the European Union have expressed their astonishment that voting to leave the European Union means Britain will now leave the European Union.

"I thought it just meant that Polish bloke from Number 43 who puts his bin out on the wrong day would be sent home," said one upset Leave voter.

"I thought it just meant that I'd no longer have to phone up to get an appointment at the doctor's because the NHS would have all that extra money," said another worried Leave voter.

"Apart from it specifically saying on the ballot paper that we were voting on whether or not to leave the European Union, how were we supposed to know this was a vote about leaving the European Union?" said one (cont. p94)

"This must be the new Single Market"

BRITISH GOODS

Lady Macbeth Fury Over Vine Slur

by Our Political Staff, Jane Thayne and Henry Porter

LADY MACBETH hit out angrily last night at suggestions that she was in some way similar to Sarah Vine, who notoriously incited her weedy Scottish husband to murder his old friend.

Lady Macbeth was said to be furious at attempts to compare her responsible political strategy over the Scottish throne with what she called Sarah Vile's "vaulting ambition".

Lady Macbeth told friends, "My slogan was the perfectly acceptable 'Out! Out! Damn spot', whereas the evil Gove came up with 'Out! Out! Damn foreigners'.

"Mr and Mrs Gove were against Freedom of Movement Across Europe, whereas my husband and I merely wanted to restrict the movement of trees from Burnham Wood to Dunsinane. There is no comparison."

She continued, "And the key difference between myself and the ruthless, scheming Mrs Vile is that I am sane and have a conscience, which will haunt me until the end of my days, whereas she HAS GONE

COMPLETELY MAD!!!

"She believes she is the power behind the throne and writes hundreds of vain pieces about herself in the Daily Mail (see p7, 8, 9 tomorrow, tomorrow and tomorrow). I, on the other hand, modestly kept myself out of the Daily Chain Mail for the whole of my husband's career."

She concluded, "Unlike the amateurish Goves, my husband and I have faith in experts and we consulted the Three Witches at every point and followed their advice.

"Sarah Vain is no Lady Macbeth. She is much worse. She is nothing but a hubble-bubble-toil-and-trouble-maker."

FARAGE CELEBRATES TAKING BACK CONTROL FROM ELITES

(with Mr Lebedev and Mr Murdoch)

Nice Union Jackboots, Nige

D I A R Y

OUR BREXIT JOY

LORD JULIAN FELLOWES: If one were to employ one's soup spoon to eat a blancmange, then others might complain that one had committed the most frightful *faux pas*. And rightly so. Might I refer you to Lord Grantham's immortal *apercu* in Series 3 of *Downton?* "I fear, Carson, that the employment of an improper eating iron has been the downfall of far greater men than I."

And so it goes with those who voted to Remain. They opted for the wrong spoon, and as a result they should not expect to resume their positions at the top table. Call one old-fashioned, but, like so many things, it's all a matter of good manners.

CHARLES MOORE: One of the most pernicious lies of the defeated Remain camp is that the Vote Leave campaign failed to convince the young. Far from it: when the dawn sun lit London on that morning after Independence Day, I enjoyed a series of delightful encounters with lusty young patriots.

As I crossed Lambeth Bridge at 6am, groups of youthful, revelling Leavers, many of them chanting a selection of hits by "chart-topper" Lonnie Donegan, recognised me and came up and kissed me. Two or three of them were wearing cutting-edge cravats and jazzy gold-buttoned blazers, which suggests they were very young indeed.

When I reached the Vote Leave offices, I found a room full of empty bottles, discarded all-British pork scratchings, and a sea of joyful young faces.

I was particularly struck by a red-headed, intellectual young man, still in shorts, a pair of sturdy Start-Rite sandals on his feet. It was Simon Heffer, bright as a button, one of our ablest and bravest thinkers, and still barely fifty years of age.

Funny how the BBC refuses to acknowledge this youthful surge. I am reliably informed by Lord Lamont, an acknowledged expert in these things, that three quarters of the young at the recent festival of popular music at Glastonbury were fervent Leavers. Disgracefully, vast unscaleable fences had been erected around the site so as to coop them in until the polls had closed. It comes as no surprise that the "official broadcaster" of the festival was the BBC. With its hatred of parliamentary democracy, it turned a blind eye to this mass-imprisonment, concentrating its resources on forcing the public to believe in the fantasy of a "falling pound".

JAMES DELINGPOLE @JamesDelingpole 12m: Have I got this right? Shitty wankertwats back the pongy Remain vote – then think they can be PM? Learn some sophistication, arseholes!

ALLISON PEARSON: I'm very sorry, but is British self-loathing now so rife that it's OK for our so-called national broadcaster to talk down our country?

Auntie Beeb got her moth-eaten knickers in a right old twist, with professional boo-hooey gloomsters Laura Kuenssberg and Kamal Ahmed (silly old yours truly, to expect a trusty Smith and Jones delivering our news!!) poring over yet more good (oops, sorry, bad!!) news of economic turmoil with which to dampen our spirits.

So they whip up panic about "UK stock market plunges!", "UK credit rating downgraded!" "Pound Sterling drops against US dollar!" as if this meant anything at all.

Welcome to the national nervous breakdown. The want of perspective is staggering. "Things have got worse" they say.

What, worse than 9/11, when innocent men and women fell hundreds of miles to their tragic deaths?

Worse than the Somme, where literally billions of brave soldiers courageously sacrificed their own lives so that the rest of us could vote Leave?

Worse than Bhopal, whatever that is when it's at home?

Worse than my Victoria Sponge, which – oops! – has just come out of the cooker all flat and soggy (memo to self: bin that recipe!)?!?

No, I don't think so. The ordinary, decent folk where I live know that when push comes to shove, the economy is just numbers, numbers, numbers.

But people are people.

And – sorry! – but, in my book, it's people – lovely, decent, men, women and kiddies – that matter most.

SIR TIM RICE: *"Yes, our world is a great big glorious UNIVERSE!*
And if we'd voted Remain things would be much much WORSE
For – dah! di! dah! dah! our PLANET!
By which I mean every Jack, Jill and JANET!
So let's rejoice we voted LEAVE!
'Cos it a truly brilliant thing WE'VE
Voted the right WAY
Not just for tomorrow but also for toDAY!"

MELANIE PHILLIPS: Frankly, it makes me want to weep.

It begins with voting Remain.

It ends with prostitution, alcoholism and a lifelong addiction to crack cocaine.

Last month, hundreds of millions of uneducated young men and women descended on the polling booths – high on illegal drugs, their minds warped by crystal meth – and voted to be ruled by a foreign superstate hell-bent on destroying all that is great about our precious country.

They failed in their murderous quest.

But the rest of us are left reaping the whirlwind.

The Remainers are on the rampage of revenge.

And the statistics bear it out.

Vomit in our streets.

Pools of urine in our shop doors.

Unsavoury hard core porn in our primary schools.

Old folk knifed in their own front parlours.

Is this Gomorrah? Is it Sodom?

No. This is Britain in 2016.

And, frankly, it makes me want to weep.

As told to
CRAIG BROWN

"Which side of the family – Brexit or Remain?"

"It's Volte McVolte-face!"

Boris Johnson, brother of the famous Rachel Johnson, gives the inside story of the most historic week ever in British Politics

Cripes! I didn't see that one coming! There was I, thinking "We've had our fun, fought a top-hole campaign and made friend Dave look like a prize chump – and then the jolly old voters will do their stuff and let him scrape home by the seat of his pants..." But then, blow me down, Mr and Mrs Britain got a bit carried away and went way over the top.

So BoJo was out on the tiles, raising a few glasses of Bolly to our honourable defeat, when suddenly he sees that Dimbleby chap on the telly putting on a solemn voice and telling us that we'd won!

Blimey! That wasn't the idea at all! Then, blow me down again, what do I see on the old gogglebox, but Defeated Dave blubbing on the steps of Number Ten, telling the nation that he was packing it in as soon as poss and leaving the whole wretched shambles to be sorted out by someone else, ie us!

Or, to be more specific, yours truly, who romped home with his 17 million votes and ended up with the worst poisoned chalice in the history of the world.

Cripes and double cripes! This really wasn't in the script at all! It was meant to be crowds cheering me outside the house, as Mr Gallant Loser, shouting, "Bor-is, Bor-is, Bor-is... in, in, in".

Instead of which, they're all screaming, "You scumbag, Boris. Look what you've done. It's all your fault."

So I rang the Gover in a bit of a flap, to ask whether he'd heard the dreadful news.

I got his groggy Missus on the blower, who said she and Michael had conked out and gone to bed early having had a skinful the night before, celebrating our glorious non-victory, and were having a well-deserved lie-in.

"For Gawd's sake, Sarah," I shouted in exasperation, "you've got to wake him up. We're in a hell of a mess. It seems that not only have we won this effing referendum mullarkey but now Dave's done the dirty on us and everyone will be expecting us to clear up the shitfest!"

A minute later, a bleary-sounding Govester stumbled onto the line. "This can't be happening, Boris. It can't be true." I told him that for once I wasn't lying! It was far too serious for that.

Sounding thoroughly brown-trousered, Michael said, "So what's the plan then, Boris?" At which point, alarm bells started to ring in BoJo's head, and I said, "Hang on, Govester – I thought you had the plan. You're meant to be the clever one."

At this point, the Wonkster went deathly quiet, then stammered, "Don't worry, Bozza, you can trust me. I'll bring the plan along to your campaign launch."

"Good man, Gover," I said, remembering not to call him The Gopher on account of him being oiky and jolly chippy when us OEs ask him to do all the heavy lifting. "I'll leave it to you – but don't forget to put in your contact lenses, so you don't look too nerdy, and put a confident and not too miserable smile on your chops ready to face the cameras."

And double blow me down, I didn't see the next bit coming either! I was just preparing my brilliant ad libs about how Govey and I were the dream team and the EU nightmare was over now the dawn of freedom was breaking and other Churchillian style crowd-pleasing piffle when chum Lynton burst in to tell me that the Governator had announced his plan. "And the plan is to shaft you up the Brexit, cobber. You're toast!"

Cripes, cripes and triple cripes!!! Govey had betrayed me! Before I could betray him! It's like the Roman chaps I keep going on about – the noble Borisius Maximus being knifed on the Capitol steps by the scheming assassin Govus Minimus!

What to do? Do I stand and fight and honour the 17 million who supported me? Or does gallant Bozza run away, bravely leave everyone up shit creek sans paddle and live to fight (or possibly run away) another day?

No brainer!

Bye!

The Rt Hon Boris Johnson, *MP for the Daily Telegraph.*

PARTY LEADERSHIP: HOW IT WORKS

Claimed to back Remain but campaigned half-heartedly

Favourite to lead

Claimed to back Remain but campaigned half-heartedly

Utterly unfit to lead

Pollsters were right again, say pollsters

by **Crystal Balls**

ONCE again, Britain's polling organisations were totally vindicated by their predictions of the result of the EU referendum.

Said YouGove's Peter Kellner, "We were 100% right in forecasting a very narrow margin between the two sides, and that the result would be well within the margin of error.

"As all our surveys found, both online and via phone polling, right to the last minute, the result could have gone either way – and it did."

When asked why YouGove, ComRong, Ipso Non Facto and all the other pollsters had predicted a win for the Remain camp, Mr Kellner said, "We have conducted a future poll amongst all our fellow pollsters, and 99 percent of them agree that the voters were lying to us, and were deliberately trying to make it seem that we are not very good at our job."

POST-BREXIT BRITAIN

OUR BREXPERTS ANSWER YOUR QUESTIONS

Dear Brexpert
As a fervent one-nation Tory, I am deeply concerned that Brexit may tear this country apart. Will the North-South divide be even greater than ever?
IN, NEASDEN

Dear IN
Don't worry, Brexit will unite the country as never before, as it will be as grim down south as it is up north.

Dear Brexpert
How will Whitehall cope with the extra bureaucracy needed to extricate ourselves from the thousands of laws, treaties, directives and EU agreements, and negotiate new ones?
SIR HUMPHREY, WHITEHALL

Dear Sir Humphrey
No problem. You will simply have to recruit thousands of extra civil servants with European expertise, most of them probably coming from Brussels. They may have to spend a lot of time handling their own visa requirements, but there should be a few hours left for them to sort everything out.

Dear Brexpert
I didn't bother to vote. Will I regret this?
STU DENT, 23 ½

Dear Stu
That depends on which side you didn't bother to vote for. Still, wasn't Adele great? Awesome!

Dear Brexpert
I think we've all heard enough from experts. They're useless, aren't they?
MG, NOTTING HILL

Dear Mr Gove
In my expert opinion, you are an unprincipled opportunist masquerading as a patriot. But what do I know?

Dear Brexpert
That sounds like a foreign name. Why don't you go home?
NIGEL FARRIGHT, THANET

Dear Mr Farright
I refer you to my previous answer.

LATEST SHADOW CABINET APPOINTMENTS

IN COME

Ajiit Prop 23, Shadow Minister for Elderly

Doug Grave 94, Shadow Minister for the Young

Diane Abbott 62, Shadow Minister for Still Being Jeremy's Only Friend

Des Pratt 37, Shadow Minister for Defence, Foreign Affairs, Fisheries and Women

Will Fayle 42, Shadow Minister for Enterprise

Sue Pine 27, Shadow Home Secretary

Diane Abbott 62½, Shadow Minister for Still Being Jeremy's Only Friend

Mo Mentum 34, Shadow Minister for Everything Not Mentioned Previously

Dee Team 56, Shadow Minister for Selecting Shadow Ministers

OUT GO

Bea Team 34 *(resigned)*

Lou Selection 58 *(sacked)*

Hope Fool 83 *(deceased)*

POETRY CORNER

In Memoriam Jeremy Corbyn, leader of the Labour Party

So. Farewell
Then Jeremy Corbyn.

You were leader
Of the Labour Party
Until all your MPs
Deserted you.

Oh. Hang on.
You still are leader
Of the Labour Party.

So. Farewell
Then the Labour Party.

E.J. Thribb (17½)

A Psychotherapist writes:
The Five Stages of Grief for Remainers

1. Denial
2. Bargaining
3. Anger
4. Depression
5. Theresa May

Engineers to try turning Britain off and on to see if it will come back on again

TECHNICAL support specialists will attempt to turn Britain off on and on again over the weekend to see if they can get the country to restart its normal functions again.

For the past two weeks, engineers have been busy checking why there is no sign of power in the country.

"All normal functions seem to have ceased," revealed a tech support worker. "We've been checking all the usual power sources, but it looks like everything has shut down, and remote access to Europe seems to have been disconnected, even though we were operating in a multi-user environment. It seems that someone has just yanked a plug out.

"If it means a forced reset, we could have huge losses," he warned.

"Take me to anyone who remotely resembles a leader"

Nursery Times

Friday, Once-upon-a-time

TRAGIC END OF THE LEGENDARY WIZARD OF OSBORNE

by **Richard and Judy Garland**

THE bells of the Emerald City last night pealed in joy at the news that the long reign of the fabled Wizard of Osborne had at long last ended.

For years, the Wizard had regularly amazed the simple Munchkins with his parade of seemingly magical tricks, as he conjured money out of nowhere and made vast financial deficits disappear in a puff of smoke, and every time the little Munchkins would happily sing "Somewhere over the rainbow there's a huge pot of money that will make everything alright".

But each year it turned out that the Wizard's promises failed to come true, and his tricks were shown up to be no more than smoke and mirrors.

And so it came about that he eventually produced his last trick which exposed him once and for all as no more than a hopeless fraud, hiding away behind his curtain.

What the Wizard did was tell all the Munchkins that unless they voted the way he told them to do, the whole Land of Oz

would descend into chaos, with the Wicked Witches turning everyone into frogs and causing a collapse in house prices.

But the Munchkins did not listen to the Wizard and told him to fly off in his balloon and never return to the Land of Oz again.

But the best thing of all was that the Land now had a new and very different ruler – the modest, sensible, down-to-earth girl Dorotheresa, with her magic kitten-heel shoes. And everyone lived happily ever after (or at least for a few days).

IS IT 'HAPPY EVER AFTER' FOR JEMIMA PUDDLEDUCK?

by Our Showbiz Staff **Harry Beatrix Potter**

WILL love last this time for the unluckiest duck in the puddle, the much-romanced Jemima Puddleduck? The heiress to the fortune of the late Sir Jammy Fishpaste and contributing editor of the *New Stoatsman* has had a string of doomed relationships with unsuitable farmyard Romeos.

First, there was the predator Mr Imran Fox, who turned from lovable playboy into a hard-line political activist, "The Fanatic Mr Fox".

Then there was the thespian pig, Hugh Grunt, who escorted Jemima on both sides of the pond but who in the end she found to be "a bit hammy".

After that it was a return to Puddleduck's usual type, the Fantastic Mr Fux, aka Russell Randy, the loquacious lotharlo.

But that too turned sour when the hyper-sexed vulpine revolutionary couldn't resist all the other birds.

Now, the *Nursery Times* can exclusively reveal, Jemima has been seen around the duck houses with none other than top rat Matthew Fraud!

A friend of Ms Puddleduck's quacked to me in confidence, "This time it's different because, unlike her previous beaux, Matthew is not a known love rat with a string of failed relationships and adulterous liaisons behind him... oh, hang on, perhaps he is."

A friend of the rat, however, squeaked, "Matthew is a reformed rat. He won't just duck off. When he sees another chick, he won't be up the drainpipe like a rat up a... er..."

"Congratulations! And celebrations!"

THE ENGLAND FOOTBALL TEAM – IS IT A JOB FOR A FOREIGNER?

by Our Sports Correspondent
Owen Goal

FOLLOWING England's ignominious exit from Euro 2016 after their humiliating defeat to the minnows of Iceland, pundits are questioning whether now is the time for the England team to cast the net wider and look abroad, if they want to win a major tournament.

"Yes," said FA spokesman Hugh Sless. "We need to swallow our pride and bite the bullet. There are some jobs that foreigners just do better, which is why we are now looking to replace all the English footballers with foreign ones."

He continued, "Sturridge, Vardy and Kane did their best, but frankly, we'd be better off with the likes of Messi, Ronaldo and Payet donning the famous white shirt with pale blue bits and three lions proudly promoting Nike.

"Joe Hart would, of course, keep his place as the face of Head & Shoulders shampoo, though between the sticks we'd probably replace him with a five-year-old Azerbaijani apprentice fisherman, who has at least some cursory knowledge of nets."

Hugh Sless also defended England manager Roy Hodgson, pointing out that he had in fact come back from the tournament with some silverware, namely a poisoned chalice to hand over to his successor.

Mr Hodgson is confident of more success as a football manager in the future, having gone part-time, taken up dentistry and changed his name to Roy Hodgsonsson.

Police in new historic abuse arrest

by Our Crime Staff
Hugh Tree

The South Yorkshire police made a dramatic arrest last night when they stormed into their own police station and apprehended the entire force on a charge of "wasting police time".

Said Chief Inspector Dawn Raid, "We have had suspicions about ourselves for years and now, following a tip-off from the Crown Prosecution Service, we decided to act."

She continued, "The CPS told us that they were dropping all the charges against Sir Cliff Richard and indeed everyone else we investigated. This was the vital piece of evidence that we needed to nail ourselves not only for time-wasting, but for the grotesque abuse of public money and trust."

She concluded, "There may be further charges of impersonating a police officer, since I and some of my lads have looked more like a pack of idiots than a law enforcement agency."

FEMALE RUSSIAN ATHLETE DENIES TAKING TESTOSTERONE

I've never taken drugs

Southern Rail to cancel all hope for commuters

by Our Railways Correspondent
Dee Lais

SOUTHERN Rail is to axe three hundred and fifty services a day under an amended timetable drawn up in response to it being unable to run a decent service.

"It's not right that commuters who pay huge amounts for a season ticket can be arriving at the station not knowing whether their train will be cancelled or delayed or terribly over-crowded," said a Southern Rail spokesman. "So we want to give our commuters the certainty of knowing that there will be no trains running at all."

The Department of Transport admitted that the current situation was unacceptable and had decided after very little thought to give permission for this emergency timetable, which would ensure profits *(surely "service to the passengers"? Ed)* were maintained, having rejected as eminently too sensible an emergency timetable to strip Southern Rail of its franchise, as demanded by all its long-suffering passengers.

"Southern Rail is an embarrassing and disgraceful shambles," said a Transport Department spokesman. "Luckily these are the three attributes we value most when awarding a rail franchise."

Mr Greedy faces select committee

MR Greedy has to go and answer some tough questions today. Poor Mr Greedy. Or rather "rich" Mr Greedy. Because he's got lots and lots of money. Although it's all in Mrs Greedy's name. Clever old Mr Greedy!

"Hello, Mr Greedy," says Mr Cross, the MP. "The name's Mr Green and stop staring at me," replies Mr Greedy. "You look like Mr Orange to me," jokes Mr Cross. "That's because I spend so much time on my yacht!" snaps Mr Greedy, who doesn't like being asked questions about his money! "You're Mr Rude," he shouts at all the MPs.

When they ask him about some of the details of his business activities, Mr Greedy becomes Mr Forgetful!

"I'm not a liar," he says. In fact, he says it so often he becomes Mr Long Nosey. "I live in a tax haven for health reasons," he adds, becoming Mr Even Longer Nosey.

"Well, your bank accounts are extremely healthy!" says Mr Cross. "That is bang out of order!" says Mr Greedy Bastard, and he promises to make everything alright. "Just leave it with me!" he says, "the money I mean!"

Then Mr Greedy goes back to Monaco and is never seen again, turning BHS pensioners Mr Happy and Mr Angry into Mr Unhappy and Mr Bloody Livid.

WILL RUSSIA LOSE THE 2018 WORLD CUP?

No, we will win it, trust me

POETRY CORNER

**In Memoriam
David Cameron,
Prime Minister of the
United Kingdom**

So. Farewell
Then David Cameron.

Your greatest political
Mistake was to have
A referendum.

Little did you realise
That when it was over
It would be you who
Would not "Remain",
But would have
To "Leave".

Now, we are looking
Back at what you
Achieved in your
Six years in power,
And realising that
You haven't got a
Legacy to stand on.

　　　E.J. Thribb (17½)

DAVID CAMERON: THAT PRIME MINISTERIAL LEGACY IN FULL

■ Allowing marital union for same-sex couples

■ Breaking up every other union

■ Er... That's it.

Lives of the Saints and Martyrs No.94
Mother Theresa

AND IN THAT land there dwelt a holy woman called Theresa who had given up her worldly life amongst the money-lenders in order to devote herself to public service. Theresa became known far and wide for her good works, looking after the poor and needy who travelled from all over the world to be welcomed by her and looked after with kindness and grace.

In fact, so many came from distant lands that some uncharitable folk said, "Why can't you turn some of them away? Not being racist, just asking." And they expected Theresa to perform miracles, such as turning 330,000 people into just tens of thousands.

Other wicked folk looked on her good works with jealousy in their hearts and said, "You are not Mother Theresa. You are not a Mother at all. And this makes you incapable of caring for others and being concerned about the future. Obviously, I don't want you to take this out of context, as I will then have to claim I have been misquoted and resign in disgrace."

And so it came to pass that her foes were defeated and Theresa became the Anointed One and she forgave them all, proving her saintliness once again.

The people loved Mother Theresa and still believed in her goodness, so that when she said, "I will heal this nation," they all rejoiced and said, "Look! The pound has risen from the dead! It's a miracle! Truly, Theresa is a saint."

And so she was canonised (but not water canonised as her foolish tormentor-turned-acolyte Boris would once have liked) and all the world gave thanks that Mother Theresa of Calculata was leading them to salvation and not into the wilderness for the next forty years.

　　　© *Liam Fox's Book of Martyrs*

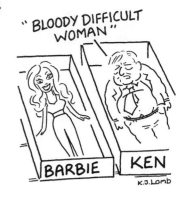

" BLOODY DIFFICULT WOMAN "

BARBIE　KEN

K.J.Lamb

News in brief

Brewery piss-up — lawyers called in

■ The organisers of the Labour Party's Summer Brewery Drinks have been forced to seek legal advice after a disagreement as to who should be in charge of the occasion.

Supporters of Jeremy Corbyn insist that he has all the skills necessary to run an alcohol-fuelled event in the alcohol brewing establishment, but his critics say he has already had nine months to prove his worth, and the brewery doesn't even have a record of his making a booking.

Both sides are now seeking legal representation, but can't decide which lawyers to go with, or even a process by which they would make that decision. The case continues...

Now out on DVD

Angie The Eagle

Hilarious biopic of Britain's most-loved amateur. Enjoy the endearing tale of shy Angie the unlikely star who decides to compete at the highest level of the Labour Party against the ruthless professionals who belittle her performance! Don't miss the scene where she goes downhill very fast, before losing control and discovering that she is for the high jump. Will this plucky Brit prove the doubters wrong? Will the Eagle soar? Or will her poor vision lead to disaster and a broken leg (*surely "party"? Ed*)?
Eye rating: Zzzzz

Dave Snooty

HELLO READERS, I JUST WANTED TO SAY SOME GOODBYES...

SO GOODBYE EU, GOODBYE UK, GOODBYE PROSPERITY, GOODBYE TOLERANCE, GOODBYE DECENCY AND GOODBYE SANITY!

10

A WEEP IS A LONG TIME IN POLITICS

SURVEY
Do you think drinking should be banned at airports?

Yes
23%

No
14%

How dare you, as soon as I've finished this pint I'll have you
42%

Bleurrghhhhh!
85%

Daily Mail

FRIDAY, JULY 8, 2016

YES! IT'S SOARAWAY BRITAIN!

by Our Political Staff
Polly Anna

BRITAIN's historic decision to break the shackles of Brussels and escape the clutches of the European superstate has immediately had an extraordinary effect on this country.

Yes, overnight it's become one big happy nation, breathing a sigh of relief that the miserable years of EU tyranny are finally over and the people of Britain are once again free to eat whatever shaped bananas they want, whilst boiling a powerful British kettle and telling their nice Polish carers to go back home and leave them to die. *(Is this right? Ed.)*

The brave decision to leave the EU, backed by this newspaper, has already resulted in the pound not falling, share prices not tumbling, pensions not being cut, growth not being slowed, our AAA rating not being cut and, best of all, house prices being in no danger of falling whatsoever.

The Establishment has lost. Project Fear is over. From now on, it's "Project Cheer". And who is better placed than your upbeat, positive, benign Daily Mail, with its long history of seeing the best in every situation, to make you feel better about the catastrophic decision you've just made. *(You're fired. Ed.)*

US GUN CRIME

Why weren't the police armed? laments NRA

AFTER a spate of American police officers being gunned down in surprise attacks, the National Rifle Association have said serious questions need to be asked as to why the murdered officers were unarmed.

"This is madness," said a spokesman. "For years we have said that the only thing which can stop a bad guy with a gun is a good guy with a gun. Sadly, these deaths prove that beyond all doubt, and officers must be armed now."

Why didn't the police have more guns? laments NRA

THE NRA have announced, on discovering the officers murdered in surprise attacks were armed, that the only possible solution to restore peace to the streets of America is to provide the police with more guns.

"We have now learned that the police shot in these surprise attacks were already armed", said a spokesman. "But what is rapidly becoming clear is that the old adage 'the only thing that can stop a bad guy with a gun is a good guy with a gun' is no longer fit for purpose in modern America. We have, as a result, concluded that the only thing that can stop a bad guy with a gun is a good guy with

a gun and also with another gun."

Under the NRA's proposed scheme, each officer will be given a supplementary gun as well as their main gun, which they will be required to be holding, loaded and cocked, at all times. "That way, if a bad guy with a gun starts shooting, he should only be able to kill one or two people before a good guy with a gun gets there and blows away the bad guy with the gun", explained the NRA. "Really, when you think about it it's surprisingly obvious."

In the event that bad guys start carrying two guns, it is understood the NRA will urge police to carry three fully loaded guns at all times.

NEW PRIME MINISTER MEETS QUEEN

"How low can you go?"

"I've appointed Boris as Foreign Secretary"

'I've Always Admired Theresa' Say All Tories

by Our Political Staff
Peter O'Bornyesterday

AS Theresa May last night assumed the leadership of the Conservative party, not a single Tory in the country could be found who did not believe that she was the greatest prime minister since Mrs Thatcher.

Said all of them, "Theresa has done a superb job at a very senior level of government and I have never imagined for a moment that there could be any other candidate to succeed David. It is true that originally I gave my support to Boris and then to Michael and then to Liam and then to Andrea. But I only did this for tactical reasons, to ensure that Theresa came through in the end."

"I have been waiting all day," they all continued, "hoping for Theresa to reward me for my longstanding and loyal support, but of course I recognise that she has been very busy choosing her shoes… Whoops, you won't put that bit in, will you? *(Yes, Ed.)*

B. JOHNSON FOREIGN SECRETARY

UGANDA UGANDA UGANDA

grom

EYE SUMMER POLL

☐ Should Sir Philip be stripped of his knighthood?

☐ Should Sir Philip be made to put his shirt back on?

David Davis Hails Trade Deal With Narnia

by Our Fantasy Correspondent
Fawn Britton

DAVID Davis has hailed his first trade deal since the referendum vote, declaring the exciting news in a hastily arranged press conference.

"I am delighted to tell you now that Narnia will be the first non-EU country to have a trading agreement with the UK.

"This vindicates everything I've said about Brexit," said the minister. "Narnia has been excluded from our shores because of our membership of the EU. The Brussels bureaucrats assumed that, just because it didn't exist, it had no right to have access to our markets, which is just the kind of petty over-regulation I've been fighting all my life.

"But now, in return for their imports of Turkish Delight and snow, we can make the UK world leader in exports of hand-knitted scarves for talking animals.

"This shows that we don't need France, Germany or Italy now. We have the makings of a world-class trading block. With Narnia on our side, it's only a matter of time before Brigadoon, Lilliput and the Island of Sodor follow."

"Now then, let's be 'aving you!"

CHILCOT REPORT ASTONISHES NATION

by Our Political Staff **W.M. Deedes**

BRITAIN was rocked to its foundations last night by a report on the Iraq war which was not just a whitewash.

"We've never known anything like this," said stunned observers. "The report names names, apportions blame and finds that the government and the army made a whole string of utterly disastrous and unforgiveable mistakes, every one of which should have been foreseen and avoided if those responsible for them had been remotely competent or honest.

"All of us who have read this report are still in shock. For years, we have been predicting that Chilcot would produce nothing but another bland, anodyne pile of civil service waffle, letting everyone off the hook, but when we actually read those two millions words, we just couldn't believe what we were reading. Or rather, we could, which is what makes this report unique."

ROYAL TRIBUTE TO LONG-STANDING RELATIONSHIP

by Our Social Staff **James Lifelong-Bond**

THE Queen and the Duke of Edinburgh last night saluted the extraordinary staying power of the relationship between actor Tom Hiddleston, 35, and singer Taylor Swift, 26.

Said the Queen, "In an age of uncertainty and change, there can be nothing more comforting than the stability and durability of a union such as that between Hiddie and Swiftie."

The couple have been together now for almost 25 minutes and have defied the sceptics who said that theirs was a partnership that could not survive the media spotlight.

But, as they celebrate their 26th minute together, "Hiddleswift" *(surely "Swiftleton"? Ed)* provide an enduring example to couples everywhere as a model of commitment, sending out a message of hope to all.

As they stroll hand-in-hand along the golden sands of the beach at Aldeburgh, who can doubt that at some time in the future we will be raising a toast to their historic 27th-minute anniversary? A remarkable achievement in this day and age!

God Save the Night Manager! Long Live the Queen of Pop Rock/Country!

TRUMP VISITS GOLF COURSE

What's your handicap?

I'm an ignorant, racist, sexist megalomaniac

Channel 4 defends 'Naked Attraction'

by Our TV Staff **John Thomas** and **Koo Starkers**

A HUGE row erupted, largely in the pages of all newspapers, when Channel 4 aired their new dating show "Naked Attraction", featuring all-nude contestants.

Newspaper editors were unanimous in condemning this kind of nudity and insisted that it should not be shown, illustrating their point by showing lots of disgusting pictures (*see right – more online, not pixelated*).

Gogglecox

C4 Controller Jay Hunt defended the nude series, saying, "We are not embarrassed by this show. I'm proud that Channel 4

has nothing on. Nothing at all. I've taken everything decent off, and now there's nothing at all left."

She continued, "This is a naked attempt to get more viewers, and what could be more natural than that?! We are fulfilling a social need as a national broadcaster, which is to help adolescent boys who live in areas with slow broadband. Which, let's face it, is most of Britain."

Parents horrified by Pokémon Go

PARENTS previously horrified that video games were turning their children into couch-potato zombies are now horrified that the new, best-selling, augmented reality app, *Pokémon Go*, is exposing their children to the outside world.

Said one parent, "We're horrified that a video games company like Nintendo has reacted in a wholly indefensible way to decades of us moaning that our kids are growing obese sitting in front of screens, by creating a video game that takes them outside and exposes them to perverts and weirdos that, according to my television, inhabit the real world.

"Nintendo needs to redesign this app immediately, so it neither encourages our children to sit inside and grow obese in front of the computer nor go outside and be snatched off the street and abused by predatory paedophiles." *Reuters*

We Must Protect Turkish Democracy, Erdogan explains

Turkey's president, Recep Tayyip Erdogan, has explained in a televised address that Turkey's democracy is so fragile that he must be granted the authority to save it. Steps to preserve Turkey's embattled but sacred parliamentary system include:

● All judges to be protected from risk in deep, soundproof, lead-lined cells

● Newspaper websites to be replaced by pictures of democratically elected president

● Everyone to go home before 8pm, to spend time thinking about voting for the president

● Elections to be safeguarded by being scheduled in advance

● Next election slated for June 2035

● Immediate hanging for anyone looking at the president in a funny way

● Er…

● That's it.

● Or else.

TURKEY HOLIDAY THREAT

> I decided to upgrade the hire car, darling

LATE NEWS

'NOT ENOUGH POLICE TO STOP TERRORISTS' SAYS TOP POLICE CHIEF

INSPECTOR Sir Bernard Hogan–Howe of the Metropolitan Police today told journalists that there are, in his opinion, insufficient police to stop the inevitable terrorist attack on Britain.

He told reporters, "My officers are simply too stretched at the moment to ensure the surveillance of all the potential terrorists in Britain. This is due to so many of them having to take part in raids on Sir Cliff Richard's home and the various related investigations into everyone who was famous in the 1960s, '70s or '80s."

(Rotters)

The noise modern sirens make

PAE-DO PAE-DO PAEDO!!

Boris Johnson, the Secretary of State for Foreign and Commonwealth Affairs, writes exclusively for Private Eye about another historic week in politics

Cripes! I didn't see that one coming either! There was old Bozza, head in hands, drowning my sorrows with flat fizz left over from the non-victory bash, thinking yours truly had blown it for good, having wasted a lifetime of greasy-pole climbing by backing the wrong nag, ie myself, in the championship hurdles, when – blow me down – *tring! tring*! someone's on the blower.

My first thought was, "I'm not in. It could be chummy publisher asking for his half-a-million quid back for the book on the Bard I haven't written. Oo-er!" But then my second thought was, "Hang on! It might be the good old Daily Torygraph renewing my bish-bosh-any-old-tosh money-for-old-rope column for another year."

So, heart-in-mouth, I answered. A woman's voice came down the line, asking me if I'd like to be Foreign Secretary. "Who is this?" quoth I, thinking this is mighty fishy. "May," she replied. "Sounds like April the first to me!" I batted back, thinking I was being pranked.

"No, this is the Prime Minister," she continued, "and I want you to be Britain's international ambassador and most senior diplomat."

"If that's you, Mrs Gove," I interrupted, getting quite baity, "this is not bloody funny. Now get off the line and go back to your broomstick."

Well, to cut a long story short, which I don't normally do but I've got rather a lot on my plate now, Mrs T (Theresa) was not joking, because *entre nous* she is somewhat lacking in the funny bone department and she was deadly serious, as ever, about giving me this top job. Foreign Affairs, eh? Bojo's hardly going to say "No, thank you" to that. And something about a secretary to boot? Hello! Ding dong!

So, faster than Gove off a shovel, I said, "Yes, count me in, Ma'am. Can't wait to start buzzing round the world, flying the flag and teaching Johnny Foreigner some manners!"

At this, Mrs T laughed delightedly. (You see…? Bounder Bozza can charm the pants off any of the fairer sex, even Ms Grumpy Drawers herself!) "Carry on, Boris," she said, still laughing, "what can possibly go wrong?"

I promised her I would get on the job asap (not that sort of job – Bojo's a good boy now, scouts' honour, no flies undone on Boris, etc), but just had to make one very important call first. I had to break the news of my appointment personally to Mr Gove. Haw! Haw! Haw! eh, readers?! What japes!

Cripes and double cripes! It's the end of week one and this job hasn't turned out to be quite the lark I thought it would be – chaps with big plumed hats, endless cocktail parties with the president of Bongo-Bongo Land, native handmaidens dancing topless, singing "Bozza Rules the Waves", etc, etc.

Instead, there's yours truly getting booed by the Froggies at an embassy shindig and the next day the Bozmeister has to put on a serious face because Johnny Islamist has gone completely loco on the Riviera. No jokes there!

And no sooner had I finished my ultra-sincere speech about how Britain stands beside France, spirit of unity, common European values… (er, before we bid you adieu and split off to do our own thing, sorry old bean!) than news comes through from the gogglebox that our Ottoman friends have gone berserkers in Turkers.

My new FO minders told me it was probably best not to say that sort of thing in public – so instead I've written a solemn poem which reflects on the gravity of the situation in President Erdogan's post-coup Turkey:

There was an old fellow
From Ankara
Who was attacked by the army
With tankerers.
They attempted a coup,
Ended up in the stew,
Leaving the democratically
Elected President Erdogan
Back in control,
For which we give
Half-hearted thankerers.

I think that says it all, don't you? Bingo! International crisis solved! Perhaps the job isn't so hard after all!

Toodle-pip!

Boris J

DIARY

DONALD TRUMP: MY PRESIDENTIAL CHECKLIST

A is for APRICOT, I never liked apricots, never. They're nasty, stupid little fruit, 'fact you can't call them a real fruit, they're like a peach but not a peach, more like a total loser peach, second you start eating one, it's all over, there's nothing there, nothing! And you know what? It's an amazing thing, but I read somewhere they're what ISIS eat, I'm telling you, apricots are what ISIS feeds its terrorists on, and that's what sends them mad, it's true. So why do we let those guys eat these disgusting apricots? You know what? Just so you understand, in the Trump White House there will be no apricots, no apricots at all, total and complete ban on all apricots. Security guys, if they find an apricot in someone's bag, too bad, you know what, they'll explode it. And I want to tell you, that's going to send out one helluva message to the world, so they'd better take notice because

B is for BOMB and you know what? Under our African-American President – and, by the way, that guy Obama still makes his speeches facing Mecca, that's what they tell me – under our African-American President, our military have been ordered not to bomb our enemies, can you believe it – and, by the way, I'm worth what, 100, 200, 300 billion, I could bomb my friends any time I wanted, and believe me I gotta lot of friends, and I could bomb them a hundred million zillion times over if I wanted to, but I don't, right, right, because I'm not that kinda guy, I look after my friends, they're valuable to me – but what's the point in not bombing your enemies? So, first day I'm President, I plan to put in an express order for extra bombs, thousands and millions of brand new bombs, and I'm going to call in our top Generals and I'm going to tell 'em, you guys, you just bomb whoever you want, particularly those guys with beards, I'm telling you, they're hiding something, I read it somewhere. Oh, and by the way, don't go all gooey on the babies, sure, some babies are fine, but what about the others? What about the babies who hate us, all crying and bawling and bent on revenge, they just want their own way, gimme this, gimme that, kill, kill, kill, they're just like the

C is for CHINESE. I love the Chinese, 'cos they're people just like us, right? Well, not just like us, don't let 'em fool you, guys, they're not like us at all – have you seen the state of their so-called Great Wall recently? I tell you, that wall is a disgrace, total loser wall, all crumbly, so many steps, not one elevator – not one! – they should be ashamed of themselves, but you know what I'll do, first day in White House, I give the order, right? We airlift that Great Wall from China, we buy it at a knockdown price, top negotiators, right? and we fly it all the way to our Mexican border and place it right there, right there! And then we say to the the Mexicans, OK, guys, until you build a new wall AT YOUR OWN EXPENSE, we're going to have this shabby old Chinese wall standing there, one hell of an eyesore, no good for anything, full of termites probably, but you guys better get used to it. So that takes us to

D is for DALMATIANS because I don't like a spotty dog, spotty dogs they give me the creeps, they're supposed to be so cute, so cute, but you know what I don't call it cute to have black spots and white spots all over your body, like some disgusting incurable disease, like they got AIDS or something, and the smart people, the smart people they realise those spots mean something, they know they're not just any old spots, let's be honest, folks, they're spots in CODE because the experts are telling me they're sending secret messages to our enemies in ISIS, that's what I read somewhere, so on my first day in the White House I'm going to appoint the most incredible, unbelievable team of dog catchers, thousand, millions of them, and they're going to scour this country top to bottom for dalmatians, and let me tell you if there's any dalmatian thinks it can get away with bleaching itself or tippexing those horrid spots and pretending to be a labrador don't worry, we'll see through his evil disguise with our infra-red radar devices, we won't let those spotty dogs fool us, and when we've rounded all them up, believe me, we'll teach them a lesson, kill, kill, kill, they'll never forget and that's a promise, you see what we need to make America great again is

E is for ENTERPRISE, because I've made billions and billions, literally billions from enterprise. I own buildings. I'm a builder. I know how to build. Nobody can build like I build. Nobody. I build the best product. First day in the Trump Oval Office, I'm going to build the best spaceship ever built. And you know where I'm sending this spaceship? Not the moon. No way. Who wants to go to the moon? It's dark, it's dusty, it's got no attractions. Mars? Boring as hell. No. Stand by, America, for – Destination Sun. Let's think big! Let's think bright! The sun's a great place, it has sun the whole year round, that's why it's called the sun, stupid, because it's the total number one hotspot, so the experts assure me. And as your President I will send America's most expensive spaceship to land on the sun, by the way, no Muslims or Mexicans or undesirables permitted on voyage. And the Trump White House will be staffed by many, many, women because, unlike Crooked Hillary, I'm a 100 per cent

F is for FEMINIST – and – you know what? we're talking classy, great-looking feminists, 36-24-36, totally fit and obliging and not just in the Oval Office, but up to the very highest reaches of the Trump White House, taking your orders on the exclusive Trump White House Roof Terrace, which we plan to develop big-time, so you can relax with an ice-cold refreshment and an all-over leisure-pamper, I look after my friends, right? Right? And that's why we need more

G is for GUNS because, let's be honest, there's too many human beings alive today, just going nowhere, doing nothing, getting in the way, lazy good-for-things, taking our taxes, maybe planning to rob our banks, right, or kill our old folk, least that's what our brave crimefighters tell me, so, it makes sense, right, we've got to take these guys out before they commit their horrendous crimes, we've got to shoot 'em dead, right between the eyes, kill, kill, kill, before they shoot, and that's why we need more guns, and – by the way – what's all this about safety-catches, we don't need safety-catches, we got to ban these no-good safety-catches, these terrorists are relying on our safety catches, and we gotta kill them before they kill us, let's be honest there's no such thing as safety first when it's time to kill kill kill.

As told to
CRAIG BROWN

Who should be the next Ukip leader? You choose who should fill Britain's number one far-right hot seat

| Douglas Carswell | Neil Hamilton | Christine Hamilton | A kipper | Marine Le Pen | Mike Read | Bernard Manning | Nigel Farage again |

Text, email or ring in to Nick Ferrargi's LBC show and drone on for several hours with your opinion

81

Made in Spain

A book of recipes by Miriam González Durántez (NOT Mrs Clegg)

Recipe No.94

Venganza

This is a dish, like gazpacho, best served cold. It is a traditional Spanish dish and one that I particularly enjoy serving up to all the snotty, stuck-up English people like the Camerons who, due to my husband's job, I was forced to meet occasionally (as occasionally as possible!) at their ghastly dinners, where they put Hellmann's Mayonnaise on the table(!) and the men wore red trousers with holes in them and the women discussed their holiday cottages instead of their jobs as high-powered feminist lawyers and former advisers to the European Foreign Affairs Committee.

The recipe is quite simple – a mix of bitter and sweet (but mostly bitter!) – and the important thing to remember is to let everything stew for as long as possible before stirring it all up and presenting it to the public in a rather unattractive light.

Venganza ("Revenge" you would probably say in your country!) is best left for a few years to cool and then served up in small slices inside an expensive hardback cookery book.

BRITISH SCHOOLS TO TEACH CHINESE-STYLE MATHS

THOUSANDS of primary schools in England will copy the Chinese style of teaching maths, the Department of Education has confirmed.

"International tests show that in China the percentage of 15-year-olds who are functionally innumerate (unable to perform basic calculations) was more than 10 percentage points lower than in England," said schools minister Nick Gibb.

Sample Questions

If a lone Tiananmen Square protestor has a shopping bag, how many tanks are needed to crush his illegal protest?

A) 1
B) 5
C) All of them

If a human rights activist posts an article online criticising the Communist Party, how many years will he remain in jail before trial?

A) 3 months
B) 2 years
C) 15 years

How old do you need to be to start working in the Apple factory?

A) 5 years
B) 7 years
C) What time can you start?

If your parents are senior members of the party and decide to buy one more London penthouse, how many empty penthouses do they now own?
(you're under arrest, Red Ed.)

21-Hour Bombing Window In Aleppo 'Far Too Short' Say Russians

THE Russian government has issued a communique condemning the limited window of only 21 hours a day to bomb civilian populations in cities across Syria.

"These three-hour daily ceasefires and humanitarian food corridors in places like Aleppo severely limit and cause unnecessary breaks and delays to our civilian bombing campaign," a spokesman for President Assad's Russian-backed regime said.

From The Message Boards

Members of the online community respond to the major issues of the day...

Tattoos raise awareness

Just as I'd got used to David Dimbleby and the "rise of the middle-class tattoo", events overtake me once again! The in thing now – or should I say "ink thing"? – is to raise awareness. An Aussie mum had a hearing aid tattooed behind her ear in support of her deaf daughter, and then a DJ from Wiltshire stole a supermarket trolley in protest against the carrier bag charge, and had "5p bags! Fu#k that £1 trolley" inscribed on his arm. The man claims that bants are "all I live for" and says he had it done in order to "push the banter to the next level". Bants or pants, what say you guys? *– Bogbrush*

not bein funny but some deaf peple dont look deaf cos they dont ware hearing aid's? maybe give them face tatoo's sayin i am deaf to make it more clearer? *– Hayley 321*

I'm afraid face and hand tattoos remain strictly taboo, Hayley. A highly qualified professional lady had a job offer withdrawn recently because her body art extended beyond her wrists. *– Queen of Herts*

totely ridiclous 😊 think of the money us mum's coud save on face paintin if you we was aloud to tatoo kid's face's *– Darling Deneyze*

I have a borstal tear (not a solid one, I'm not an animal!) on my face, two dots and a swallow on my left hand and ACAB on the knuckles. Some soppy plod asked me what that meant. All coppers are bastards, I replied, and he said, "Thank goodness it's not racist or I'd have to nick you!" Do I regret my youthful brandings? Yes. ACAC would be better! *– Bermondsey Bob*

As a boy I always had trouble spelling "Hitler", and my history teacher once made me write it 500 times. In the end I got so fed up that I had it tattooed on my wrist, so if I ever needed to check, I could lift my watch and see it underneath. Unfortunately the tattooist decided to do a swastika below it, and this is visible even when I'm wearing a long-sleeved shirt. It sometimes prompts a hostile reaction, but when I show the Hitler part, most people understand the point of it. I had trouble with von Ribbentrop too, but decided not to get that done, because it's a name you rarely need to use and it might seem a bit weird. *– Malcolm*

Tattoo a poppy on traitor Jeremy Corbyn's face. *– Last Briton standing in Britainistan*

he would just ware a berka to cover it up 😊 shithouse *– Broken Britan*

send him to stoke and we will kick his fuckin head in *– stokie steve*

HARRY POTTER TICKETS ON SALE FOR £8,000

Extortiarmus!

KEY

"I'VE JUST ABOUT HAD ENOUGH OF YOU"

GIN

DAVID CAMERON RESIGNATION HONOURS SHOCK NO ONE

by Our Political Staff

WE CAN exclusively reveal today that the former Prime Minister is preparing to reward a number of his closest supporters by giving them honours in what is already being known as "the Resignation List" – due to the fact that everyone is resigned to the fact that it will be full of Tory donors, time-servers, personal friends, hairdressers and people who don't deserve an honour at all.

That List In Full

George Osborne, politician *(Companion of Dave)* for services to losing the referendum

Sir Andrew Cooked-Goose, businessman *(Knighthood)* for services to giving money in order to lose the referendum

Sir Ian Failure, businessman *(Knighthood)* for services to giving even more money in order to lose the referendum

Will Strawpoll, campaigner *(OBN)* for services to getting the Labour Party to help lose the referendum

Isabel Blow-Dry, stylist *(OMG)* for services to Samantha Cameron looking good while losing the referendum

Thinna Rogers, stylist *(LOL)* for services to George Osborne looking thin while losing the referendum

(That's enough honours. Ed.)

Are You A Blairite?

???? TAKE OUR QUIZ!

1) I think Jeremy Corbyn is:

a) An absolute unmitigated disaster and a distinctly nasty piece of work

b) A divisive figure with some controversial aspects but ultimately a well-meaning guy

c) The best thing since Lenin and a Christ figure who will purge the sins of the party and win a 200-seat majority at the next election

2) Given he's lost the support of 170 of his own MPs, Corbyn should:

a) Resign immediately. For Christ's sake, man, it's over. Are you insane?

b) Appoint a steering committee but ensure the members' voices are heard going forward

c) Sack the 170 Judases, lock them up, and replace them with 170 true believers. If anyone objects, lock them up too.

3) The idea that the leadership challenge is a conspiracy by shadowy forces is:

a) Absurd, paranoid hysteria of the sort I thought we left behind in the 1970s

b) Unfounded, but shows the strength of feeling among party members

c) I can't speak about this here. Meet me behind the Walthamstow UNITE offices at midnight. The password is 'BLAIR OUT'.

Mostly a) *YOU ARE A BLAIRITE. Get out of the party now, scumbag, and join the Tories.*

Mostly b) *YOU TOO ARE A BLAIRITE. You have no place in our progressive movement. Why don't you just go and join the BNP?*

Mostly c) *YOU ARE STILL A BLAIRITE. You have been filling in this questionnaire to trick the true believers. Resign before we put a brick through your window!*

NEW CELEBRITY BIG BROTHER SCANDAL

by Our TV Staff **Des Pratt**

THIS week Christopher Biggins was thrown out of the Celebrity Big Brother House in one of the most sensational evictions since the last one.

Biggins was discovered to be an actual celebrity who people had heard of, which was deemed "totally inappropriate" for Channel 5's ratings flagship. A fellow contestant, someone who was once on Hollyoaks or possibly Geordie Shore, said, "It was very insensitive of Biggins to be a celebrity, when the rest of us barely know who we are, let alone our fellow housemates."

Biggins tried his best to blend in and play down his fame, but footage came to life linking him with a quality sitcom called Porridge, and a number of still photos emerged showing Biggins smiling next to Joan Collins.

A spokesman for Channel 5 said, "This is the kind of thing that gives the Big Brother House a bad name. We don't mind people presenting Nazi theme shows and being bi-phobic, but we really object to them being household names."

Christopher Biggins will be appearing in Panto at the Michael Barrymore Theatre in Solihull, as Dame Hitler Twanky in *Snow White and the Seven Transgender Dwarves*.

Sarah Vain
I'm back and I'm twice as modest!

Why have all these women leaders got bob haircuts? Because they are trying too hard to look serious, that's why! Hillary Clinton and Angela Merkel and Nicola Sturgeon have ALL got hair that's too short. (I won't mention Mrs May here as, unlike ME, my hubby ISN'T back in favour yet!) So take a tip from yours truly – powerful women CAN have longer hair, CAN show their sexy side and CAN still be taken seriously about world affairs. Or they can have short hair – just see photo byline above!

* * *

Did you see Michelle Obama speaking at the Democratic Convention, wearing a sleeveless dress and showing off her upper arms? Bingo wings alert for normal women! I certainly wouldn't have done that if it had been me as the wife of the leader of a country (which it WON'T be, due to my hubby being in the Dog House rather than the White House!).

* * *

Sir Philip Green has been shown up to be nothing more than Sir Shifty Green! (Great nickname coined by this newspaper. Well done, Mr Editor!) The fact that he was up to no good was totally ignored by everyone in the fashion world and all those silly models, like Kate Moss, who fell at his feet and sucked up to the leathery old sugar daddy instead of writing pieces about low wages and pension contributions like the excellent Daily Mail is doing! *(It's ok, you're still hired. Ed.)*

Eye Fashion Week
THOSE POLITICAL BOBS IN FULL

TICK ✔

TICK ✔

CROSS ✗

YES, IT'S THE ISIL-LY SEASON!

by **All Staff**

THANK goodness summer is here and at last there is some light relief from all the rest of the year's depressing news.

July and August have thankfully provided something else to read after months of non-stop politics and arguments about the EU. That's why they traditionally call this time of the year "the Isil-ly season" because, instead of carrying on with all the predictable heavyweight stories focusing on world economics and such like, the newspapers and TV stations can shift their focus and concentrate on the really deeply unpleasant stories about murders and attempted murders by deranged people claiming to be members of IS.

No wonder the Isil-ly season is such a popular time for *(You're fired. Ed.)*

My commuter HELL
Your stories from the frontline...

Dr Miriam Stern, 51
Little Scowling to Paddington via Market Sodborough

Annual season ticket: £9,400

Time lost over week's travel: 94 mins.

"My journey was AWFUL. Incredibly HOT in the carriage, I almost fainted, felt like a cattle train. Luckily I had a seat. NO free papers at the station again. They say keep things in perspective but this service is DISGUSTING."

Alan Angry, 43
Port Wrath to London Bridge via Umbrage

Annual season ticket: £9,494

Time lost over week's travel: 994 mins.

"This route is an unmitigated NIGHTMARE. It makes me so FURIOUS EVERY SINGLE DAY. Southern Rail are a complete joke – they need to GET A GRIP and sort this MESS out. NOW!"

Anonymous commuter, 34, Aleppo suburbs to city centre
Annual season ticket: n/a. Time lost over week's travel: 9,994 mins.

"I went to get some bread from the centre, as my family were starving. The Castello Road was closed by Russian air force jets, so everyone went on another route recommended as a safe corridor. But then the heat from a barrel bomb incinerated us all."

PRESIDENT PUTIN ANSWERS YOUR QUESTIONS ON THE OLYMPICS

Q Mr Putin, were you surprised when some Russians were allowed to compete by the Olympic Committee?

A No, I always said that the only dopes were on the IOC!

Q Did you think all along that they would accept your case?

A Of course. It was a strong case with $3million in it!

Q Is Russia really strict about taking drugs?

A Yes, we make sure they take the right ones!

Q Don't you think a Russian presence will demean the Games?

A No, it will inject a little unpredictability into the events!

Q Are you taking the piss, Mr Putin?

A Yes, and then exchanging it for clean samples of urine!

Q I'm sorry to ask this, but why have you got a pistol in your hand?

A On your marks... get set... run...!

THOSE RUSSIAN COMPETITORS (STILL) TO WATCH

Sonya Switchpissova

4 x 4 Underwater weightlifting

Don't miss her trademark move, the squat and thrust, as she emerges from the cubicle and thrusts a test-tube of someone else's urine into the lab assistant's hands.

Mikhail Dummiprik

Synchronised shot putt

Incredible accuracy, as he fills his beaker from a record-breaking 20 metres away, using someone else's urine stored in a fake plastic penis.

Sasha Runoff

Modern Biathlon

The fastest woman on the planet – see her break the record for jumping out the window and running a mile as soon as the drugs testers come knocking on her door. *(That's enough. Ed.)*

ENJOY YOUR MEAL

"Don't tell me what to fucking do!"

NEW ENGLAND MANAGER SAM ALLARDYCE APPOINTED

Those future tabloid headlines in full

Match 1
SAM-TASTIC!

Match 2
SAM-SATIONAL!

Match 3
AWE-SAM!

Match 4
Sam-thing's wrong!

Match 5
DO SAM-THING!

Match 6
Oh what a Sam-bles!

Match 7
SAM-AGEDDON!

Match 8
THE SAM OLD STORY!

Match 9
AUF WIEDER-SAM!*

Match 10
ENGLAND SEEK NEW MANAGER

*vs. Germany – lost on penalties

Fracking protests grow

by Our Environmental Staff
Doug Big-Hole

THERE were nationwide protests last night at the news that fracking would begin throughout the country, and residents in specific locations would be offered compensation of up to £15,000.

Hundreds and thousands of angry home-owners who will not be affected took to the streets to say, "It's not in my backyard! Why not?!"

These so-called IMBYs are threatening to stop other home-owners from mining a rich seam of money, and are demanding that drilling begin in their back gardens immediately.

Said one, "Just because we are in an area of outstanding natural beauty, with no natural gas anywhere near us, we have been totally overlooked. This is completely unfair!"

Protestors jumped up and down, causing minor tremors around the country, releasing dangerous shale gas, and causing frackers to complain about the appalling noise.

LORD LUCAN FOUND

'Moustache Disowns Farage' Shock

by the Editor of the Financial Times
Lionel Barber, Légion d'Honneur
(deuxième classe)

A prominent moustache was publicly embarrassed last night by being linked to the discredited former leader of Ukip, Nigel Farage.

"What was the moustache thinking of?" said one prominent facial hair specialist, Professor Mary Beard. "I am afraid that it has made a fool of itself by becoming attached to Mr Farage's face."

There was fevered speculation last night that the moustache would split from Farage, who has been involved in numerous scandals over the last few years.

The question now remains: Can the moustache salvage its reputation?

Said top ex-moustache wearer, the late Enoch Powell, "I think it will be a close shave. You know what they say about politicians – hair today, gone tomorrow."

Nursery Times

···················· · Friday, Once-upon-a-time · ····················

ANTI-TROLL SQUAD LAUNCHED

By Our Social Media Staff **Tweety Pie**

THE Metropolitan Nurseryland Police Force (the Boys in Blue) today announced a new taskforce to crack down on trolling.

Costing a huge pot of gold, the force will monitor all bridges in the land over which billy goats are likely to go trip-trapping.

Any troll lurking underneath the bridge, threatening to "gobble them all up", will now be arrested.

Trolls will not be allowed to claim that their abusive and threatening remarks were just "banter between mates".

Instead, the troll will be charged with hate crimes and will be sentenced to having his eyes poked out by the largest goat and to being "crushed to bits, body and bones" before being tossed into the river.

On other pages
● Children of Woman in Shoe witness birth of yet another child – Jools criticised for "not knowing what to do" **2** ● Owl and Pussycat shocked as their Olympic boat "turns pea-green" **3** ● Cataract operations cancelled: Three Blind Mice furious. "What will they cut next?" they ask Farmer's Wife **94**.

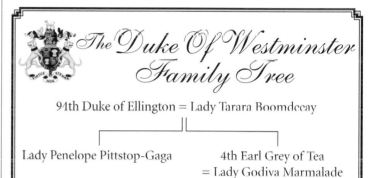

The Duke Of Westminster Family Tree

94th Duke of Ellington = Lady Tarara Boomdeeay

Lady Penelope Pittstop-Gaga

4th Earl Grey of Tea = Lady Godiva Marmalade

Gerald, 7th Duke of Earl

The Duke of Yesminister = Lady Inred

Lord Screaming of Sutch = Lady Inbred

Lady Vajazzle-Growbag, Lady Fruitella-Mayfair, Lady Bird of Book, Lord Hugh of Hee – 95th Duke of Westeros, Lord of the Isles, Father of Dragons *(Have you checked this? Ed.)*

"It's the way he looks at other women"

RELATE

HOW THE GLORIOUS GB GOLDRUSH UNFOLDED

10.31am
The Aquadrome

Team GB's Tracy Lycra wins gold in the 800m pursuit butterfly, while Charlie Speedo and Andy Budgie-Smuggler romp to victory in the synchronised underwater trampolining, following their double-bronze in last year's Rangoon Commonwealth All-Comers.

11.15am
Copacabana Marina and Sewagedrome

Team GB's newest sailing phenomenon, Freddie Anorak-Jones, medals in the Nimbus 2000 class, smashing the record set by New Zealand's Kris Windcheater and has moved up a class since winning silver at the Gobi Desert Asian Games in 2014. Meanwhile, Sid Floater, Britain's top C3PO steeplechase kayaker, double-golds and single-silvers to make a record canoeing medal trawl.

12.16am
The Zika Gymnasiadrome

No one in the world can stop Team GB's Larry Backflip from snatching gold in the freestyle parallel peloton pommel, with his daring, innovative reverse stretch triple-bypass somersault to the theme of Downton Abbey.

2.08pm
The Pele Judodrome

Sandy Greenbelt from Heckmondwike beats her British teammate, herself, in the 33kg downhill keirin final, bettering her performance in last year's Pyongyang sudoku world tournament, to bronze triumphantly.

3.32pm
The Ipanema Arenadrome Park

The Team GB septet of beach badminton Olympians, under veteran Captain Jenny Shuttlecock, dominate the new Olympic event of seven-a-side omnium beach badminton and, in a thrilling final, crush the Saudi Arabians in their distinctive black-and-black burkinis after the French withdraw in protest.

4.53pm
Christ the Redeemer Rowing Lake-a-drome

Having dominated every aquatic contest since the Battle of Trafalgar, there was no stopping Britain's all-conquering rowers in the 2,000m cross-country mixed coxless sculls, featuring Sally Croptop and Johnny Singlet who only started rowing together that morning. Team GB triple-golds, double-silvers and multiple-medals.

7.28pm
The Favela Dromadrome

Concluding an epic day of sport, the climax of the 8-day modern octathlon sees Team GB sweeping to victory in all the events, with Lizzie Leotard and Jim Jockstrap effortlessly outscoring the opposition in the 20,000m hurdles, the clay-pigeon modelling, the 5k monocycle dressage, the freestyle parachuting from a hot-air balloon, the synchronised chess, the sideways quadruple jump, the archery on waterskis and the all-important egg-and-spoon race.

On other pages

- Bolt wins third 100m gold **27**
- Phelps wins 94th swimming medal **39** ● Fijians win Rugby **43**
- Other countries do other things **86** ● But we don't care **93**
- Nouns to be "verbed" in irritating way by all sports commentators **94**

WHAT YOU WILL SEE

THE OLYMPIC WEEK IN FULL

- *Marvellous* Monday
- *Terrific* Tuesday
- *Wonderful* Wednesday
- *Thesaurus* Thursday
- *Fantastic* Friday
- *Sizzling* Saturday
- *Supercalifragilisticexpialidocious* Sunday

Rio2016 ⬮⬮⬮⬮⬮

Monet's Olympic Diving Pool

Exclusive to all BBC channels

NEWSREADER: And here are today's news headlines from the BBC (the British Brazil Corporation)...

SECOND NEWSREADER: It's gold, gold, gold all the way! History is being made, as Britain's golden boys and girls surge to glory in the most exciting Olympic Games ever to have been held! Over now to Clare Balding for the latest Olympic record to be smashed by a Brit!

CLARE BALDING: Hi, I've just broken the World and Olympic record for being constantly on television without a break. I've just notched up 738 hours, 12 minutes and 38 seconds. Clare, how do I feel?

CLARE BALDING: Well, Clare, after all the training and all the hard work, I just can't believe I've made it this far, it's like a dream come true.

CLARE BALDING: Would you like to cry, Clare, because then we can put that in the highlights package?

CLARE BALDING: Boohoohoo.

CLARE BALDING: Brilliant, Clare, back to the studio...

FIRST NEWSREADER: News just in... Clare Balding has just wept as she broke her own record.

SECOND NEWSREADER: In other news... There have been some bombs in Thailand, there's some siege or other going on in Syria, and something is happening in Ukraine which may lead to the end of the world. Now, back to Rio where the entire BBC is reporting on the latest news from the Olympics, which you've probably just seen because there isn't anything else on TV unless you want to watch the Bourne Identity on ITV again.

FIRST NEWSREADER: Coming up shortly, it's the big showdown between John Inverdale and Sir Steven Redgrave in the Men's Throwing a Hissyfit.

But first the weather where you are... if you're in Rio *(continues for 94 days until closing ceremony and then continues some more when Paralympics open)*

WHEEEEE

Diver's mother angered by lack of coverage

■ The mother of a bronze medal-winning Olympic diver was furious yesterday when she saw the coverage of her son in Britain's national press.

"I looked at the front page," she said, "and the coverage was miniscule. Tiny doesn't begin to describe the trunks that my son Tom was forced to wear. They left nothing to the imagination! He may as well have been naked! And as for the other one who's name I can't remember, he wasn't wearing much either!

"Frankly," she concluded, "the entire coverage of my son was pants – and not very big ones!"

New song for diver who didn't get any coverage

■ The Olympic Village was swinging to the sound of a new song specially composed to celebrate the success of Britain's medal-winning synchronised diver, Dan Goodfellow.

Neglected by the press, his fellow athletes have come up with a rousing chorus to compensate for the fact that everyone thinks he's just the bloke standing next to Olympic poster boy Tom Daley.

So, start up the Bosanova rhythms and sing along:

For he's a jolly good diving
partner of Tom Daley,
For he's a jolly good diving
partner of Tom Daley,
For he's a jolly good diving
partner of Tom Daley,
And so say all the papers.

SHOCKING SCENES IN THE AQUATIC CENTRE

Have you seen what Helen Skelton is wearing?

That skirt's so skimpy you can almost see her knees!

OLYMPICS 'COULD INSPIRE A NEW GENERATION'

IT's hoped that the amazing scenes of Team GB in Rio will inspire a whole new generation of young people to watch television.

"The last thing my kids, glued to their iPhones and tablets, would ever have considered doing would be to watch television," said all parents, "but there were the 13 and nine-year-old on the sofa with us, cheering along as the gold medals poured in.

"I really hope that this means future generations will now occasionally join their father and me in the living room, and not be on their iPhones 24/7 in their bedrooms."

BRITAIN'S ATHLETICS IN CRISIS

by Our Athletics Correspondent
John Alpha-male

WITH yet another impressive haul of medals achieved by British athletes in Rio, there are already concerns that Team GB will lose its official status as "plucky".

"It's a very real concern," said one patriotic onlooker. "Britain's status as 'plucky' has been hard-earned over the years, through a devoted programming of underfunding.

"Our 'plucky' status was achieved by surprising everyone by winning one, or maybe two gold medals by a sheer bloody fluke by a rank amateur, or by someone in Swindon taking up a sport that no one's ever heard of.

"With this disgustingly large number of gold medals being won in the last two Olympics, by highly trained, well funded athletes, there is a real danger that we could lose our 'plucky' status to Mongolia, or even a country we've never heard of. It's that serious."

The government strongly disputed the concerns, claiming that there were already plans to preserve the "plucky" status by stripping funding from all major sporting venues and selling off the last remaining playing field in preparation for 2020.

Britain Edges China to Second Place in Table Glory

by Our International Affairs Correspondent **Jack Union**

BRITAIN can hold its head up high after a stunning performance, in which our boys and girls were beaten only by the mighty Americans in the only table that really matters – International Arms Sales 2016.

Yes, Team GBH proved that British hardware can go faster, higher and kill more people indiscriminately than almost any other country.

Surely this is something to be proud of, despite the killjoys who claim that too much public money is spent to get these results?

As we watch the fireworks at the end of the fierce competitions round the globe, the reputation of our highly trained hard-working merchants of death has never been higher. With sales rocketing up, we've beaten Russia, we've beaten China, and the Saudis have beaten a lot of protestors over the head with our batons. Yes, it's boom time for Britain! On your marks, get set, bang!

GLENDA SLAGG

She's back! Fleet Street's Olympic Truth-Zika!! (Geddit?!?)

■ SHAME on you, Mr Lloyds Bank!!?! Or rather Mr Lloyds Bonk!!? It's you I'm talkin' about, António Horta-Osório!!?!!!! Fancy doin' the dirty on your lovely missus with Blair babe Wendy Piatt in steamy Singaphwoar!!!! And all at our expense?!!? (Time for Mrs Horta-Osório to "bail" out!!?? Geddit?!?) Why don't you stick to screwing your customers, António??!?!?? Tell you what, Senhor Lothario, they should change the Lloyds logo of the black horse to something more appropriate, ie a love rat!?!?! (Geddit???!?)

■ HATS and trousers off to hunky Horta-Osório, the Lloyds Bank boss who is not afraid to show a gal his interest rate is going up!!? (Geddit?!?) Thank gawd there's one bonker who doesn't just screw his customers!!?! They must have modelled the Lloyds logo on you, Senhor Sexy!!? Because when it comes to extra-marital performance-related malarkey, you're clearly a stallion (Geddit??!?) from Phwoartugal!?!!! Talk about hung like a Horta (That's enough of this filth. Ed.)

■ SO it's boo-hoo-hoo for Break-up Beatrice!!!? There is to be no happy ending for this little Princess because her beau has given her the heave-heau!?!?! (It was a mutual decision to split, with both needing space to contemplate the future. Ed.) Anyway, since Dave dumped her, it looks like the Duchess's daughter is going to be as unlucky in love as Forlorn Fergie??!? All together now... "Who cares?" (Surely "Aaaah!"? Ed.)

■ TOM DALEY??!?? Mmmmm!??!!? He's the munchy Mr Macho of the Olympic Diving Board!!?? With his teeny trunks and his tanned torso, he's one guy this gal could dive in and (I've got a disappointment for you – Mr Daley is engaged to Mr Dustin Lance Black. Ed.) No matter, Aunty Glenda can "turn" Dishy Daley faster than Mr Bronze can perform a reverse triple pike somersault with a double flip and fries to go!!!?! Mmmmm!!!?!!!! Fancy a quick tuck and a smooth entry, Tom??!? (This is terrible. Ed.)

■ Edward Ling???!?!?!?! Bronze-winning farmer-turned-Olympic trap shooter!?!!?? Is that a gun in your pocket, Ed, or are you just pleased to see me???! Oh, it's a gun!!! Bet you're not firing blanks though, Mr Ding-a-ling??!? (You're fired. Ed.)

Byeee!!

"It makes it more like actually being there"

— PILBROW —

CORBYN AND BARONESS CHAKRABARTI LATEST

I'd like you to clear the party of claims of anti-Semitism

I'd be honoured

Labour cronyism outrage

THE Labour party has promised a full and independent investigation into claims of cronyism after suggestions that Shami Chakrabarti was awarded a peerage in return for chairing an inquiry that cleared Labour of anti-Semitism.

"This full and independent inquiry will be chaired by the distinguished human rights campaigner Shami Chakrabarti," Jeremy Corbyn told reporters.

"A woman so respected that she was recently awarded a peerage for services in getting me out of a very tight spot."

Speaking to reporters from inside a toilet at Westminster, Ken Livingstone praised Jeremy Corbyn's handling of the debacle, saying even Hitler himself would be hard pressed to find fault with his behaviour.

(Rotters)

WE'D LIKE TO BUY A PLACE TO LIVE AND START A FAMILY

YOU'RE SUCH CRAZY, HEADS-IN-THE-CLOUDS DREAMERS!

SPOT THE DIFFERENCE

Sir Philip Sidney

Knighted by Queen Elizabeth I

Inspired by Penelope, Lady Rich of Rochford Hall

Created romantic poem *Arcadia* for the benefit of mankind

Famous last words: *"Thy necessity is yet greater than mine"*

Sir Philip Green

Knighted by Queen Elizabeth II

Inspired by Tina, Lady Rich of Monaco

Created retail consortium *Arcadia* for the benefit of himself

Famous last words: *"Fuck off, it's my money, I earned it"*

A Doctor Texts

AS A doctor, I'm often asked, "Doctor, what's wrong with me?"

The simple answer is "I don't know. I'm not there."

What happens is that the patient starts to feel ill and then types their symptoms into their smartphone, thus accessing the new NHS 111 website or *Appus Cheapus Chippus,* to give it the full medical name. The website then responds by texting the patient back with a full diagnosis.

This may read "Lose some weight", "Give up smoking" or "Go to A&E at once, for God's sake".

WARNING: Do not use phone to text symptoms whilst driving, as this could result in your medical emergency becoming much worse due to a crash.

© A. Doctor 2016

ME AND MY SPOON

THIS WEEK

JUDGE PATRICIA LYNCH QC

Do you have a favourite spoon?
Don't be a cunt.

Do spoons feature prominently in the judicial process?
You are a cunt, aren't you?

Do you come across a lot of spoon-related crime?
What a stupid question, you stupid cunt.

As far as spoons are concerned, do you have anything to say other than the C-word?
Go fuck yourself…

Thank you, you cunt.

NEXT WEEK: *Usain Bolt "Me And My Bolt".*

POETRY CORNER

In Memoriam Eric "Winkle" Brown, aviator

So. Farewell
Then Eric Brown,
Test pilot
Extraordinaire.

You flew more
Types of plane than
Anyone else ever.

Now you have
Taken off for the
Last time and
I hope you have
A happy landing.

You have earned
Your wings.

E.J. Thribb (17½)

In Memoriam Cynthia Payne, suburban brothel keeper

So. Farewell
Then Cynthia Payne,
70s celebrity Madam.

"Would you like to
Go upstairs?"'
Yes, that was
Your catchphrase.

Now you have
Gone upstairs
Or downstairs,
Depending on your
View of Cyn.

E.J. Thribb
(17½ luncheon vouchers)

In Memoriam David Jenkins, former Bishop of Durham

So. Farewell
Then David Jenkins.

You were famous
For being the bishop
Who hated Mrs Thatcher
And supported
Arthur Scargill in
The miners' strike.

You were even more
Famous for saying that
You didn't believe in
The Resurrection.

Now you can
Put your theory
To the test.

E.J. Thribb (17½)

Daily Mail

FRIDAY, SEPTEMBER 2, 2016

BRITAIN'S BREXIT BOOM

By Our Financial Staff **Dick Tation**

IT'S OFFICIAL! Britain has banished the post-Brexit blues – figures now show that the economy is doing better than ever before.

Unemployment is down to a new low, spending is up to a new high, borrowing is breaking new records and business confidence is going through the roof.

So much for all those moaning minnies who said that leaving the EU would result in financial disaster! Well – look what's happened! As soon as Britain freed itself from the shackles of the unelected bureaucrats in Brussels and took control of its own destiny, everything's turning up roses – and we haven't even left the EU yet!

Oh, hang on. Perhaps that's why. Oh. Er… perhaps we should stay in after all and not upset the apple *(You're fired. Paul Dacre)*

LATE NEWS

● Unemployment up by one. EU to blame.

Daily Mail Campaign

BAN THESE TOXIC BEARDS NOW!

They're everywhere! You can't escape them! Slowly but surely they have infiltrated every aspect of our lives! But we say enough! It's time to stop the creeping beard menace from polluting everything before it's too late! From Paul Hollywood's mini-beard to Evgeny Lebedev's micro-beard, beards have become the greatest threat to society *(It's meant to be "beads", you idiot. You're fired. Paul Dacre)*

BALLS ON STRICTLY

He's got two centre-left feet

ITALIAN EARTHQUAKE

'Bake Off' Not Affected

by Our Entire Staff **Lemon Drivel**

THERE was widespread relief across the UK this morning when it became clear that the tragic earthquake in the mountainous region of Umbria in Italy would not disrupt the BBC's hugely popular prime-time reality cooking show which has returned triumphantly to our screens continuing its heartwarming, ratings-busting, nation-building, soaraway success story that *(cont. p94)*

THE FANTASTIC MR FOX

I'm going to travel the world looking for trade

Cheeky!

Are You Being Served? The Remake

That Script In Full

(Interior Comedy Department Store BBC. Theme tune with lift attendant voice-over)

Attendant Voice-over: Third floor: Ratings – going down!

(Enter viewer)

Viewer: I'd like a new television programme, please.

Mr Lucas: I'm afraid we don't have any of those.

Miss Brahms: I do have a couple of things you might like.

Mr Lucas: I'll say!

(Live canned laughter from 1980s)

Miss Brahms: I meant I've got a couple of stonkers.

Mr Lucas: Phwooar!

(Live canned laughter from 1970s)

Miss Brahms: Cheeky! I meant I've got a couple of old sitcoms – *Porridge, Till Death Us Do Part, Keeping up Appearances…*

Viewer: They look a bit past their sell-by date.

Mrs Slocombe: What – like my pussy?!

(Live canned laughter from 1870s)

Miss Brahms: I can wrap them up for you as though they were new.

Viewer: Haven't you got anything a bit less 1970s?

Mr Lucas: Mrs Brown's boys?

(Live canned laughter from 2010s)

Viewer: I said, haven't you got anything a bit less 1970s?

Mrs Slocombe: What – like my pussy?!

Viewer: Look, if I want some cheap innuendo I can watch Mel and Sue on *Bake Off.*

Mrs Slocombe: I've got a soggy bottom!

(Live canned polite applause from 1930s)

Viewer: This is terrible. What self-respecting actor is going to appear in this kind of pointless rehash?

Mr Humphries: I'm free!

Rest of Cast: So am I!

Viewer: Has the BBC really got no new comedy at all?

Mr Peacock: You'll have to ask young Mr Hall.

(Mr Tony Hall emerges from elevator with a gorgeous pouting Yentob on each arm)

Mr Hall: You're all doing very badly!

THE END
(it really is)

I DISAGREE WITH WHAT YOU SAY,

THEN YOU'RE NO-PLATFORMED

Voltaire Goes to Uni

TRAINGATE Day 94
Those entirely plausible explanations so far

▶ All the seats were taken

▶ Some of the seats were taken and all the others were reserved

▶ All of the seats were taken by luggage

▶ Or by small children

▶ Or by bags containing small children

▶ Or by Pokémon Go figures, visible only to Jeremy on his phone

▶ All the seats were taken by his wife

▶ All the seats were taken by his other wives

▶ All the seats were deliberately taken by Blairites, to deprive Jeremy of much needed rest before taking on the might of Owen Smith

▶ All the seats were reserved by Richard Branson, in a deliberate attempt to undermine renationalisation of the railways

▶ All the seats were taken by midget journalists from the

Corbyn: "Getting seats is impossible, or it will be if I win the leadership election"

mainstream media in a deliberate attempt to discredit Jeremy

▶ Jeremy had a seat but gave it up to a blind leper who, when he touched the hem of Jeremy's jacket, was miraculously healed

▶ The train was so ram-packed with excuses there was no room for the truth.

TRAINGATE Day 95
The mystery deepens

11:07

11:29

LOYAL Corbynites have flooded onto social media to insist that photos supposedly showing empty seats on a train where Jeremy Corbyn staged a sit-down protest are part of a much wider conspiracy.

"Traingate is bigger than the JFK assassination carried out by the CIA and the faked moon landings put together," said Twitter user @MoMentum1456. "The Establishment are so scared of Corbyn, they are determined to destroy him."

Those Questions That Must Be Answered

● Why on the CCTV footage does Jeremy cast no shadow?

● And why do the pages of *Private Eye* "flutter" when everyone knows there is no breeze on a Virgin Train?

● Why does the first photo claim Jeremy has travelled to the year 1107?

● Are the numbers 11 and 29 in Photo 2 Illuminati code used by Branson and Blair (B&B!) in their ongoing Corbyn smear campaign?

● Why is the woman in Photo 1 ALMOST identical to a woman seen on footage taken moments before JFK was shot in Daley Plaza?

● Why does the hair colour in the two pictures not match? Are these in fact two separate train journeys?

● Was the train switched mid-journey? Is the Jeremy Corbyn in Photo 2 a lookalike recruited by the security services?

If you slow down the video footage of Jeremy on the train and watch it frame by frame, you can clearly see how much of your life you've wasted.

"Why's that girl got weird brown hair?"

HERNEMAN

Notes&queries

Mr Corbyn described his train as 'ram-packed', but what does 'ram-packed' actually mean?

● Ram-packed is an old Welsh expression used by hill farmers when sending their sheep off to market in carts. Visitors to the Brexit Beacons can still find "ram-packers" loading up their carts in the traditional way in order to get EU subsidies.
The Reverend Seumas Milne

● The Reverend Milne is of course wrong, as he is about most things. The "Ram Pack" was the term used to describe the infamous gang of gambling, hard-drinking hell-raisers who turned Las Vegas into their own personal playground. The Ram Pack, led by Frank Sinitta, and including the Dean of St Martin's and David Davis Junior, gave their name to the expression "I am absolutely ram-packed".
Lady Diane Abbott

● Lady Diane and Seumas are yet again trying to mislead the public (unlike Mr Corbyn). The expression "ram-packed" derives from the mispronunciation over time of Mrs Alistair Beaton's phrase "jam-racked" – indicating jars of jam which have been placed so tightly on a shelf that there's no room for any more, and the only place to put one is on the floor by the toilet next to a copy of *Private Eye*. (That's enough shameless self-promotion. Ed.)

Answers please:

Is anything smaller than a microbead? Is River Rocket the name of Jamie Oliver's son or a type of salad? Why isn't Clare Balding on television more often?

BRANSON HITS OUT AT CORBYN

If there's one thing I can't stand, it's lame, half-arsed publicity stunts by some beardy the public hates

Diary
Sarah Ferguson @SarahTheDuchess

Tweets All / No replies

Sarah Ferguson @SarahTheDuchess   Jul 16
So proud to become Professor of Philanthrepeneurship at totally brill @HuddersfieldUni. I ♥ all ships, also boats.

Sarah Ferguson @SarahTheDuchess   Jul 14
OK, they've just told me he's been dead for years. But that makes it even sadder, surely.

Sarah Ferguson @SarahTheDuchess   Jul 14
So sorry to hear of the death of Dr Martin "Luther" King. What a horrible way to go. Deepest sympathy to his lovely family. 😢

Sarah Ferguson @SarahTheDuchess   Jul 14
They're going on about new PM forming her "cabinet" but you'd think she'd get a handyman in for that, surely.

Sarah Ferguson @SarahTheDuchess   Jul 13
Some people say tomorrow is the first day of the rest of your life. But for me the first day is when you are born.

Sarah Ferguson @SarahTheDuchess   Jul 12
Memo to @LabourParty. Breaking up can be very painful. Been there, done that, got the T-shirt. Hugs and sympathy to lovely lovely Angela and Jeremy! 😢

Sarah Ferguson @SarahTheDuchess   Jul 8
Also to my two gorgeous gorgeous girls for those fabby big lovely warm huggies they gave me yesterday 😊. Love ya!

Sarah Ferguson @SarahTheDuchess   Jul 8
Big thank you to all the police officers in the US and everywhere who so bravely risk their lives every day to safeguard our streets 😊 and sometimes get killed for their troubles 😞

Sarah Ferguson @SarahTheDuchess   Jun 24
UK voted Remain. So now will we remain out of Europe? Sorry! Can't get my head round it.

Sarah Ferguson @SarahTheDuchess   Jun 22
Remember to cast your vote in Refrendum! As Royal can't say how I'd vote but tbh I've had totally brill free hols in Italy Austria etc etc

Sarah Ferguson @SarahTheDuchess   Jun 21
So excited. Referendum is going to be literally the biggestest vote in the world ever!

Sarah Ferguson @SarahTheDuchess   June 3
RIP Muhammad Ali. So much more than just a wrestler.

Sarah Ferguson @SarahTheDuchess   May 19
It is every child's right to go to a good hairdresser. But some kids don't even know what a hair extension is. Please give generously.

Sarah Ferguson @SarahTheDuchess   Apr 21
Seriously, though! Dead Prince was great singer, used to love boogying to his totally brill Can't Stop Til You Get Enough. RIP.

Sarah Ferguson @SarahTheDuchess   Apr 21
Devastated to hear of the untimely death of Prince. Durh! Not talking about you, lovely ex-hubby Andrew @TheDukeofYork!!!!!!

Sarah Ferguson @SarahTheDuchess   Apr 20
Sorry! Meant to say the other way round. Silly Sarah!

Sarah Ferguson @SarahTheDuchess   Apr 20
Let's make a joly good #education something for the few, not the many.

Sarah Ferguson @SarahTheDuchess   4 Apr
So sad 😞 to hear of death of lovely TV personality and former husband of @lizaminelli #DavidGestRIP. Forever in our ♥♥♥s.

Sarah Ferguson @SarahTheDuchess   4 Apr
Just heard David Gest dead. Definitely rings a bell. Remind me, someone?

Sarah Ferguson Retweeted @JacquiP   17 Mar
Fantastic to meet @SarahTheDuchess today on Platform 9 at Guildford. Very natural, down to earth.

Sarah Ferguson @SarahTheDuchess   17 Mar
Still waiting for train at Guildford station. Available for a selfie if anyone wants one.

Sarah Ferguson @SarahTheDuchess   17 Mar
Just posed for ANOTHER selfie this time with June and Jacqui from Farnham! How much L♥VE can one girl get????

Sarah Ferguson @SarahTheDuchess   17 Mar
Love you, Surrey! Glad to see I'm still popular! Wooh! Posed for selfies with lovely, lovely, total strangers Sue, Bob and Sally. 😊

Sarah Ferguson @SarahTheDuchess   17 Mar
Looking forward to an amazing day in Surrey. Keep an eye open for Sarah! Happy to pose for selfies, etc! 😊😊

Sarah Ferguson @SarahTheDuchess   6 Feb
So proud of big-hearted @Tamara_Beckwith for buying a fabby new @Gucci bag, 5% goes to charity for poor homeless kiddies in Africa. 😊

Sarah Ferguson @SarahTheDuchess   6 Feb
Giving is so important. Support @TheDukeofYork.

Sarah Ferguson @SarahTheDuchess   10 Jan
Welling up at the news of the death of s. There's a starman da di da di dah. Unforgettable.

Sarah Ferguson @SarahTheDuchess   Dec 14 2015
Flattering sugestion from @piersmorgan but have greatest respect for remarkable dignified ex-mumsy-in-law @HMtheQ so I would insist on having her gracious permission before accepting top job.

Sarah Ferguson Retweeted Piers Morgan @piersmorgan   Dec 14 2015
Paging @SarahTheDuchess! When your ma-in-law pops her proverblals, you should take her place on throne. Go for it, gal!

Sarah Ferguson @SarahTheDuchess   Dec 14 2015
Thrilled to see good friend @PiersMorgan at @PlanetHollywood tonight. Total hero!

Sarah Ferguson Retweeted Piers Morgan @piersmorgan   Dec 14 2015
Great to catch up, @SarahTheDuchess. FYI, you were looking totally babelicious!!!

Sarah Ferguson @SarahTheDuchess   11 Sep 2015
Falling from tall building not a nice thing to happen to anyone, esp. when you're hard at work. 😞

Sarah Ferguson @SarahTheDuchess   11 Sep 2015
Remembering all those who so tragically lost their lives on this day yonks ago, I don't know how many – sorry no good at sums!!!

As tweeted to CRAIG BROWN

That EU Big Three Statement In Full

WE, the leaders of the only three countries which matter in Europe – Germany, Germany and Germany *(surely Germany, France and Italy? Ed)* – have met on this tiny but historic island of Ventotene to plan the glorious future of the EU without having to worry about the other tiny but irrelevant island of Britain, which has unfortunately decided to abandon ship just as we were sailing onto the rocks *(surely into an even more glorious future? Ed)*.

Whatever the people of Europe may think, the dream of the EU is by no means finished. We are honest enough to recognise that we have a few little problems: the impending collapse of the euro, the unprecedented debt mountain, the ever-growing flood of immigrants, the ever-growing threat of terrorism.

But we have every confidence that we will confront these problems with exactly the same resolve and imagination that we have shown in the past – ie none. *(Surely "by coming up with a whole range of new initiatives and strategies which will soon bring everything under control"? Ed.)*

Meanwhile, we have approved the following historic resolutions:

1. That we will meet again on some other significant island, to be photographed walking resolutely back to the future.

2. We will then issue a further resolution identical to this one, containing those inspiring words "unity", "peace", "hope", "vision", "dream", "grapefruit segments"... *(Is this right? Ed.)*

3. Er...

4. Das ist it! A.M.

Late News

Juncker lashes out

■ The President of the European Commission, Jean-Claude Juncker, last night astonished waiting reporters by claiming that all the troubles of the world can be blamed on the ridiculous idea of countries having national borders.

"We in Luxembourg," he said, "are very happy to allow huge quantities of money to come into our country with no controls or questions asked. This money is entirely free to flow into our banks, where it can live safely without having to pay any tax to the so-called 'countries' where the money comes from. That is what I mean by the freedom of movement – the freedom of capital to move out of everywhere else and into Luxembourg."

NEW NICK CLEGG BOOK
The ten biggest revelations

1 I don't like the Tories very much.

2 And when I started working with them, they turned out to be Tories!

3 Isn't my wife fabulous?

4 Not like Michael Gove. He's awful.

5 Absolutely awful.

6 The thing is, they just can't be trusted.

7 Er...

8 Can I be Deputy Prime Minister again, please?

9 Er...

10 That's it.

"It's not a burkini, officer – I'm a Carmelite nun"

BURKINI-CLAD WOMAN FINED ON FRENCH BEACH

We're here to stop you being told by men what to wear

NEW FRENCH VALUES
Liberté... Égalité... Nudité

Mr Bumble 'to overhaul workhouse'

by Our Business Correspondent
Charles Dickens

After being widely pilloried in the press, Mike Bumble has announced a total overhaul of work practices and conditions at his "Orphans Direct" workhouse in Mugfog, the conditions of which were described in *Oliver Twist* as being little short of a workhouse.

"I'm raising the minimum working age to 11, I'm scrapping zero hours contracts and the lads will no longer be beaten with sticks for asking to go to the loo during working hours," Mike Bumble told reporters. "I really am all heart.

"Obviously mistakes have been made and I want to see them put right. I'm not a heartless man, for example the practice of shooting employees who don't doff their cap to me immediately when I enter will also be phased out over the next few years."

However, the pugnacious and controversial "Orphans Direct" workhouse owner refused to comment after shocking new footage emerged of a small boy named Oliver being refused additional gruel, after asking Mike Bumble: "Please, sir, can I have some more?"

A spokesman for Mike Bumble hit back at critics, pointing out that gruel doesn't grow on trees, as it's mostly gravel mixed with a little cesspit water.

Gigi

Rio 2016

TEAM BRITANNIA RULES THE WORLD

ONCE, Britain turned the map of the world pink with her mighty empire. Today, Britain has turned the world gold with the exploits of her all-conquering Olympians.

However we look at it, Britain is once again a world superpower, winning respect from every other nation on earth.

A tiny group of windswept islands off the coast of Europe has produced a generation of supermen and superwomen such as the world has never seen before. Across every discipline, our athletes demonstrated their awesome mastery – from kayaking to taekwondo, from skateboarding to origami.

And this is why we say that every single medal winner from Team GB must immediately

be given a peerage. Arise Lord Peaty of Greenpool and Lord Mo of Mobot. Step up Baron and Baroness Kenny-Trott of Keirin!

And while the Queen is at it, it would only be fair to give out knighthoods as consolation prizes to all those gallant sportsmen and sportswomen who only just missed out on a medal by coming fourth (usually as a result of being cheated by foreign judges or secret dope-takers).

This would show the world just how much we appreciate all that Team GB has done to transform Britain into a nation truly second to none (except of course America, which doesn't really count because it is so much bigger and richer and generally takes winning at sport far too seriously).

THEN AND NOW

1 AD	2016 AD

	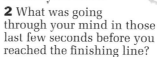
Circuses and Bread	**Olympics and Bake Off**

RECORDS TUMBLE AS BOLT HITS TOP FORM AGAIN
by Our Athletics Staff **Mark Getsetgo**

USAIN BOLT tore up the record books once again, with a series of personal bests which will live long in many people's memories – but probably not his.

The world of athletics had never seen anything like it, as he beat his record time again and again.

First it was 3am, then it was 4am, then 5am when Bolt emerged from the nightclub. And the records didn't end there, as Bolt sped from one woman to another, amazing on-lookers as he achieved a

unique "triple triple" – three lots of three women. With his track record never in doubt, Usain stretched his legs and showed his class, and according to one of the spectators, "It was amazing to watch, and all over in less than 10 seconds!"

There was a photo finish with a selfie, as Bolt came first, again and again and again. *(That's enough of this filth. Ed.)*

He's now preparing for the high jump, when he goes home and explains this all to his girlfriend. *(You're fired! Ed.)*

Those BBC Questions We Shall Be Very Pleased Not To Hear Again For Another Four Years

1 How did it feel to be standing there with a gold medal around your neck?

2 What was going through your mind in those last few seconds before you reached the finishing line?

3 Can you reconstruct your emotions as you waited for the judges to give you the scores?

4 Can you talk us through what you were thinking when you realised that a precious gold medal was within your reach?

5 Can you describe for us how amazing it was to win that amazing medal in that amazing time, that was not only a personal best but also a new Commonwealth record and only just outside the British record which has stood for an amazing six months?

6 Can you say just how much it means to you to have won

gold for Team GB here in Rio, after all the years of hard work and training and all the amazing support from your family, including your Nan in Heckmondwike, whose tweets about how much she hoped you would win were trending in 87 countries and now you have?

7 Could you take this opportunity in front of a BBC audience of millions to celebrate your amazing gold medal by proposing live on air to your amazing Team GB partner and then can you talk us through your emotions and how you were feeling in those vital few seconds when you were at last popping the most amazing question you will ever ask in your life... and then can you reconstruct just what you were thinking when *(cont. until 2094)*

YET ANOTHER TRIUMPH FOR POST-BREXIT BRITAIN

BRITONS can be truly proud today at the news that we are to build the world's greatest wall around Calais.

This remarkable infrastructure project will be over 300 miles long and 700 feet high, and will be capped with two million tons of British-made barbed wire made from Chinese steel.

This astonishing structure will be clearly visible from the planet Jupiter, and pictures of it will be beamed back to Earth by space probes of the future.

Compared with other countries' walls, such as the so-called Great Wall of China or the Trump Wall along the US-Mexican border, this British achievement will be viewed by the rest of the world as living proof that post-Brexit Britain is a global superpower like no other.

And if there is one thing we have learned from the great walls of history, it is that it can often take up to several months before people work out how to go around the side of them.

TRIAL OF THE CENTURY
Was Radio 4 guilty?

by Our Criminal Correspondent
Jeffrey Archer

THE radio story that has gripped the nation finally reached a conclusion, as Radio 4 was found guilty of "coercive control".

For the past year, listeners had been subjected to a sustained campaign of mental cruelty as they were cynically manipulated into staying awake during episodes of the Archers.

Mrs Dull of Ditchwater, Herts, said, "I couldn't resist the mind games. I felt powerless, trapped in a living hell where I was unable to turn the radio off."

The case against the BBC included systematic and relentless mentions of the Archers everywhere.

Exhibit A: **That Radio 4 schedule in full**

6.30am *Today*: Top barristers are asked how they would defend talking about a fictional case on a current affairs show.

1.30pm *I'm Sorry, I Haven't a Clue*: In-depth examination of the jury's verdict using a swanee whistle and a kazoo.

3pm *Gardeners' Question Time*: If

Helen had murdered Rob, what would be the best type of soil for burying the body?

4.30pm *The Food Programme*: If Helen had been sent to prison, what would have been her dietary option? And Sheila Dillon samples organic porridge production in Borsetshire.

7pm *The Archers*: An everyday story of barristers, a judge and 12 angry luvvies.

8pm *Feedback*: Looks back at the Feedback from previous Feedbacks in a special Feedback feature in response to the last Feedback. Is there too much talk of the Archers on Radio 4?

Listeners are now worried that the story might not be over, as Rob's final remarks to Helen clearly indicate that the cruelty will continue on long wave forever.

"Do we have to equip ourselves with tools for the future? Can't we just learn stuff instead?"

TORIES DISAGREE ON GRAMMARS

It's an embarrassing split, Theresa!

Prime Minister Introduces New Kind of Grammar School

THE Prime Minister has insisted that the proposed Grammar Schools would not be like the old-fashioned Grammar Schools, but would in fact be "Grammar Schools of the future".

"For a start, these new-style Grammar schools will not be allowed to exclude any pupils," she said forcefully. "They will be far more inclusive, and will have places allocated for children from poor backgrounds, children from the north, and children who aren't clever enough to go to Grammar schools.

"These new-style Grammar schools, called 'schools' for short, will be the start of a new revolution in selective education, where I select the phrase Grammar Schools, and use it in a selective context to gain support in certain sections of my party."

"Are you actually trying to left swipe my face?"

HIDDLESWIFT 'NO LONGER AN ITEM'

by Our Showbiz Staff
D.J. Taylor-Stone

IT's official! The romance of the millennium between *The Night Manager's* **Tom Hiddleston, singer Taylor Swift and the world's newspapers is over.**

Only a few weeks ago, the glamorous couple were "an item" on page one, two and three to ninety-four of every publication on earth.

But now the love affair of the media and the wannabee Hollywood power couple is finished and devastated newspaper editors all over the globe are weeping inconsolably about what they call "a terrible hole" in their lives and their front pages.

Said one, "Once, these two celebrity sweethearts were very much in the papers. Now they

have fallen out and will have to be replaced by pieces about *Poldark*, *Bake Off* or Rufus Sewell.

"It's a tragedy," said the editor, "but we must move on and find another celebrity couple whose names we can run together in a really annoying way."

Late News

● **Hiddleliddle**? Is the star of The Night Manager having an affair with the Spectator's top political columnist, Rod Liddle?

● **Liddleswift**? Is the Spectator's top political columnist Rod Liddle romancing prize-winning literary novelist Graham Swift?

● **Liddlelidl**? Is the Spectator's top political columnist Rod Liddle going down to the supermarket to stock up on cheap fags and booze? *(You're fired. Ed.)*

VAZ WELCOMES IMMIGRANTS

I'd like these to take away, please

Aren't you going to finish your coffee first?

'I AM GENUINELY SORRY' SAYS VAZ

by Our Political Staff **Alex Rentboy**

THE Chairman of the Commons Home Affairs Committee, Mr Keith Vaz MP, said yesterday that he was "genuinely sorry" that he had been caught.

Mr Vaz continued, "It is truly regrettable that I am no longer able to continue my very important work for the nation as chair of this very important committee which I have been proud to serve with immense distinction over so many years.

"I think it would only be fair to say," Mr Vaz added, "that my departure from the centre of British public life is an enormous and possibly irreplaceable loss, as will be ever more widely realised in years to come.

"I would emphasise that this decision was entirely mine and mine alone, and nothing at all to do with the fact that the committee was about to sack me.

"For the record," he went on, "I have always been extremely passionate about the issues of drugs and prostitution, and I would like to make it clear that the alleged episode which was so grossly misrepresented by a certain Sunday newspaper, only arose because, in my dedication to the work of the committee, I needed to carry out some first-hand research into both these complex issues."

Mr Vaz then expressed his "deep regret" that he would no longer play his unique and vital part in helping members of the ethnic Asian community.

"Who, in future, will people like the poor Hindujas be able to turn to when they are in desperate need of a British passport?" he concluded. "My departure is nothing less than a tragedy, which will leave the nation infinitely poorer, not to mention myself."

British Businessmen 'Shockingly Lazy'

by Our Business Correspondent **Noah Shame**

TRADE Secretary Liam Fox has defended his comments lambasting British businessmen as being lazy, citing the example of hard working lobbyist Adam Werritty.

"Have any of these lazy businessmen shown the get-up-and-go spirit Werritty displayed in 2011 by sharing a hotel room with me on foreign trade visits?" Liam Fox asked reporters.

"Have any of these businessmen gone the extra mile by handing out business cards at meetings falsely suggesting they were Government advisors? Have any of these titans of industry attended Government briefings with me, despite them not having the necessary security clearance as Mr Werrity did?

"The answer to all those questions of course is no, and what a damning indictment of British business that is.

"Adam Werrity showed me what 'get up and go' meant, as he would often get up at 4am to go back... (*That's enough, Ed.*)

THOSE TOP GIRLS' AND BOYS' NAMES IN FULL

Once again, we are delighted to record the most popular children's names recorded in Private Eye's Births column in the past year.

Girls	Boys
1. Demelza	1. Ross
2. Victoria	2. Albert
3. Sue	3. Mel
4. Mary	4. Berry
5. Helen	5. Rob
6. Mentum	6. Mo
7. Jezza	7. Jeremy
8. BB8	8. Sir Killalot
9. Pink	9. Floyd
10. Taylor	10. [To be announced]

The most popular name has unfortunately been disqualified after it was considered inappropriate for both boys and girls – "Namey McNameface".

DAVID CAMERON RESIGNS AS AN MP

I'm going to spend more time with my family's money

"So how are you adjusting to gender-neutral toilets?"

Oxford English Dictionary
2017 PREVIEW

Brexit *(see Brexit)*.
Brexit *(see Brexit)*.
Brexit *(see Brexit)*.
Brexit *(see Brexit)*.
Brexit *(see Brexit)*.
Brexit *(see Brexit)*.
Brexit *(see Brexit)*.
Brexit *(see Brexit)*